Eastern Europe since 1970

We work with leading authors to develop the
strongest educational materials in history,
bringing cutting-edge thinking and best learning
practice to a global market.

Under a range of well-known imprints, including
Longman, we craft high-quality print and electronic
publications which help readers to understand and
apply their content, whether studying or at work.

To find out more about the complete range of our
publishing please visit us on the World Wide Web at:
www.pearsoneduc.com

SEMINAR STUDIES   IN HISTORY

Eastern Europe since 1970

BÜLENT GÖKAY

Longman

An imprint of **Pearson Education**

Harlow, England · London · New York · Reading, Massachusetts · San Francisco · Toronto · Don Mills, Ontario · Sydney
Tokyo · Singapore · Hong Kong · Seoul · Taipei · Cape Town · Madrid · Mexico City · Amsterdam · Munich · Paris · Milan

Pearson Education Limited
Edinburgh Gate
Harlow
Essex CM20 2JE
England
and Associated Companies throughout the world.

Visit us on the World Wide Web at:
www.pearsoneduc.com

First published 2001

ISBN 0-582-32858-6 PPR

British Library Cataloguing-in-Publication Data
A catalogue record for this book is
available from the British Library

Library of Congress Cataloging-in-Publication Data
Gökay, Bülent.
 Eastern Europe since 1970 / Bülent Gökay.
  p. cm. -- (Seminar studies in history)
 Includes bibliographical references and index.
 ISBN 0-582-32858-6 (pbk. : alk. paper)
  1. Europe, Eastern--History--1945–1989. 2. Europe, Eastern--History--1989- I. Title.
 II. Series.

 DJK50 .G628 2001
 947'.0009'045--dc21   2001022349

Set by 7 in 10/12 Sabon Roman
Printed in Malaysia,LSP

CONTENTS

INTRODUCTION TO THE SERIES

Such is the pace of historical enquiry in the modern world that there is an ever-widening gap between the specialist article or monograph, incorporating the results of current research, and general surveys, which inevitably become out of date. *Seminar Studies in History* is designed to bridge this gap. The series was founded by Patrick Richardson in 1966 and his aim was to cover major themes in British, European and world history. Between 1980 and 1996 Roger Lockyer continued his work, before handing the editorship over to Clive Emsley and Gordon Martel. Clive Emsley is Professor of History at the Open University, while Gordon Martel is Professor of International History at the University of Northern British Columbia, Canada, and Senior Research Fellow at De Montfort University.

All the books are written by experts in their field who are not only familiar with the latest research but have often contributed to it. They are frequently revised, in order to take account of new information and interpretations. They provide a selection of documents to illustrate major themes and provoke discussion, and also a guide to further reading. The aim of *Seminar Studies in History* is to clarify complex issues without over-simplifying them, and to stimulate readers into deepening their knowledge and understanding of major themes and topics.

NOTE ON REFERENCING SYSTEM

Readers should note that numbers in square brackets [5] refer them to the corresponding entry in the Bibliography at the end of the book (specific page numbers are given in italics). A number in square brackets preceded by *Doc.* [*Doc. 5*] refers readers to the corresponding item in the Documents section which follows the main text.

LIST OF FIGURES AND TABLES

ACKNOWLEDGEMENTS

We are grateful to the following for permission to reproduce copyright material:

British Broadcasting Corporation/Czech Radio for an extract from a speech by Alexander Dubček on 21.12.68 taken from *Summary of World Broadcasts*, 1968; Greenpeace International for an extact from the article 'Is Poland lost?' by Sabine Rosenbladt in *Greenpeace* 13 (6) November–December 1988, article courtesy of Greenpeace USA; Quartet Books for an extract from *Poland: Genesis of a Revolution* editied by Abraham Brumberg; Quartet Books/Harcourt for an extract from *Antipolitics: An Essay by Gyorgy Konrad* 1984 translated by Richard E. Allen 1984; Scribner, a Division of Simon & Schuster for an extract from *Germany and Eastern Europe since 1945* Copyright © 1973 by Keesing's Publications Limited; Taylor & Francis Books Ltd for an extract from *Charter 77 and Human Rights in Czechoslovakia* by H. Gordon Skilling 1981: Taylor & Francis/ M.E. Sharpe for extracts from *The Power of the Powerless* by Václav Havel, published by Routledge (Unwin Hyman); University of California Press for an extract from KOR: *A History of the Workers' Defense Committee in Poland* 1985 by Jan Jozef Lipski and *Letters from Freedom: Post-Cold War Realities and Perspective* 1988 by Adam Michnik.

We have been unable to trace the copyright holder of *Perestroika Annual* edited by Abel A. Ganbegyan and would appreciate any information which would enable us to do so.

Figure 1 from *Communist Regimes in Eastern Europe*, Third Edition, Hoover Institution Press (Staar, R.F. 1977); Table 2 from *Comecon Data 1990*, Macmillan Ltd (Vienna Institute for Comparative Economic Studies, 1991).

We have been unable to trace the copyright holder of *Nationalism and Communism in Romania* by Trond Gilberg and would appreciate any information which would enable us to do so.

Plate 1 reproduced courtesy of Gilles Peress Magnum Photos; Plate 2 reproduced courtesy of The Associated Press Ltd; Plate 3 reproduced courtesy of Smithsonian Institution Traveling Exhibition Service, from *Art as Activist: Revolutionary Posters from Central and Eastern Europe*; Plate 4 reproduced courtesy of Agence France Presse.

While every effort has been made to trace the owners of copyright material, in a few cases this has proved impossible and we take this opportunity to offer our apologies to any copyright holders whose rights we have un-wittingly infringed.

Map 1   Physical features of Eastern Europe

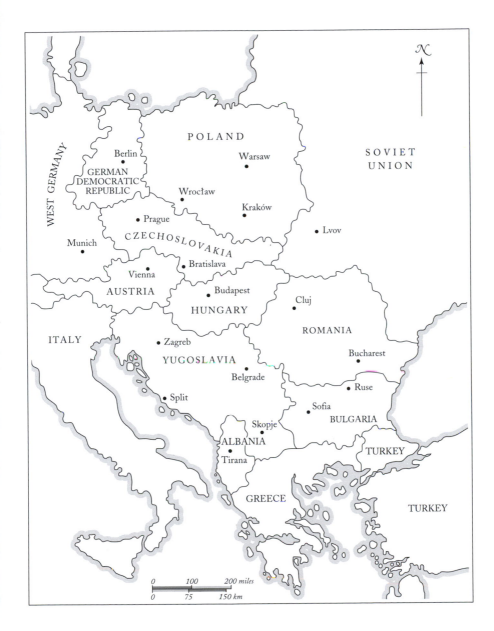

Map 2 Eastern Europe, November 1955–October 1990

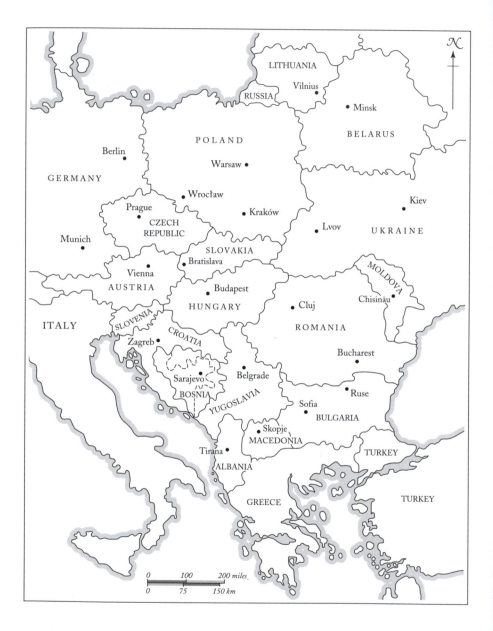

Map 3 Eastern Europe, 1996

CHRONOLOGY

1968

January
Alexander Dubček replaces Novotny as Czechoslovak Party leader.

March
Novotny is also ousted from the presidency.
Student demonstrations in Poland.

April
Action Programme of basic reform is announced in Prague.

June
Warsaw Pact warns Czechoslovakia against excessive reform.

Soviet and Czechoslovak leaders reach a temporary agreement.

Student demonstrations in Yugoslavia.

20–21 August
Invasion of Czechoslovakia by Soviet and other Warsaw Pact troops.

September
Soviets proclaim doctrine of limited sovereignty, which is confirmed later in the year by Brezhnev at the Polish Party Congress.

1970

Croat nationalist unrest in Yugoslavia.

December–
January 1971
Price increases in Poland lead to the 'Baltic Crisis'.

1971

May
Honecker replaces Ulbricht in the GDR.

September
Four Power Agreement on Berlin.

1972

22–30 May
Nixon visits the Soviet Union. The arms control treaty is signed.

November
Measures that partially recentralize the economy are approved by the Central Committee in Hungary.

December
Basic Treaty between the GDR and German Federal Republic is signed.

1975

August   The permanent Conference on Security and Cooperation in Europe is set up under the Helsinki Final Act. It is signed by 35 countries, including Bulgaria, Czechoslovakia, East Germany, Hungary, Poland, Romania and Yugoslavia.

1976

June   Price increases in Poland result in strikes and demonstrations.

September   Foundation in Poland of the Committee for the Defence of Workers (KOR).

1977

January   Foundation of Charter 77 in Czechoslovakia.

1978

July   China suspends foreign aid to Albania.

1980

July   Price increases in Poland.

August   *Solidarity* (a free trade union) is founded in Poland.

13 December   General Jaruzelski declares Martial Law in Poland.

29 December   President Reagan announces sanctions against the Soviet Union in response to the declaration of Martial Law in Poland.

1981

March–April   Ethnic disturbances in Kosovo.

1982

         Debt crisis in Yugoslavia.

May   Hungary joins the International Monetary Fund (IMF).

31 December   Martial Law in Poland is 'suspended'.

1983

July   Martial Law is lifted in Poland.

5 October   Lech Walesa is awarded the Nobel Peace Prize.

1985

March   Gorbachev becomes General Secretary of Central Committee of CPSU. Kohl meets Gorbachev and Honecker at Chernenko's funeral.

19–21 November   First Reagan–Gorbachev summit meeting, in Geneva.

1986

26 April   Disastrous accident at a nuclear power plant in Chernobyl, Ukraine.

May   Slobodan Milosevic becomes leader of Serbian League of Communists.

June   Poland rejoins the IMF.

1988

August   The Polish government decides to negotiate with *Solidarity*.

December   Gorbachev announces unilateral troop withdrawals from Czechoslovakia, East Germany and Hungary by the end of 1991.

1989

June   Elections in Poland. Solidarity wins a vast majority of seats available to it.

August   Solidarity-led government is formed in Poland.

September   Hungary allows GDR citizens to emigrate via Austria. Government and Opposition Round Table Talks are concluded.

October   Warsaw Pact foreign ministers confirm the effective renunciation of the 'Brezhnev doctrine'; in what is popularly known as the 'Sinatra doctrine', East European countries can now 'do it their way'.

9 November   Berlin Wall is breached.

November   Demonstrations in Prague. Todor Zhivkov resigns in Bulgaria.

December   Government of National Understanding is formed in Czechoslovakia.

21 December   Ceausesçu rally is disrupted. Fighting breaks out between demonstrators and *Securitate*.

25 December   Nicolae and Elena Ceausesçu are executed.

1990

January   Poland implements 'shock therapy' programme.

March–April   Elections in Hungary. Right-of-centre coalition government is led by the Hungarian Democratic Forum.

April–May	Elections in Croatia are won by the nationalistic Croatian Democratic Union.
May	Elections in Romania are won by the National Salvation Front which is dominated by former communists.
June	Elections in Czechoslovakia are won by the Civic Forum and Public Against Violence.
	Elections in Bulgaria are won by the former Communist Party.
	Miners break up an opposition demonstration in Romania.
	Hungary withdraws from the Warsaw Pact.
1 July	German currency union.
24 September	East Germany withdraws from the Warsaw Pact.
25–27 September	Bulgaria and Czechoslovakia join the IMF. Albania is now the only non-member in Eastern Europe.
3 October	Germany is reunified.
6 November	Hungary joins the Council of Europe, the first former-communist country to do so.
November–December	Presidential elections in Poland (Walesa is elected).
	A communist-led government in Bulgaria resigns following a wave of strikes.
	Elections in Macedonia, Bosnia-Herzegovina, Serbia and Montenegro. Former communists win in Serbia and Montenegro. A weak coalition government wins in Bosnia and Herzegovina. A nationalist coalition wins in Macedonia.
December 1990–January 1991	Anti-government demonstrations take place in Albania.

1991

25 February	Warsaw Pact member countries agree to disband the Pact as a military alliance from 31 March.
April	Elections in Albania are won by the former communists.
June	The Albanian communist-led government resigns after a wave of strikes.
	The last Soviet troops leave Hungary and Czechoslovakia.
28 June	COMECON is formally dissolved.
June–July	Slovenia establishes *de facto* independence after a brief outbreak of hostilities.
	Relations between Croatia and Serbia degenerate to fighting. The United Nations imposes a peace of sorts.
1 July	The Warsaw Pact is formally dissolved at a meeting in Prague.

September	The Romanian government resigns after demonstrations led by miners. A broad-based interim government is formed.
October	Elections in Poland produce no clear winner. Elections in Bulgaria are won by the Union of Democratic Forces with small majority.
December	The Albanian Democratic Party withdraws support from the coalition government.
26 December	The Soviet Union is formally dissolved following Gorbachev's resignation on Christmas Day.

1992

15 January	The European Community recognises the independence of Slovenia and Croatia and hence the break-up of Yugoslavia.
March	The Bosnian War starts.
	Elections in Albania bring the Democratic Party to power.
	Romanian elections give victory to the anti-reform candidate, President Iliescu.
June	Elections in Czechoslovakia result in the decision to dissolve the state into the Czech Republic and Slovakia – the 'Velvet Revolution'.
October	The fall of the Union of Democratic Forces (UDF) government in Bulgaria.

1993

May	Former communists and allies return to power in Poland.

1994

May	Former communists return to power in Hungary.
September	Socialists return to power in Bulgaria.

1995

November	Walesa is replaced as Polish president by a former communist.
	The Dayton Accord ends the Bosnian War.

1996

June	The conservative government in Czechoslovakia loses its overall majority; a banking crisis follows.
	The disputed election in Albania returns the Democratic Party to power.
November	Reformists win the Romanian elections.

December	Widespread demonstrations against President Milosevic take place in Serbia.

1997

Spring	The socialist government in Bulgaria collapses and the UDF returns to power.
	Albania descends into anarchy after a pyramid selling crisis; foreign troops restore order.
May	There are demonstrations in Slovakia after the collapse of a presidential referendum.
June	The Czech Republic faces financial crisis.
	Socialists win the Albanian elections.
September	Former communists lose power in Polish elections.

1997

16 November	85 per cent of the participants in a binding referendum vote in favour of NATO membership in Hungary.

1998

28 February	Some 80 Albanians are killed in ferocious fighting between the Serbian police and the Kosovo Liberation Army (KLA) in the Drenica region of central Kosovo.
July–August	A Serbian counter-offensive, using indiscriminate forces, re-takes most of Kosovo from the KLA forces.
September	The UN Security Council calls for an immediate ceasefire and political dialogue in Kosovo.
4 October	The Russian government issues a statement on Kosovo. It says that any NATO bombing would be a gross violation of the UN Charter.

1999

4 January	Clashes take place between Serb and Albanian forces in Klina.
16 January	A Kosovo Albanian news agency reports that 38 Albanians have been killed by Serb security forces near Racak in Kosovo. The OSCE (Organisation for Security and Cooperation in Europe) verification mission confirms the killing of at least 23 Albanian civilians. The Kosovo Albanian leadership calls for NATO intervention.
6 February	Kosovo–Serb talks begin in Paris, chaired by Britain and France.

9 February	The Hungarian Foreign Minister visits Moscow. Russian Deputy Foreign Minister warns him that NATO novices must observe the restrictions following the Russia–NATO Founding Act on the non-deployment of significant armed forces on their territory.
17 February	Soviet President Yeltsin sends a message to US President Clinton expressing his opposition to the use of force in Kosovo.
20 February	Clinton responds to Yeltsin saying that NATO reserves the right to make appropriate moves.
11 March	Russian Ministry of Defence spokesman says that Moscow plans no military measures in response to Poland, Hungary and the Czech Republic joining NATO.
12 March	Poland, Hungary and the Czech Republic become members of NATO.
24 March	NATO Secretary-General Javier Solana gives the go-ahead for NATO bombing of military targets in Yugoslavia. 'Operation Allied Force' begins. The Yugoslav government declares a state of war in Yugoslavia.
25 March	Yugoslavia breaks off ties with the USA, the UK, France and Germany. It expels journalists from these states.
25 March	Hungarian television reports that the Serbian authorities have ordered a general mobilisation in Vojvodina and Hungarian conscripts are being taken from their homes by force.
26 March	The Albanian Minister of Information says that Albania's airspace is at the complete disposal of NATO.
30 March	The Macedonian Foreign Minister meets the Secretary-General of NATO in Brussels and demands early membership of NATO.
1 April	The Serb Deputy Prime Minister attacks Romania, Hungary and Bulgaria for aiding NATO.
6 April	A British Ministry of Defence official says that 1.1 million inhabitants of Kosovo have become refugees since the ethnic fighting began in Kosovo in 1998.
9 April	UN Secretary-General calls for Yugoslav authorities to withdraw forces from Kosovo and accept an international military presence to oversee the return of refugees. He says if Yugoslavia agrees to this, then NATO should suspend air strikes.
14 April	NATO admits it accidentally bombed Kosovo refugees between Prizren and Djakovica.
23 April	A massive attack smashes open the building that housed Serbian State Television in the centre of Belgrade. At least ten people die.

27 May	In The Hague, the International Criminal Tribunal for the former Yugoslavia indicts Milosevic and the Serbian leadership for war crimes.
3 June	Following the mediation of the European Union (EU) special envoy and the Russian special envoy, Milosevic and the Serbian parliament approve a peace plan that puts the UN in charge of Kosovo, with NATO as the occupying force.
10 June	The Serbian withdrawal from Kosovo begins. NATO's air strikes end after 79 days.

CHAPTER ONE

INTRODUCTION: UNDERSTANDING THE CONTEXT OF CHANGE

THE GEOPOLITICS OF EASTERN EUROPE

Eastern Europe has long played a crucial role in modern European history and is destined to be the focus of some of the most far-reaching changes in global politics. It has had a stormy and eventful history. At no point in history has it been easy to define the region in any other than geographical terms. What constitutes Eastern Europe has varied with time, as have the forces operating within the area. For centuries, trends in Eastern Europe have served as a litmus test for the ebb and flow of the competition between Eastern and Western worlds. The complicated history of Eastern Europe is grounded in geography. The developments in Eastern Europe have been much influenced by its physical, economic and human geography. The distinctive geopolitics of Eastern Europe derive from the region's perceived location on the borderlines between Europe and Asia. One important feature of the region's spatial location is its comparative closeness to Asia. For centuries, Eastern Europe has been considered to constitute a 'crush zone' between Europe and the Eurasian heartland, and has been subjected to periodic waves of invasions [9; 23].

From a geographical point of view, one outstanding feature of the area is its mountainous character. Eastern Europe is cut in half by the Carpathian Mountains. Although the mountains contributed to particularism and isolation among the peoples, they did not provide a natural barrier against outside invasion. To the north, the eastward extension of the North European Plain has given invaders easy access from both directions. Another invasion route was found between the Carpathians and the Black Sea. No natural barriers hindered passage from the lands north of the Black Sea, along the Danube Valley, into the Pannonian Plain. In the Balkans, the main ridge of the Balkan mountains, stretching westward from Sofia to the east, cuts the peninsula into two [23].

Eastern Europe does not have any access to the open seas, although this has not necessarily impeded economic development. The region's socio-economic development has been shaped by one major geographical feature, the River Danube. The Danube flows from Bavaria, through Austria, Slovakia, Hungary, Serbia and Romania to the Black Sea. The Danube and its tributaries played a vital role in the settlement and political evolution of Eastern Europe. Throughout history, this great river has been the principal route in this area for military invasion, trade and travel. Its banks, lined with castles and fortresses, formed the boundary between great empires, and its waters served as a vital commercial highway between nations. The Danube is of great economic importance to the countries that border it – Ukraine, Romania, Yugoslavia, Hungary, Bulgaria, Slovakia, Austria and Germany – all of which variously use the river for freight transport, the generation of hydroelectricity, industrial and residential water supplies, irrigation and fishing [24; 119] (see also Map 1 on p. x).

Eastern Europe has always been less developed than the countries further west. From the time of the Enlightenment, East Europeans have struggled to emancipate themselves from a legacy of underdevelopment and dependence. For most of its history, Eastern Europe has constituted part of the European economy's periphery. Edward Tiryakian describes Eastern Europe as an historical and cultural area that forms a double periphery [41]. It has been, historically, a periphery of two more remote civilisations, that of Moscow and that of the Ottoman Empire. It has also been a periphery of more accessible Western civilisation. One result of this situation of structural dependency has been that Eastern Europe, for the greater part of the modern period, has lacked autonomy in the economic as well as in the political sphere [41].

Today most of Eastern Europe remains relatively backward, under-capitalised, under-productive and under-employed. Politics in Eastern Europe also reflects the region's relative economic backwardness and more traditional social structure. Eastern Europe had not been greatly affected by the ideas of the Enlightenment of the eighteenth century. Nor did the liberal revolutions of the nineteenth century take root in the mostly rural societies of Eastern Europe. The political culture is, therefore, less developed than it is in Western Europe, and provides opportunities for demagogues and populists. Notions of consensus-building, tolerance and compromise politics are less widely accepted. Ideas associated with the classical liberal tradition are much weaker in Eastern Europe than in the West [23; 36].

A constant theme in the politics of Eastern Europe in the twentieth century has been the close linkage between domestic economic and political developments, social structures and culture on the one hand, and the external environment, that is changes in the wider global system, on the other. The linkage between domestic and international affairs has grown rapidly in both directions in the late twentieth century. There is a complex interdependence between the regional and the global, which provides us with an essential background for analysing the changing dynamics of international politics in this region. On the one hand, fast-changing domestic dynamics and new demands have become increasingly dependent upon international politics. On the other hand, the historical and cultural traditions of the East European states have remained important in determining the main focus of international affairs in the region [36; 69; 70].

Until relatively recent times, Eastern Europe did not exist as a distinct geographical or political notion. After the First World War the northern part and the southern part of Eastern Europe were united into a single geographical unit. After the Second World War the geographical notion of Eastern Europe merged with the ideological notion to form the contemporary political-geographical concept. For all practical purposes, Eastern Europe meant communist Europe, except for the USSR. It meant a group of countries sharing state socialist regimes and having antagonistic relations with the capitalist states in the West. Thus, geographical Eastern Europe and political Eastern Europe were not perfectly compatible. This definition excluded Greece, Turkish Thrace, Finland and the European non-Russian republics of the Soviet Union, which are geographically part of Eastern Europe, and included the German Democratic Republic and the former German provinces of Pomerania and Silesia (then parts of Poland), which traditionally were not considered to be part of the geographical Eastern Europe [33; 79].

Eastern Europe is a mosaic of peoples and cultures of very different origins and varied historical experience. It is only the experience of 'communism' between 1945 and 1989 that imposes a unity on the area. Communist Eastern Europe had a stormy and eventful history. Beginning in 1944, relations with Moscow were at first flexible. However, after a short-lived flirtation with 'national roads to socialism' from 1944 to 1948, a Stalinist assault took place from 1948 onwards. Stalin's system of control over Eastern Europe encompassed the creation of command economies and centralised bureaucratic state apparatuses controlled by the Communist Party. From that point on, Soviet influence and the firm control of Moscow over the whole region remained the crucial fact of life until 1989, the historic year of geopolitical transition. It is this common communist experience that justifies the collective use of the term 'Eastern Europe' for societies whose pre-communist histories were very varied [66; 80].

Elements of history, culture and ideology combined after the Second World War to shape Soviet policy towards Eastern Europe. That policy has undergone many changes since that time, but it was always motivated by core Soviet interests, interests determined by geography as much as by ideology and power politics. The Soviet Union saw Eastern Europe as a buffer zone, a base and a laboratory: a military and ideological buffer zone against the West; a base for the protection of socialist power and Soviet influence over the rest of Europe; and a laboratory for the exoneration of

Soviet ideological aspirations of internationalism and proletarian dictator-ship. The relative weight reserved for these factors has of course changed over time, but the importance of the East European interstate system, and Moscow's control over it, was central to the strategic thinking of the Soviet leadership [33; 49].

Ultimate control of Eastern Europe was exercised by Moscow against the backdrop of the threat of force. The military organisation uniting the Eastern European socialist countries under Moscow's domination was the Warsaw Treaty Organisation (WTO), or Warsaw Pact as it is commonly known. The Warsaw Treaty was signed in Warsaw on 14 May 1955, by representatives of Albania, Bulgaria, Hungary, the German Democratic Republic, Poland, Romania, the Soviet Union and Czechoslovakia. A com-bination of internal and external factors was at work at this early stage. However, the most immediate cause was the accession of the Federal Republic of Germany (FRG) to the North Atlantic Treaty Organisation (NATO). This is the event most frequently cited by Soviet commentators as the origins of the Warsaw Pact. The preamble to the Warsaw Treaty identi-fied the reintegration of West Germany into the Western Bloc as giving rise to the need for a counter-balancing alliance. In some points of phrasing the Warsaw Treaty mirrored that of the North Atlantic Treaty of 1949, which established NATO. On the same day as the Warsaw Treaty was signed, an announcement was made on the formation of the Joint Armed Forces of the Warsaw Pact signatories. In effect, the signing of the Warsaw Treaty legiti-mised the presence of Soviet troops in Hungary and Romania, since they would otherwise have had to withdraw once Soviet forces withdrew from Austria with the signing of the Austrian State Treaty. The Warsaw Treaty therefore provided a broad legal basis for the stationing of Soviet troops in Eastern Europe [66; 81; 94]. Indeed, Molotov, then Foreign Minister of the Soviet Union, saw the Warsaw Pact primarily in terms of safeguarding the military security of the socialist camp.

Apart from the brief period of Hungarian withdrawal in 1956, only Albania withdrew, in 1962, from the Pact. No other state joined. The nature and extent of Soviet control in Eastern Europe was altered over time yet the Warsaw Pact continued to provide a complex mechanism for coordinating military and foreign policy for the Soviet bloc states, with the USSR being the ultimate arbiter [51] (see also Figure 1).

With the end of the Cold War, the reasons for the region's continuing importance have radically changed. European politics have taken on a new meaning following the fall of the Berlin Wall. Eastern Europe has opened up at its Western side and is no longer the front line for an authoritarian superpower. Instead, it finds itself acting as a 'buffer region' between the European Union and Russia. Eastern European countries are now at the core of the process of integration across the Cold War European divide [74].

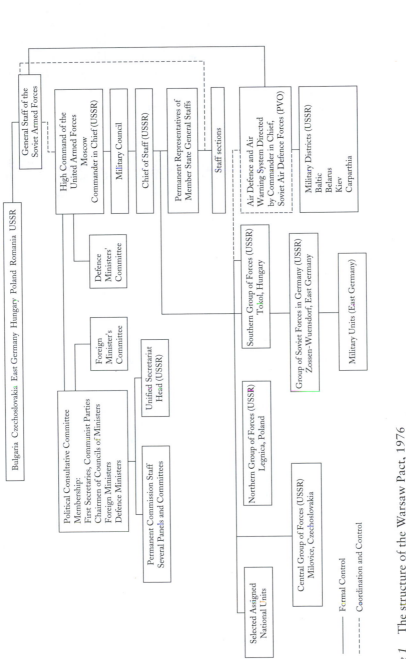

Figure 1 The structure of the Warsaw Pact, 1976

Reprinted from *Communist Regimes in Eastern Europe* by Richard F. Staar, with the permission of the publisher, Hoover Institution Press. Copyright © 1977 by the Board of Trustees of the Leland Stanford Junior University.

This book is an enquiry into the factors that have shaped Eastern Europe's development since 1970 and have given it the character it has today. In many ways, 1970 was a watershed in the history of the region. The Eastern Bloc was slowly getting over the trauma of the invasion of Czechoslovakia by the armies of the Warsaw Pact. The ruling parties seemed to believe that rapid economic development would allow the regimes simply to grow their way out of political, social and economic difficulties. By looking at the developments in this important period, this book focuses on the forces that led to the revolutionary changes which occurred in Eastern Europe in 1989, and the subsequent process of transition now unfolding in the new post-communist societies there. In a way, this is an attempt to provide a general explanation for the collapse of the Soviet-style communist regimes in Eastern Europe.

THE CONTROVERSIES OVER THE CAUSES OF COMMUNISM'S COLLAPSE IN EASTERN EUROPE

Much has been written on various aspects of East European history and some on the collapse of the communist regimes there. Most of the publications are, of course, monographs concerned with limited aspects of East European history and politics. But some general works provide useful background material and a general overview on the region.

Many reasons have been advanced for the collapse of communism. These can be summarised under two general categories: the first category is related to the inherent weaknesses and internal structures and developments of the communist system; the second is related to external factors and global developments. Some writers in the first category explain the collapse as an inevitable result of the inherent problems and internal mechanisms of the socialist state system. In this view, the evolution of communism contained within itself its own rejection [41]. These authors emphasise that a political system based on rigid single-party rule creates no real support. Repressive regimes, they say, are inherently vulnerable. Communist political systems in Eastern Europe collapsed at the end of the 1980s because of long-standing internal weaknesses that denied them the popular legitimacy needed for long-term survival. According to this view, the collapse was caused by dictatorship and popular demands for liberal-democratic rights. Eastern Europe rejected communism, it is contended by authors such as Wandycz, because it was contrary to freedom and because it was foreign [124]. Ralf Miliband, similarly, writes that it was the authoritarian nature of communism that must, above all, be sought as the reason for the regimes' collapse, for the lack of democracy and civic freedom affected every aspect of life, from economic performance to ethnic strife [11]. Richard Pipes, in his book, *Communism: The Vanished Specter*, claims that communism collapsed because it contradicted human nature [83].

Other authors emphasise the failure of the economic system of the socialist states as the reason for collapse. In this view, the command economies of socialist states were increasingly incapable of providing labour incentives, efficient allocation of capital and stimulants to innovation. The collapse was, Philip Longworth asserts, above all a consequence of economic failure [70]. Change happened in Eastern Europe first, says Charles Gati, because all communist regimes there were dissatisfied with the performance of their economies [37]. To the authors in this group a serious dissatisfaction with the performance of East European economies is the key to understanding the historic changes of 1989 [44].

It has also been argued by some commentators that other internal factors played as big a role here as economics. Boris Kagarlitsky says psychological factors were equally important. The instability of communist social structures, the destruction of former institutions and the deep crisis that emerged as a result of disappearing traditional networks, all helped to make social psychology an important factor [58]. It has also been claimed that behind the collapse of the East European regimes lay their 'moral hollowness'. This, according to Gale Stokes, made the role played by ideas particularly important. In this view, political ideas have an autonomous strength that is not necessarily rooted in social relations and economic development [108].

The communist parties, paradoxically, played an essential role in their own collapse. According to Poznanski, communist party leaders lacked belief in their own mission. During the 1970s and 1980s, party leaders stopped believing in what used to be perceived as the historic mission of the apparatus [84]. When the party lost its power to command the polity, says Robert Skidelsky, the system stopped working [72]. Ernest Gellner explains this as the major failure of the Brezhnev period. The sleazy but relatively mild squalor of the Brezhnev years proved far more corrosive for the image of the faith than the total, pervasive, random and massively destructive terror of Stalin. When the *nomenklatura* switched from shooting each other to bribing each other faith evaporated [38].

Other authors, like E. P. Thompson, emphasise the role of popular unrest and the protest movements in Eastern Europe in bringing about the collapse of communism [11]. Similarly, as Alan Mayhew says, citizens became more and more convinced that the corrupt and inefficient system of one-party rule and central planning must be swept away, and they freed themselves, at great cost and with practically no outside assistance, from communist rule [74]. The change of regimes came, in the view of Berglund, Hellen and Aarebrot, from within and mainly as a result of an alliance between the working class and the intellectuals [9]. According to Norman Davies, it seems that a generation which had lost the pervasive fear of the Stalinist era suddenly decided that enough was enough [24].

In the view of the second category of authors, the collapse of the communist regimes of Eastern Europe should not be attributed simply to the internal factors, that is the severity of the economic, political, social and ideological crises over which the regimes presided during the 1980s. According to this view, external factors were critical in understanding the timing and particular patterns of the collapse. The most popular reason for the collapse, according to this category of historians, was the leadership of Gorbachev in the Soviet Union. Nothing would have happened if Gorbachev had not tried to reform socialism in the Soviet Union, says Karen Dawisha [25]. Michael Waller writes, in *The End of the Communist Power Monopoly* (1994), that the path to 1989 was laid by a reforming Soviet leadership under Mikhail Gorbachev. In Waller's view, Gorbachev's policies undermined state socialism economically, ideologically and politically. The organising principles of the centrally managed and controlled economy were cast in doubt. The party's dominant role was destroyed as a result. Collapse of the monopoly in the Soviet Union meant collapse across the region [122].

Other authors tend to attribute the historic changes of 1989 to the policies of the Western leaders – to the 'renaissance of the market economy' under Reagan and Thatcher and to the uncompromising and confrontational policies of the West towards the Soviet Union [20]. It has been claimed by Leslie Holmes that the determination of the United States to proceed with the Strategic Defence Initiative ('Star Wars') in the 1990s was an important reason for the deepening of the crisis of the Soviet bloc. The Soviet Union had neither the technological nor the pecuniary wherewithal to move to this new stage of the arms race [52].

Finally, there are some authors in this category who explain the collapse of the communist system in Eastern Europe in the context of wider global developments in the late twentieth century. The state socialism collapsed, says Attila Agh, because of the globalisation of the world system [4]. It is important, says Robin Blackburn, that one has to set the communist failure into an international context. In this view, the socialist system did not fail in any absolute sense. It was rather a comparative failure that provided the basis for the collapse [11]. Similarly, what was determinant was, says Fred Halliday, the global context, and in particular the relative record of communism compared with its competitor, advanced capitalism. Halliday argues, in his *Revolution and World Politics* (1999), that communism competed with capitalism on a world scale, and that the factors leading to the collapse were in considerable measure international in character [45].

The affects of globalisation have been observed at different levels as well. Zbigniev Brzezinski points to increased communication and travel, and the resulting spread of new ideas. He also emphasises that the proliferation of East–West civil association and media accessibility has been an important factor in the collapse of the socialist state systems [15]. In his view, the countries of the Soviet bloc could not insulate themselves from the capitalist world any more. In the most obvious field of all, communications, it became increasingly possible for people within communist states to hear and see what was happening in the outside world. This 'demonstration effect' accelerated the momentum of change and made each revolution faster than its predecessor, effecting a 'domino collapse' of Soviet-dependent regimes across Eastern Europe, says Raymond Pearson [81]. Writing in 1990, George Steiner claimed that it was a 'TV-revolution' and a rush towards the 'California-promise' that America has offered to the common man [in 43 *pp. 129–32*].

The events of 1989–90 were clearly too multi-faceted to be subject to simple explanation or attributed to any single variable. It is not surprising that there are many different approaches in explaining an historical change of such magnitude and complexity. Each of these approaches is valid in so far as it grasps fragments of the overall picture of change in Eastern European states. This book is based on this rich and colourful literature. Much of it has proved invaluable in the preparation of this volume. It is contended here that there was no one single cause or set of causes to explain the collapse. The approach adopted in this book is that the fall of communism has to be considered as a multi-causal phenomenon involving internal and external factors, some being long-term and structural while others are contingent.

AIMS OF THIS BOOK

The primary aim of this book is to provide a general narrative, in one single volume, to explain the process of change in Eastern Europe since 1970. In doing this, emphasis has been placed on understanding the forces and general patterns that made the historic changes in 1989 possible. My main concern is, therefore, with the process of change. How did it occur? Why did it occur when it did? How is one to describe the internal logic of this failure? What earlier developments prepared the ground for change? Why did it take different forms in different countries?

I have not sought to provide a detailed narrative. It is practically impossible to describe national developments in each East European state in detail in one single volume. However, the tremendous variety of national experiences and the increasing diversity in Eastern Europe in the 1970s and 1980s make it difficult to generalise and require a particular attention to the national differences. An effort has been made here to follow the general aspects of change in each East European state and identify the similarities as well as differences. The main chapters are arranged in a country-by-country basis so that it should be possible to refer easily to the relevant experience of an East European country at any point. In doing so, I hope to expose the particularities of each society more clearly.

An analysis of the process of change in Eastern Europe since 1970 involves many factors of variable weight, working in changing combinations. It is easy to write that all factors were important and that one should not attempt to arrange them according to degree of importance. In fact, decisions about their relative importance and the structure of the account are inextricably linked. The chapters that follow provide a framework for investigating the forces driving the process of change in Eastern Europe since 1970.

The main text in this book is divided into three parts. Part One, Background, looks at Eastern Europe between Stalin's death in 1953 and 1969, and aims to give an overview of the region as a whole and to the individual countries around the end of the 1960s. Part Two is divided into three chapters. The first, Politics, explores the political developments of Eastern Europe during the 1970s and 1980s. The next chapter, East European Economies, is devoted to an investigation of economic issues during the same period. This chapter will provide an understanding of the process of economic decline since this is considered to be the most important long-term underlying cause of the collapse of the socialist state systems. Chapter 5, The Collapse, addresses the origins, reasons and the actual process of the collapse of the East European state-socialist regimes at the end of the 1980s. It is in this chapter that I aim to provide a clear analysis of the interaction of the structural, long-term and contingent factors leading to the collapse of the communist regimes of Eastern Europe. Chapter 6 in Part Three, Post-Communist Transitions: Old Patterns, New Trends, deals with the period after the collapse of the regimes and looks at the major problems and dilemmas that have had to be confronted during the transition to democracy and the market economy.

PART ONE   BACKGROUND

CHAPTER TWO

EASTERN EUROPE AFTER STALIN, 1953–69

Stalin's death in March 1953 was an important event for Eastern Europe. De-Stalinisation, the change of leadership in Moscow and in most Eastern European countries, had important repercussions for the social, economic and political order in all of the East European countries. The new Soviet leadership began to pursue a more tolerant policy towards Eastern Europe. In 1955, Nikita Khrushchev and Georgi Malenkov, party leader and head of state, respectively, visited Belgrade and apologised to Tito for expelling Yugoslavia from the Cominform (the Communist Information Bureau which was founded and controlled by the Soviet Union in 1947 and dissolved in 1956). In Hungary, the Soviet leadership moved to end the Stalinist practice of placing the offices of both prime minister and general secretary in the hands of one man, Matyas Rákosi, head of the Hungarian party. All these steps and serious encouragement from Moscow initiated a series of new trends in Eastern Europe. The Stalinist uniformity of the political and economic systems of the East European states gave way to increasing diversity. The worst excesses of the police terror came to an end. Economic concessions to the people became more acceptable and feasible. In this new climate of relaxation, many in Eastern Europe wanted to go further, and in two countries (Hungary and Czechoslovakia) they came close to succeeding [6; 33].

When Stalin died, the economic resources of the Soviet Union and its European satellites were dangerously overstretched. Stalin's heirs received calls for help and warnings of impending disaster from the East European states within months of taking office. They were quick to react to the worsening situation. In April 1953, Moscow began to evolve a new line which provided for concessions to the farmers, workers and consumers, and for foreign policy initiatives aimed at bringing about a relaxation of tension in international relations with a view to slowing down the arms race. The resulting relaxation Stalin's successors announced after his death had different echoes in Eastern Europe. Leaderships were shuffled, concessions were made to popular discontent, secret police powers were curtailed and a limited degree of democracy was introduced in some countries. The essential system, however, remained the same: the communist parties led; the police were empowered to intervene as a last resort; and the final word on major decisions remained with the Soviet leaders in the Kremlin [70].

Although Eastern Europe, as a regional label, encouraged facile gener-alisations where a less aggregative perspective might be more appropriate, the region was never uniform. It was, in fact, divided into two tiers: the Balkans in the south-east, and East-Central Europe in the north-west. At the beginning of the communist period, those Balkan countries were less urban and more rural than the East-Central Europeans – Poland, Hungary, Czechoslovakia and the GDR. There were marked differences in the political cultures as well. During the communist period, geopolitics and different political cultures created further profound differences in the way the communist regimes operated in the region [69; 76].

EAST-CENTRAL EUROPE

The German Democratic Republic (GDR)

Walter Ulbricht, a communist leader who had been in exile in the Soviet Union since 1933, was a dominant figure in the GDR. The Ulbricht regime in the German Democratic Republic was one that resisted the calls for reform, the so-called 'New Course' (a relaxation in the drive for the socialisation of the economy). Instead of adopting measures calculated to ease the situation of the population, the ruling elite in East Germany imposed new and higher work norms accompanied by corresponding wage increases. From the 1960s onwards, the GDR's economic planners placed a continuing emphasis on consumer goods, attempting to satisfy the demand for improved living standards, and on social policy, education and welfare provision.

In 1963–64, various observers of the GDR expected that the economic reforms would sooner or later bring about basic political changes. Others believed that the economic reforms were themselves to be equated with po-litical liberalisation. Still, with increasing living standards and an improved economy, the East German state seemed firmly placed without any serious challenge on the horizon.

When the Warsaw Pact forces moved in to crush the reformist move-ment in Czechoslovakia in 1968, East German troops were among them. The 1968 constitution described the GDR as 'a socialist state of the German nation', referring to the goal of unification 'on the basis of demo-cracy and socialism' [185 p. 205].

Hungary

The impact of Stalin's death and the ensuing relaxation of the more arbitrary forms of repression was felt everywhere in the bloc but nowhere more dramatically than in Hungary. Only three months after Stalin's death a group of Hungarian leaders were invited to Moscow to discuss the possibilities of a 'New Course' in Hungary. This was a reaction to the popular protests and strikes in Hungary in August 1953. The Soviet Politburo attacked the Stalinist leader of Hungary, Rákosi, and pushed for change from all sides. Although Rákosi retained his position as First Secretary of the Party, a reform-minded person, Imre Nagy, was appointed premier on the spot. Nagy was strongly supported by Malenkov. He spoke for those who welcomed the so-called 'New Course' and he immediately initiated some economic reforms, following Malenkov's similar economic policies in the Soviet Union. The peasants were given permission to leave the collectives, the number of private farms increased, investment in heavy industry fell dramatically, and the real wages of the industrial workers increased reasonably. There were some developments on the political and social side as well. The internment camps were closed and the '*kulak* lists' were abolished.

By early 1955, however, the wind from the east changed direction. In Moscow, Malenkov's star began to wane, and Khrushchev's to rise. In January 1955, the Hungarian leaders were called to Moscow again. This time, Nagy was reprimanded for encouraging factionalism in the Party. His stance was too liberal for the old guard of the Party. When, in February 1955, Malenkov was demoted in Moscow, Nagy was condemned as a revisionist and right-wing opportunist, and was urged to resign. He was dismissed as prime minister and expelled from the Party. Now Rákosi, back in power, tried to reverse the 'New Course'. But a return to Stalinist economic policies was not easy to implement. Khrushchev's economic policies and political programme in the Soviet Union were not yet clear. Having pushed out Malenkov, Khrushchev too proceeded to initiate his own version of de-Stalinisation. When Rákosi attempted to arrest 400 of his opponents, Moscow pushed for his resignation. Eventually he was replaced by Ernö Gerö, another member of his team. Soon Gerö proved to be unable to control the situation in Hungary. There was a number of sources of strong opposition: the revolt of the press against censorship and despotic methods in the cultural field, student protests around the 'Petofi Circle', which was originally set up as the official Party youth organisation, and a wave of workers' protests and strikes.

When the Party failed to control the protest movement, the impact of the movement extended much further. New aims were added by the now even more optimistic protesters. Extreme demands, like 'Soviet forces to leave our homeland', or 'democratically elected party leadership', appeared. On 23 October 1956, large numbers of demonstrators besieged the Hungarian Parliament and surrounded the radio building. All this resulted in a full-scale gun battle between demonstrators and the security forces. Soon after, serious street fighting spread throughout the country. Revolutionary councils sprang up everywhere and power passed into the hands of the councils at local level [198].

The Warsaw Pact was little more than a year old when the Hungarian crisis erupted, and the organisation as such played little part in its resolution. The Soviet Union used mainly its own forces to restore authority. There seems to have been no coordination through Warsaw Pact channels, as opposed to Soviet consultation with other East European leaders.

On 4 November 1956, 2,000 Soviet tanks, supported by 150,000 soldiers, went into action in Budapest. Scattered fighting occurred. But soon, with no serious armed opposition, the Soviet soldiers were in control. Between November 1956 and October 1957, 20,000 people were arrested, 2,000 were executed and thousands were deported to camps in the Soviet Union [201; 206].

'The Hungarian uprising of 1956' showed that the country desired to emerge from Stalinism with national independence, the restoration of democracy and a full disintegration of the leading position of the Communist Party. However, this path failed. After the suppression of the uprising, the ruling party re-instituted a large part of the old Stalinist political system [33; 198].

Czechoslovakia

As in Hungary in 1956, the Czechoslovak reform movement began within the ruling party. The crisis arose out of a combination of several factors, the most important of which related to the economic problems the country faced. The accumulated problems of a distorted industrial structure, an adverse trade situation, an ageing or obsolete production base, relatively low labour productivity and wasteful utilisation of production resources had, by the early 1960s, assumed such huge proportions that any quick resolution of Czechoslovakia's economic problems seemed out of the question. The structural deformations were inextricably linked with the centralised bureaucratic system of economic control. Ultimately, it was the command system of administration, with its tight control over planning and the allocation of supplies, and its counterproductive and distorting initiatives, which had become the insurmountable obstacle to any structural reform.

The discontent was felt by every stratum in the country, and by each national component as well. There was widespread dissatisfaction among the working people, and a number of economists openly began to criticise the existing economic model. The role of Slovakia and Slovak nationalism was central to the crisis. Slovakia, which was less economically advanced and culturally different from the Czech lands, had always felt exploited by the Czechs and the Slovaks became openly hostile to the ruling Czechs. A growing number of political and economic figures, openly supported by large segments of the population, came to realise the necessity for radical economic reform. Václav Havel, then a young dissident playwright and essayist, was among those intellectuals who thought that 'socialism with a human face' was possible in Czechoslovakia. Many authors, too, agree that 'reform communism' in Czechoslovakia in 1968 had a better prospect of success than anywhere else in Eastern Europe [33].

As a result, a majority of the Communist Party of Czechoslovakia's (CPC) Central Committee adopted a reform programme in 1965. The reform was to eliminate some of the centralised bureaucratic system of planning and administering the economy by commands from the centre. The reform anticipated the revitalisation of some of the economic functions of the market, of prices and of money. Socialist enterprises were to be transformed back into independent, profit-oriented market entities, and the state was to limit itself to blocking monopolistic tendencies among the enterprises and seeing to it that pressures of domestic and foreign competition acted to force enterprises to operate efficiently. A system of self-administration in all sectors of the economy was key to this reform programme [173].

Despite the widespread support for the reform programme, the conservative political leadership and most of the bureaucratic apparatus resisted and obstructed all moves towards the purposeful introduction of new measures. In this way, the fight for economic reform turned into a political struggle aimed first at toppling Novotny and then at democratising the entire political system. When Novotny was replaced by Alexander Dubček, a reform communist, in January 1968, there followed the Czechoslovak 'Spring', a start at the consistent implementation of the reform programme [180] [*Doc. 1*].

In the night of 20–21 August 1968, more than half a million troops of the Warsaw Pact countries, with the exception of Romania, invaded Czechoslovakia. The invading units of the Soviet Union, Poland, East Germany, Hungary and Bulgaria met with no military resistance but with the virtually unanimous passive resistance of the population. They were confronted with a continual barrage of hostile propaganda. At the height of the crisis, when the deadlock became patent and the passive resistance of the population threatened to erupt any moment into a violent confrontation with the occupation forces, the Czechoslovak president went to Moscow to negotiate a solution with the Soviet leadership. After four days of negotiations, the Soviet leaders agreed to return the interned Czechoslovak politicians to power in exchange for the promise that the situation in Czechoslovakia would be normalised. The invasion and the following measures put a clear stop to any future developments of reform communism in Eastern Europe [179].

Why did the invasion take place? Although it still seems difficult to find a definitive answer, Ben Fowkes provides a convincing argument: the Soviet leaders feared that, as a result of the logical culmination of the reform process, the Communist Party would lose power eventually [33].

Poland

While in every other country of Eastern Europe the rulers resisted the moves towards liberalisation introduced after Stalin's death by Malenkov under the slogan of the 'New Course', the Polish party leaders introduced the New Course in Poland themselves. The fall of Malenkov, therefore, did not have the devastating impact that it had had in Hungary. The beginning of de-Stalinisation, signalled by Khrushchev's speech at the February 1956 Soviet Party Congress, was taken up with some enthusiasm in Poland [214].

The communist regime in Poland entered the 1970s with Wladyslaw Gomułka as its head. In the 1950s and early 1960s, he had rejected the Soviet blueprint for Poland and had become one of the most outspoken advocates of a 'national road' to socialism. Along this line, in January 1960, the Polish Catholic Church and state reached an accord, reportedly after a secret meeting between Gomułka and Cardinal Wyszynki. In the second half of the 1960s, however, Gomułka's regime degenerated and by the end of the decade it was hard to distinguish it from a survival of Stalinism. Poland's participation in the Warsaw Pact invasion of Czechoslovakia in 1968 was a low point in this process. By this time, Gomułka had become reliant on the support of a strongly anti-liberal element within the Party [221; 225].

THE BALKANS

Albania

After years of party infighting and extermination campaigns against the country's anti-communist opposition, Enver Hoxha and Mehmet Shehu emerged as the dominant figures in Albania. They concentrated primarily on securing and maintaining their power base and secondly on preserving Albania's independence and reshaping the country according to the precepts of orthodox Stalinism. Under Hoxha, Albania became more and more isolated during decades of hardline Stalinism, which was characterised externally by dramatic rifts with Yugoslavia and then with the Soviet Union.

Albania's economy relied heavily on foreign assistance. After Albania's break with Yugoslavia in late 1948, Albania became a client of the Soviet Union for twelve years. Having relatively easy access to capital because of generous Soviet aid, the regime doubled its industrialisation drive. Considering Enver Hoxha's obsession with heavy industry misguided, the new Soviet leadership turned down the idea of investing in large-scale industrial projects in Albania after Stalin's death. The Albanian leadership's fixation on heavy industry contributed significantly to its decision to break with the Soviet Union. There were also political reasons for Albania's steady alienation from the Soviet Union in the late 1950s. Enver Hoxha found Khrushchev's revisionism unacceptable. He was especially offended by Khrushchev's denigration of Stalin in 1956. Khrushchev's policy also implied an end to absolutist rule in Tirana, which Hoxha would not contemplate. Fearful of what Khrushchev's revisionism might do to his policies and political power base in Albania, Hoxha was quick to side with the Chinese leadership. Enver Hoxha gambled that China not only would be less likely than the Soviet Union to threaten his authority but also would be more likely to provide investment money and equipment for his industrial projects. In the 1960s, thanks mainly to massive capital inflows from China, the Albanian economy expanded considerably [135; 136].

Bulgaria

Bulgaria was under the leadership of Todor Zhivkov from 1962. Zhivkov's long period in power was characterised by loyalty to the prevailing Soviet regime. He even put to Khrushchev the suggestion that Bulgaria might join the Soviet Union. Under Zhivkov, Bulgaria distinguished itself as the most docile of all East European countries in following the Soviet line. In Bulgaria the communist party probably enjoyed more genuine popular support than in any other state except Czechoslovakia before 1968. Like the pre-1968 Czechoslovak party, the Bulgarian party had long, historic roots and enjoyed a great deal of electoral support whenever the electoral system had allowed a free vote [150].

To Bulgaria, the Soviet connection had been of enormous importance. Its rapid industrialisation from the start was carried out with Soviet technical and financial aid. Bulgaria was also dependent on the Soviet Union in terms of its energy requirements. Like the other East European states, Bulgaria had in the Soviet Union a patron prepared to subsidise it for political reasons. For the same reason, Bulgaria paid a price for its dependence on the Soviet market. Most Bulgarian goods could not be sold on world markets because production was geared to lower Soviet standards [152].

Romania

In the 1960s, Romania cultivated the good opinion of the West. This was achieved on the basis of a maverick foreign policy, an anomaly in the otherwise monolithic stance of the Soviet bloc countries. The Sino-Soviet split gave the Romanian leadership unexpected room for manoeuvre. Romania retained links with China and with Israel. Nicolae Ceausescu, who came to power in 1965, broadened the independent line into a direct appeal to Romanian nationalism in every sphere of life. He received an initial boost of popularity for defying the Soviet Union. The Romanian leadership refused to participate in the 1968 invasion of Czechoslovakia, and (together with the Albanian and Yugoslav leaders) publicly condemned it. This critical independence was probably tolerated by Moscow only because of Romania's relative strategic unimportance. From Moscow's point of view, an independent Romanian foreign policy was actually never considered a serious threat [229].

Romania based its economic strategy under the communist regime in the hope that its natural resources, particularly oil, would allow it fast industrial development. The Soviet Union, however, had a different idea for the Romanian economy: it was to be the Soviet bloc's granary. Romania rejected this and broke away from Soviet economic control in the early 1960s. It reduced its trade dependence on the rest of the Soviet bloc in the late 1960s. This was helped by the fact that Ceausescu was widely fêted in the West, notably in the United States and the United Kingdom, and Romania was admitted as a member of the international financial community in the early 1970s [237].

Yugoslavia

Following Stalin's death, the Yugoslav leaders were at first hesitant towards the developments in the Soviet Union. However, Soviet–Yugoslav relations improved regularly during the first couple of years after Stalin's death. Khrushchev, in due time, shrewdly softened the Yugoslav leadership by condemning Stalin and his secret-police henchman Beria for the past troubles. Khrushchev was hoping to be the restorer of socialist unity, which would enhance his prestige at home and increase his ability to dictate his will in the people's democracies and in China. The initial steps were sufficient to enable Khrushchev and other top Soviet leaders to be received by Tito on 26 May 1955. Each side now conceded that the other was 'socialist' and not 'degenerate' or 'fascist' as the previous polemics had charged [281].

From the second half of the 1950s onwards, nationally related tensions made themselves felt in Yugoslavia. In this category, the 'Albanian question', or the situation of the Albanians living in the Kosovo province of Serbia, appeared to be probably the most sensitive nationally-related issue in Yugoslavia. Towards the end of the 1960s and during the 1970s, the events here would try the limits of national integralism in Yugoslavia. At first, the tensions were economically conditioned. The separate power centres of the communist leadership in the individual republics had an impact for the first time. Their economic interests had come to coincide with those of the population within the individual republics. For example, general dissatisfaction predominated in Slovenia because large funds were redirected from this relatively more developed republic via the federal budget to the less developed parts of Yugoslavia. The economic discussions arising from this issue in the late 1950s led many Yugoslavs to believe that a new nationalism based exclusively on unresolved economic problems could arise. From this it followed that acceptable economic solutions would dampen ethnic stirrings.

Economically, Yugoslavia experienced success in the 1960s. By the end of the decade, growth in the Yugoslav economy was higher than in other socialist countries and, in fact, among the highest in Europe [283].

PART TWO   ANALYSIS

CHAPTER THREE

POLITICS

Two important developments of the late 1960s, one in the attitude of the Soviet leadership in the Kremlin and the other in the area of East–West relations, are important for understanding the general international political context of the 1970s. A few months after the brutal Soviet response to socialist humanism in Czechoslovakia in 1968, Soviet leader Leonid Brezhnev told a meeting of the Polish United Workers' Party that when a transition to socialism takes place anywhere, the Soviet Union considers that transition to be irreversible, and he pledged to back up that view with force. This was what in the West came to be called the 'Brezhnev Doctrine', or the 'doctrine of limited sovereignty' [171]. Although the Soviet leaders maintained that there never was such a thing as a 'Brezhnev Doctrine', until the mid-1980s most observers, East and West, believed that Brezhnev's statement constituted a fundamental principle of Soviet policy towards the communist states of Eastern Europe. The Brezhnev Doctrine threw into doubt the possibility of creating 'socialism with a human face' in Eastern Europe. It appeared that any changes undermining the dominant position of the ruling parties would be met by Soviet force, as they had been in 1956 and 1968.

In 1969, a few days after Willy Brandt's Social Democratic Party took sole power for the first time in the Federal Republic of Germany, Brandt introduced a new foreign policy initiative, his *Ostpolitik* [36]. He was a firm believer in the unavoidable need for reconciliation and cooperation with Eastern Europe [*Doc. 2*]. This new atmosphere, known as *détente* in East–West relations, sought to create a vested interest in cooperation and restraint, an environment in which competitors could regulate and restrain their differences and ultimately move from competition to cooperation. *Détente*, however, was not meant to replace the abiding American strategy of containment. Rather, it was meant to be a less confrontational method of containing communism through diplomatic accords and a flexible system of rewards and punishments by which Washington might moderate Soviet behaviour. It was a general expectation in the West that this carrot-and-stick approach would establish 'rules of the game' and recognised spheres of influence. This atmosphere of relaxation led to treaties with the Soviet Union and with Poland, and in 1973 to full mutual recognition between East and West Germany. The clearing of this roadblock also in 1973 led to the convening of the Conference on Security and Cooperation in Europe in Helsinki. In return for the acceptance of postwar European borders, the Western statesmen at the conference demanded the addition of a series of clauses to the Final Act that guaranteed certain human rights.

The signing of the Helsinki Final Act in 1975 was the high-point of East–West *détente*. Some observers in the West argued that the Helsinki Accords simply condoned an illegitimate Soviet domination over Eastern Europe. In practice, however, the acceptance by the Soviet Union of the clauses on human rights, and the creation of an ongoing process of review of the agreements, gave the Western powers unprecedented opportunities to question internal policies in the Eastern Bloc. The human rights provisions in the Final Act contributed towards legitimising the East European opposition movements and greatly facilitated their work. Even in the Soviet Union itself, Helsinki Watch groups formed to monitor human rights abuses. The best-known initiative was Charter 77 [*Doc. 3*]. The Charter was signed by 1,500 Czechs and Slovaks, as well as by many intellectuals from other countries. Despite serious repression, the Charter 77 movement continued its work in Czechoslovakia right up to the fall of the single-party regime in 1989 [167].

The Soviet Union showed increasing interest, in this period, in a relaxation of tension in Europe, both as a means of strengthening its overall strategic and political position in the continent and as a means of obtaining direct benefit for its economy. The 1970s East–West *détente* facilitated increasing inflows of western capital and technology into the socialist economies [17; 57]. In the final analysis, however, it was the Soviet presence in Eastern Europe that imposed limits to change for the states within the orbit of Soviet military might. Indigenous political forces in the region caused deviations from the Soviet model and shaped national attitudes as well as social responses to the ruling communist parties. It was this interplay of two key sets of forces – the presence and policies of the Soviet Union and social forces for change within East European societies – that shaped the way the East European societies developed in this period. Outside influences encouraged the deviant patterns [31; 70].

1970s: A PERIOD OF NORMALISATION AND THE 'BREZHNEV DOCTRINE'

The invasion of Czechoslovakia ended the 'viability' phase of Soviet policy in Eastern Europe. It was the period of the 'Brezhnev Doctrine', which justified intervention, as in 1968, to prevent socialism in any particular country and in the socialist community as a whole being threatened. In the aftermath of the invasion of Czechoslovakia, East European domestic strategies were shaped by a combination of the legacy of the Prague Spring and other reform movements of the late 1960s on the one hand, and the potential threat of Soviet military intervention to prevent change on the other. The Soviet leaders moved to restore unity and coherence in Eastern Europe by initiating an elaborate programme which affected every sphere of Soviet–East European relations. Throughout Eastern European society, to one degree or another, a deep transformation took place in the 1970s.

The suppression and the subsequent liquidation of the reform movements in 1968 and after had ended all hope for the self-regeneration of Soviet-style socialism. Pessimism and apolitical resignation grew everywhere in Eastern European societies. This was variously manifested in apathy, weariness, alienation, corruption and overt dissent. Havel's essay on 'The Power of the Powerless', written in 1978 (published in 1979), was perceptive in describing how one-party state socialisms operated at a day-to-day level [*Doc. 5*]. What was important was not that people deep down believed in the ruling ideology, but that they followed the external rituals and practices by means of which this ideology acquired material existence. Havel's example is the greengrocer, a modest man profoundly indifferent to official ideology. He just mechanically follows the rules. On state holidays, he decorates the window of his shop with official slogans such as 'Long Live Socialism!' When there are mass gatherings he takes part listlessly. He privately complains, however, about the corruption and incompetence of 'those in power', which enables him to legitimise his stance in his own eyes and to retain a false appearance of dignity. This is a wonderful example that shows how the pressures at work maintain the form of the belief even though the content is gone [171].

Following the period of drift and disarray in the late 1960s, the 1970s witnessed a comprehensive drive to promote cohesion by constructing integrative links susceptible to Soviet control and manipulation. The 1968 intervention provided a context for the articulation of the keynote of a new Soviet theory of integration. Brezhnev pursued several avenues designed to make Eastern Europe more stable, less burdensome to Moscow and easier to control. The aim was to secure the consolidation of the 'socialist system'. The integrationist drive of the early 1970s was designed to strengthen the consultative mechanisms of the Warsaw Pact and promote multilateral co-operation. This policy envisaged steps towards integration in four key areas: politics, the military, the economy and culture. New multilateral forums were created and new links were established in these four spheres.

Political integration was carried out within the party–state structural complex. New institutionalised contacts between top leaders and between lower party functionaries helped to organise policies and adjust technical points of party activities. The contacts took place at the international, national and at sub-national levels. The Warsaw Pact facilitated the harmonisation of foreign policy at the state-to-state level.

The command structure of the Warsaw Pact also served to provide the context for further military integration. All member states (with the exception of Romania) shared a Soviet-inspired military doctrine. The Military Political Administration of the Soviet Armed Forces conducted this indoctrination. Furthermore, officers from the Soviet Red Army occupied all key command positions in the Warsaw Pact hierarchy.

Economic integration was undertaken through the COMECON. East Europeans depended heavily on imports of Soviet oil and raw materials and on Soviet markets for their manufactured goods. Economically, Eastern Europe was increasingly a burden to the Soviet Union. The oil shocks of the 1970s made Moscow more aware of the value of the natural resources that Moscow was trading to its partners in exchange for poorly-made machine tools. Yet the political trade-offs involved were considered to be worth the costs.

Cultural integration implied the development of 'internationalist' and 'socialist' perspectives. This was energetically fostered by the Soviet Union, particularly in the fields of social sciences and historiography. The major instruments in this domain were the East European academies of science, which were led by the Soviet academies of science.

The new policy was executed through a largely invisible power apparatus that connected the Communist Party of the Soviet Union (CPSU) with the East European parties. Apart from the Warsaw Pact and COMECON, a host of inter-state institutions was created to coordinate further links. The regional integration policy of the 1970s relied on persuasion and incentives more than on force. After 1968, party programmes were based on an increasingly cynical combination of rigid orthodoxy and overt consumerist appeals. A promise of economic benefits and international contacts, guaranteed under the umbrella of the Soviet Union, and a re-orientation of the national economies were considered as replacements for social and economic reform. This was dictated by the conviction that socialism could only survive and dominate the world if it could win the Darwinian race in terms of material production. This policy priority – the goal of catching up with the West – was not dictated by the Marxist theory itself and turned out to be fatal in the end. To achieve the economic goals, and the much anticipated social and political harmony, the East European regimes relied heavily on subsidised oil from the Soviet Union and Western trade, credits and technology [107; 113]. These measures combined to produce a degree of balance in Eastern Europe during the early 1970s, and their effects were felt in the regional and international sphere.

Of course, there were several formidable obstacles to the overall success of the Soviet integration policy, including socio-economic pressure for democratisation, the prevalent Russophobia and forces of nationalism in the region. The 1970s was the decade in which opposition became a permanent feature of Eastern European social and political life. It was part and parcel of the same process of declining ideological commitment. Especially in East-Central Europe, dissident voices became increasingly organised. Historically, Russophobia affected most of the East Europeans (except the Bulgarians, the Yugoslavs and the Czechs). The Soviets' heavy-handed actions in 1956 and 1968 only exacerbated anti-Russian feeling [70].

Initially, many observers thought that the establishment of Communist Party rule had at last provided a solution to the issue of nationalism. There were good reasons for this optimism. In Romania, a new autonomous region was created for the Hungarian minority. In Bulgaria, minorities enjoyed unprecedented freedom in education, publication and culture. In Yugoslavia, cooperation between the constituent republics was smooth and effective. Soon, however, it became clear that this was a misleading image. Resentments and hostilities were concealed rather than removed. The re-emergence of nationality-based problems occupied the countries, especially in the Balkans, from the mid-1970s onwards. Geopolitics and nationalism created profound differences between the communist regimes in Eastern Europe. These differences took on a Balkans–East-Central Europe dimension.

East–Central Europe

East Germany (GDR) remained a tightly controlled communist state throughout the 1970s: a single-party dictatorship, severe political discipline, involving censorship, and a ubiquitous surveillance of the public by the secret police were the basis of the regime. The Honecker leadership refused to consider reform and would not relax its harsh discipline. Yet the GDR regime always stopped short of brutality, refusing to imitate the Brezhnev regime's draconian suppression of human rights in the Soviet Union in the 1970s.

Politics in the GDR during the 1970s continued to be defined by its special relation to the German Federal Republic, but the nature of the relationship changed. Although this was mainly due to the increasing importance of *détente* in the East–West relations, the change in leadership also played a role in this. In May 1971, Ulbricht had been replaced by Erich Honecker as First Secretary of the Party. Honecker was more of a pragmatist. At the Eighth Party Congress in June 1971, Honecker presented his formulation of a new foreign policy. This was more a *détente*-inspired programme in foreign affairs. The objective of re-uniting Germany under a socialist government was dropped and replaced by 'separate development'.

Implicit reference to the future unification of the two Germanies was dropped altogether. Now the GDR was presented not as an alternative socialist state for the whole of Germany, but a separate state which happened to be socialist. This was followed by a change of the constitution in 1974. The GDR became a 'socialist state of workers and peasants' rather than the 'socialist state of the German nation' as it had been since the 1968 constitution.

Relations with the West improved with a number of agreements. The Four Power Agreement on Berlin of September 1971 was followed with the Basic Treaty with the Federal Republic, which was signed in' December 1972. With these, the status of Berlin was regularised, and the two Germanies pledged to recognise one another's sovereignty. Both countries joined the United Nations in September 1973. Finally, establishing diplomatic relations with the United States in April 1974 represented a considerable diplomatic success for Honecker's regime.

Several dissident groups emerged in the GDR during the 1970s. The most important were the peace and ecology movements, the East German Evangelical Church and many other intelligentsia and youth groups. However, when comparing the political dissent in East Germany to the dissident movements in Poland or in Czechoslovakia, one can see that East German dissent was less significant. Perhaps the most celebrated dissident of the GDR in this period was Rudolf Bahro. He became well-known as the author of *The Alternative in Eastern Europe*, which he wrote during the 1970s while he was a dissident Marxist in the East German Communist Party. The government imprisoned him in 1978 for his dissident activities and writings, but in 1979 he was deported to West Germany, in part due to international protests at his imprisonment [184; 185].

Throughout the 1970s **Hungary** had the reputation, along with East Germany, of being the most successful communist state in the Eastern Bloc. Hungary was under the firm control of János Kádár (1956–88) in this period. He was intolerant of opposition, yet he avoided political and economic extremes as much as he could. He wanted Moscow to support his leadership, but also wanted the Hungarian people to accept his leadership. He managed to find a separate path for Hungary on the basis of his reconciliatory motto, 'those who are not against us are for us'. Accordingly, the Party would not demand the total allegiance of all, in the classic totalitarian model, but appreciated that there could be non-Party contributions to national life. The Hungarians enjoyed a period of relative relaxation. Kádár restored good relations with the West, managed to attract foreign investment (and therefore significant amounts of hard currency) and permitted an expansion of civil liberties. During the 1970s, the communist system enjoyed a higher level of popular acceptability in Hungary than anywhere else in Eastern Europe. In this political stability, Kádár's few limited political reforms and economic liberalisation programme played an important role by improving national economic performance [203; 206].

Czechoslovakia remained under an orthodox and thoroughly dogmatic leadership in the aftermath of the 'Prague Spring' of 1968. 'Normalisation' took two years. Dubček was replaced by Gustáv Husák as First Secretary of the Party on 17 April 1969. Between May 1969 and June 1970 all former reformists were removed from the Central Committee and important party and state positions. On 6 May 1970 Czechoslovakia and the Soviet Union signed a friendship treaty confirming that the defence of socialist achievements was a joint international duty.

The Czechoslovak communist elite showed little sympathy for reforms, fearing that any change would bring instability and foreign interference in the country's economic and political life. Most Czechs and Slovaks tolerated this re-imposed conservatism of their leaders. Indeed, Czechoslovak workers seemed to be satisfied with the security and stability that went with the Husák regime and did not initially involve themselves in any sort of opposition to the regime.

However, the political effects of the economic stagnation in the mid-1970s resulted in the formation of a new protest movement, the Charter 77 movement. Signed in January 1977 and inspired by Czechoslovakia's acceptance of the human rights provisions of the 1975 Helsinki Agreements, Charter 77 accused the government of systematic discrimination in education, employment and other areas of society against citizens critical of its policies [*Doc. 3*]. Václav Havel was the leading spokesman for Charter 77. The government's immediate response to the Charter only increased its profile. The authorities organised an anti-Charter media campaign and between 1977 and 1980 sixty-one chartists were sentenced to imprisonment and at least another 108 were arrested and detained for longer or shorter periods.

Another source of popular resentment was the Catholic Church. In the late 1970s the Church hierarchy, encouraged by Pope John Paul II, who was elected in 1978, began to show sympathy for opponents of the repressive policies of the Husák regime. Many people in this period saw in the Church a way to thumb their noses at the regime without inviting retaliation [173].

Poland's communist system remained fragile in the 1970s. This was mainly due to the reluctance of Polish communist leaders to make systemic changes to sort out the increasing political and economic problems. Due to a succession of economic, social and political crises, Poland remained the Achilles' heel of the Eastern bloc in this period. The significant number of workers' strikes and demonstrations, almost all of which started in the Baltic ports of Poland, led to this period being labelled 'the Baltic crisis'.

On 12 December 1970 the government announced food price increases averaging about 30 per cent. Soon demonstrations began in the Gdansk

Lenin Shipyard and spread to other Baltic cities. Within a few days there were further demonstrations and a general strike. Everywhere, including in Warsaw, there were clashes between demonstrators and the police. Over the weekend of 19–20 December the Central Committee removed Wladyslaw Gomułka from power and replaced him with Edward Gierek. Gomułka himself had become identified with the retention of tight party controls and with a failure to tackle the endemic problems of the industry-oriented command economy. Gierek sought to confirm the regime's orthodoxy by amending the constitution in February 1976. He pronounced Poland to be a socialist state, confirmed the leading role of the Party and strengthened Polish loyalty to the Soviet Union. The conflict generated by this constitutional change was sufficient for the demise of the independent Catholic group (*Znak*) in parliament [214; 225].

The economic situation did not improve under Gierek's leadership. When the government decided to increase food prices for basic foodstuffs, violent riots broke out in several places. The government's aggressive tactics in dealing with the opposition succeeded in uniting the students and the intelligentsia with the workers. After a number of uncoordinated protests, in September 1976 the Committee for the Defence of Workers (KOR) was formed in Warsaw to aid those workers who had been imprisoned [*Doc. 4*] [219].

The main legacy of the decade under Gierek was the growth of the *nomenklatura*, the system for the appointment of a communist bureaucracy which permeated every area of public life, from government and local administration to industrial management, media, education and the arts. The *nomenklatura* provided a broad base for corruption and favouritism.

The Balkans

Albania was one of the most reactionary Stalinist dictatorships in Eastern Europe. Following the Chinese example, in the 1970s there were ruthless purges of political moderates in and outside the Communist Party, and large numbers of people were routinely moved from the cities to the countryside.

The second half of the 1970s saw the end of Albania's special relationship with China. After the break with the Soviet Union in 1961, China had stepped in and financed the building of Albania's basic industrial infrastructure, and Tirana had shifted its loyalties from Moscow to Beijing. After Mao's death in 1975, China rejected much of his Stalinism and the Albanian communists eventually broke with Beijing in the late 1970s. For the rest of the communist era, Albania was completely isolated with very few foreign friends. In August 1975, Albania was invited to the Conference on Security and Cooperation in Europe but refused to participate. It was the only European country not to sign the Helsinki Final Act.

In 1976, a new constitution was passed which recognised the Party as the sole directing power in state and society. Enver Hoxha remained firmly in command; politically he was unchallenged. He underpinned his vision of Albania with a formidable xenophobia. Fear of invasion inspired outlandish policies that became a focus of fascinated disbelief outside the country. Hoxha used the country's geographical and political isolation to implement a policy of terror and repression. No ruling Communist Party in the Eastern bloc experienced purges like the Albanian Party. This self-perpetuating mechanism of ruthless purges was the direct result of Hoxha's intense paranoia. Albania's very isolation contributed to this rise of a kind of cultish logging of craziness. Hoxha's name, image, works and monuments became all-pervasive. He sought to glorify Albania's isolation as a mark of its integrity in pursuing the one true road to socialism. Albania remained fully Stalinist, totally collectivised and utterly isolated. Private property was banned, religion officially abolished and foreign economic assistance renounced. Opponents of Hoxha were dealt with in ruthless purges. The last of several leading Party members to commit suicide, as the official accounts described it, was Mehmet Shehu, a veteran of the Spanish Civil War, in 1981 after twenty-seven years as prime minister. He was attacked *post mortem* as an agent of both the Central Intelligence Agency (CIA) and the KGB [131; 140; 142].

Bulgaria remained a repressive authoritarian communist state in the 1970s. Communist leader Todor Zhivkov firmly controlled the state and society with harsh censorship, a ubiquitous secret police and a ruthless suppression of dissent. A striking aspect of this authoritarian system was Zhivkov's policy of assimilating the country's Turkish-speaking minority of 2 million people – 15 per cent of the total population. This policy was inspired by Bulgarian nationalism, which was fed by a hypersensitivity to national identity born of an insecurity complex caused by the several centuries of Ottoman-Turkish occupation. Bulgarians also feared that the country might eventually be overwhelmed by the Turkish-speaking minority due to the high birth rate among Muslims. The Communist Party leadership reacted by dismissing ethnic differences and claiming that all citizens of Bulgaria are Bulgarians.

In 1971 Bulgaria passed a new constitution by which it technically became an 'advanced' socialist state. The Party's role was strengthened to become the 'leading force in society and state' [23 *p. 353*]. The constitution also introduced a State Council in place of the Presidium of the National Assembly. Zhivkov took on its presidency, relinquishing the premiership.

No really significant dissident movement emerged in Bulgaria in the 1970s. Only three or four minor manifestations of open opposition to the Bulgarian Communist Party are recorded. The most significant of these came in 1978, in the wake of the Charter 77 movement in Czechoslovakia.

An anonymous Bulgarian group published a six-point manifesto entitled 'Declaration 78', but the group did not develop a significant base. The regime, however, reacted to all potential sources of opposition in a ruthless fashion. The small number of dissidents were not safe even when they left Bulgaria and settled in the West. Georgi Markov, a dissident writer, died in London in 1978, having been stabbed with a poisonous umbrella, by an unknown assailant suspected of being a Bulgarian agent.

Diplomatic relations with West Germany were established in 1973, and Zhivkov visited the Vatican in 1975. The main characteristic of Bulgarian foreign policy remained loyalty to the Soviet Union. Not only in foreign affairs, but also in all aspects of political life, Zhivkov's government followed the Soviet leadership more sheepishly than any other East European state. It used to be said that when the Soviet Union sneezed East-Central Europe caught a cold and Bulgaria came down with influenza. Jokes such as this were numerous in the Eastern Bloc and reflected the way in which the Zhivkov regime obediently followed the direction of, and directives from, the Kremlin [152; 159; 165].

Under the leadership of Ceausescu, **Romania** had already been consolidated firmly as a neo-Stalinist dictatorship by the 1970s. Ceausescu's despotism united all the elements of a typical totalitarian regime: ideological uniformity, single-party rule under a single leader, the use of terror and the state control of society, communications and the economy. Like his predecessor Dej, Ceausescu was intensely nationalistic, paying only lip service to the Soviet-led perception of 'proletarian internationalism'. His nationalism was based on the pride most Romanians have in the historical origins of their society. They claim that the history of their society goes back to the Roman Empire, which they think distinguishes them from their Slavic neighbours. This nationalism was also affected by Romania's experience of tsarist and Soviet Russia in the nineteenth and twentieth centuries. Romanians deeply resented the loss of Bessarabia, Romania's north-eastern province, to Russia in 1878. Romania regained this province in 1918, only to lose it again to the Soviet Union in 1940. Romanian nationalism reached extremes in the 1970s finding expression in the official oppression of Hungarians in Transylvania and the persecution of Jews still living in Romania following the Second World War. Ceausescu used nationalism to distract the attention of his people from the increasing harshness of daily life.

Romania continued its combination of foreign policy independence abroad and nationalistic Stalinism at home throughout the 1970s. Standing up to Moscow helped make Ceausescu a hero in Romania. He increased Party involvement in the whole society. Political institutions were subjected to much change and innovation, usually in the name of extending democracy. Workers' Councils and numerous joint Party–state organs were created, and even multi-candidate elections to the parliament were introduced in the 1970s. All these measures, however, served to increase the power of the Party. By the second half of the 1970s, the Party was increasingly becoming synonymous with Ceausescu and his family. Three of those promoted to the Permanent Bureau of the Party's Central Committee in 1977 were his relatives. Ceausescu's own personality cult was unrivalled. By the end of the 1970s, he was Secretary General of the Romanian Communist Party, President of the Republic and the Council of State, Chairman of the Front of Socialist Unity and Democracy, Chairman of the Supreme Council for Economic and Social Development, and much more.

From the early 1970s onwards, Ceausescu expanded the role and scope of the *Securitate*, his notorious security service. It employed tens of thousands of active service officers, and possibly hundreds of thousands of informers who reported on the activities of citizens in every nook and cranny of society. The role of the terror practised by the *Securitate* should not be underestimated. The Poles, the Hungarians and the Czechoslovaks never faced a police apparatus of such brutal effectiveness [228; 238; 253].

Yugoslavia enjoyed a growing political influence abroad, especially in the Third World, in this period. Its impressive economic record in the 1970s provided many Yugoslav citizens with a standard of living that compared favourably with that in other socialist countries. Politically, Tito's Yugoslavia was based on military power, communist ideology and a forceful personality. However, he respected the unique diversity of Yugoslav society.

While insisting on political conformity and a Stalinist command economy, Tito allowed the large ethnic groups that dominated the six constituent republics that made up the Yugoslav federation substantial political and administrative autonomy. In the immediate postwar period, Yugoslavia undertook a strict policy of 'brotherhood and unity', by which each national group received positions in the Party and the state proportional to its size and in which linguistic and cultural diversity was recognised and encouraged. In a new constitution adopted in 1974, Tito made changes in the structure of the federal government in Belgrade to provide further means of reconciling disagreements between different ethnic groups.

Perhaps the most serious crisis in this period happened in Croatia. Events in the late 1960s, particularly the so-called 'Croatian Spring' of 1968–71, showed how sensitive ethnic-national questions were in the Yugoslav experience. It became apparent that although economic problems and a sense of economic backwardness played a large role during the onset of the crisis in Croatia, in the final analysis these economic discussions were actually only a starting point for the articulation of a much more general and deeply felt emotional current. The perception that Croatia and the Croats were being exploited by the Serbs began to grow through the mobilisation of nationalist groups. In other words, at issue was nationalism with all its ramifications.

The uncertainty of the leadership in the face of the revival of national movements caused the Party to look for theoretical concepts that might resolve these contradictions in the multi-national state of Yugoslavia. It was felt that a 'Yugoslav consciousness' must be created that could appeal to both patriotic and ethnic feelings. That implied promoting Yugoslav national integralism. In 1967, Tito stated before the communists of Belgrade that the term 'Yugoslav' meant 'membership in our socialist community but not a nationality'.

However, it was probably these attempts to stimulate a renewed Yugoslav integralism which played a large role in the rise of the national movement in Croatia during 1968–71. This movement consisted of an emotional reaction against 'unitarism' and 'centralism' in any form. It stressed the independence and equal rights of the nations within the federal structure to the point of reviving the 'right to secede'. The Croatian crisis became a crucial turning point in the evolution of the nationality question in Yugoslavia.

Tito ordered a thorough crackdown on nationalist manifestations in 1971. Protests by militant students led to the use of riot police, and the political climate turned fully against nationalism. Tens of thousands of members were expelled from the Party. Several nationalists, including Franjo Tudjman, were imprisoned and the media, student organisations and university departments in Croatia were purged. National aspirations were, however, accorded more consideration in the ensuing years. The principle of statehood for the individual republics became accepted and was adopted first in the constitutional amendments of 1971 and then in the constitution of 1974. Even the autonomous provinces within Serbia (Kosovo and Vojvodina) were recognised at the federal level as constituent elements of Yugoslavia and were granted extensive autonomous rights, which were recognised in the federal constitution. Compared to the republics, however, the statehood of the autonomous regions was not recognised. Article 4 of the 1974 constitution merely characterised the regions as 'autonomous, socialist, self-managed, democratic, socio-political communities' in which 'the nations and nationalities realise their sovereign rights'. It was on this point that the authorities of Kosovo and Vojvodina later based their claims in the struggle against the centralising tendencies of the Republic of Serbia [260; 265].

Kosovo Albanians entered the 1970s with a high level of expectancy from the central Yugoslav authorities. This was due mainly to two factors: the ever-increasing Albanian dominance in the province and the way the Kosovo Albanians interpreted the loosely defined 'Yugoslav idea'. Outmigration of Serbs has been a persistent phenomenon in Kosovo since 1966, when the authorities and police in Kosovo were 'Albanianized' after the fall of Alexandar Rankovic, the Serb head of the state security apparatus. As a result of the Serbian outmigration and the higher birth rate of the Albanians, the population ratio has changed in favour of the Albanians. They had already won the right to fly their national flag in 1968, and in November 1969 the bilingual University of Pristine was opened, facilitating higher education in Albanian for the first time. Full cultural autonomy was achieved after the Yugoslav Constitution of 1974 [267; 283].

1980s: HESITATION AT THE TOP AND REVOLT FROM BELOW

As the 1980s opened, few predicted that it would be a decade of unprecedented change in East–West relations. Despite the careful nurturing of *détente*, its spirit did not endure. In many respects, the Soviet invasion of Afghanistan in 1979 was the catalyst to the demise of *détente*. Relations between the two superpowers deteriorated dramatically thereafter. The American elections in 1980 brought to the White House a conservative Republican, Ronald Reagan, who was more determined to compete vigorously with the Soviet Union than any president since the 1960s. He denounced the Soviet Union as 'an evil empire', and echoed John F. Kennedy in calling for America to 'stand tall' in the world again. American policy aimed to wear the Soviet Union down through an expensive arms race [13; 17; 36].

As American diplomacy recovered its self-confidence and initiative, Soviet foreign policy drifted. Early in the decade a recurrence of serious unrest in Eastern Europe, particularly in Poland, kept the attention of the Kremlin close to home. The ongoing war in Afghanistan was creating increasing pressure on Soviet resources. As a result, this mixture of deepening economic problems, political crisis and popular unrest in Eastern Europe seriously restricted the Soviet ability to manoeuvre in world affairs, and until the late 1980s, the Kremlin was less able than the White House to mount new initiatives in foreign policy [81].

In Eastern Europe, the deep division between East-Central Europe and the Balkans remained throughout the 1980s. This was the contrast between the more advanced north (the GDR, Poland, Czechoslovakia, Hungary), where the necessity of a radical transformation of the economic system was more apparent, and the still relatively undeveloped countries (Romania, Bulgaria, Albania) where communist-led modernisation had not collapsed into crisis. In addition, a second division erupted in the 1980s. This was the division between regimes which, owing to a feeling of insecurity rooted in the memories of earlier social cataclysms, were prepared to exercise a relative toleration of dissent and attempt economic reforms (Poland, Hungary) and those which continued to be founded on pure repression (the GDR, Czechoslovakia, Romania, Bulgaria, Albania). Yugoslavia does not fit well into any category, but was clearly more tolerant than the latter group [94].

East–Central Europe

In **East Germany (GDR)** the political stability of the previous decade was still the dominant mood for society during most of the 1980s. There was still some degree of popular acceptance for the communist system when most other East European countries were rife with discontent. Immediately below the surface, however, serious problems were developing. Yet these were in essence economic rather than political problems.

Determined to avoid the kind of political liberalisation going on elsewhere in Eastern Europe, Honecker tried in the second half of the 1980s to impose a kind of intellectual quarantine on the country, denying East German citizens access to information about reformism elsewhere in the Soviet bloc. Many East Germans had little direct contact with dissident groups, and accepted Honecker's conservatism with equanimity. In this, the widely feared *Stasi*, the most efficient internal security organisation anywhere in Eastern Europe, played an important role, contributing to a pervasive docility in East German society. However, during most of the 1980s, the regime became less overtly repressive than it had earlier been. Many people made explicit or implicit arrangements, or at least came to an understanding, with the regime. In their daily life they made deals all the time, at various levels, with the authorities to make life more bearable. Every one was in fact involved. There was no way around it. Obviously, differing positions in the hierarchy established differing degrees of involvement. The dialectic of threat and reward remained complicated. Herbert Marcuse's concept of 'repressive tolerance' has been used to describe the nature of relations between citizens and the state. On the one hand, these relations were based on elements of political and administrative repression towards citizens. On the other hand, some elements of tolerance can be observed [73; 189; 194].

Nearly all dissent in the GDR in this decade operated under the shelter of the Evangelical Church, which acted as a moderator between the regime and dissenters. In the early 1980s, Church–state relationships promoted a stabilising safety-valve for the regime. In the course of the 1980s, however, dissenting views proliferated, increasingly putting pressure on the regime. Many dissident groups devoted to peace, the environment and other causes were harassed by the authorities and subjected to intense surveillance. Yet they were ultimately tolerated. The strategies of repression were not designed to imprison the would-be dissenter, but to establish the boundaries within which dissent had to be confined [185].

Probably the most important peace movement of the late 1970s and 1980 was the campaign against the introduction of military instruction as a required course for ninth and tenth graders in the schools. This campaign against the militarisation of society played a major role in the peace work of the Evangelical Church as well as of the youth groups on the fringe of Church activities. In May 1981 three co-workers of the Evangelical Lutheran Church of Saxony composed a petition. This was circulated throughout the country and had collected 5,000 signatures by the autumn. In January 1982, the East Berlin pastor issued an appeal which demanded the withdrawal of all occupation forces from German soil and the creation of non-nuclear zones in Europe. In 1982, a conference of the Evangelical Church Directorates condemned nuclear weapons as morally evil. In these campaigns, the Church served as mediator between the government and critically-minded youth groups in the GDR. By 1986, it was estimated that about 200 peace groups, with thousands of members, existed in the GDR.

In the 1980s, East Germany was still regarded as the most successful in the communist camp in terms of economic well-being and political stability [189].

Hungary entered the 1980s with improved living standards and a more efficient economy, thanks to Kádár's pragmatic socialism and economic reforms of the 1970s. Towards the end of the decade, however, Hungarian communism too began to experience the same problems as communist systems in other East European countries: the development of popular discontent with communist rule and ultimately a determination to reform it out of existence. Closely related to economic stagnation, the major problem was social impoverishment. The solution required more extensive reformism than the regime could allow without being challenged fundamentally. For the vast majority of Hungarians, the second half of the decade was an era of increasing economic difficulties, chronic housing shortage and sharply declining standards in general. The strain was evident, particularly on the educated classes. Doctors or university professors on fixed salaries found their buying power eroded and frequently had to look for second jobs. Social stratification increased popular pessimism, and disillusionment eventually turned into hard-line opposition to the system [*Doc. 7*].

Some important developments took place in the political sphere during the 1980s. Multi-candidate elections had been possible since 1967; in 1983 they became mandatory. In the 1985 elections, some eminent politicians were defeated and a number of genuinely independent deputies were elected. In 1983 Hungary created a Constitutional Law Council whose primary purpose was to monitor possible violations of the constitution. This was a unique development in the Warsaw Pact countries.

By the mid-1980s, a reform movement had emerged within the Party, which led not only to the deposition of Kádár but also to the capture of the Party leadership by reform elements led by Imre Pozsgay. Kádár was ousted as General Secretary in May 1988 and Karoly Grosz was appointed General Secretary. Grosz was recognised as a pragmatist who favoured economic and political liberalisation. In February 1989, in response to increasing popular demand, the Party's Central Committee approved the creation of fully independent, non-communist political parties. In June, the powers of Grosz as General Secretary were diluted by the setting-up of a four-strong Party Presidium. In the same month, the government and opposition entered into a series of negotiations on the future of Hungary. After three months an agreement was signed to initiate constitutional reform, to create a multi-party system and to hold free parliamentary elections during the course of 1990. Parliament approved the constitutional changes in October and at the Fourteenth Party Congress, the Hungarian Socialist Workers' Party was renamed the Hungarian Socialist Party. It committed itself to a multi-party, democratic political system and a market-oriented economy [199; 204].

Czechoslovakia entered the 1980s experiencing what some called a 'happy stagnation'. The security and stability reimposed in the aftermath of the 'Prague Spring' was still providing people with a level of material well-being. In the second half of the decade, however, pressure was building for radical political reform as a result of the activities of dissident movements. The Charter 77 signatories, led by the playwright Václav Havel, sought political reforms and democratisation for Czechoslovakia. Charter 77 called on people to speak out on behalf of human rights guaranteed by the Helsinki Accords. As the economies and the regimes began to weaken, dissident groups became more active, more visible and more popular. In the course of the 1980s dissident activities broke the regime's monopoly on information, establishing an alternative communication system.

In the second half of the 1980s, as the reform process accelerated within the Soviet Union, pressure for reform increased in Eastern Europe. In 1987 Gorbachev began a series of visits to the East European capitals to press home the message of reform. There were signs of tension between Husák and the Soviet leadership. Husák and the rest of the Czechoslovak delegation left Moscow in the middle of the seventeenth anniversary celebrations of their own Independence Day, and they did not return for the important 7 November parade. In December 1987 Gustáv Husák stepped down as General Secretary – 'because of his age' (he was seventy-five years old) – and was replaced by Milos Jakeš. Husák's retirement cleared the way for further and faster change in Czechoslovakia [172; 173].

The ruling communist elite in **Poland** was faced with a crisis of legiti-macy at the beginning of the 1980s. The most serious display of popular hostility to communist rule since its beginning in the late 1940s began with the 1980 Solidarity crisis. Solidarity was a new workers' union, founded in August 1980 by Lech Walesa, an electrician in the Lenin Shipyards of Gdansk. Unlike the official trade union organisations, Solidarity was independent of the Communist Party. Solidarity campaigned against the shipyard management for higher pay, better living conditions and increased popular influence over the government. The strike organised by the union spread quickly to other workers in Gdansk and, in less than a month, Polish citizens from all sectors of society were supporting Solidarity. The authorities, in the face of this powerful campaign, were forced to make significant concessions in 1980–81. The overall demands of the Solidarity leaders were, however, too great and Walesa and his followers were too naïve and over-confident about how to obtain them. As a result, General Wojciech Jaruzelski, the leader of the Polish Communist Party, declared martial law in December 1981 and drove Solidarity underground. Jaruzelski claimed that the imposition of martial law was necessary in order to avoid Soviet invasion. This claim now appears to be false, but this was not widely known at the time. The declaration of martial law, however, could not stop the opposition. Solidarity's network of supporters were able to mobilise workers and other groups within society against the practices of the communist leadership. As the decade was nearing a close, a large majority of Polish workers were again on strike, demanding improved living conditions and political liberalisation [*Doc. 6*]. The election of a Polish pope in June 1979 only encouraged the Poles to express their dissatisfaction with the regime more loudly. Walesa shrewdly benefited from the symbiotic relationship that existed between the Church and Solidarity [210; 212].

The political instability in Poland in the 1980s gave rise to the belief that Poland's main problem was a lack of political authority. However, on closer inspection, it is clear that each political crisis was caused by an increasingly deteriorating economic situation. The Polish case was one of economic difficulties, rather than political discontent, although clearly the former led to the latter [221; 224; 226].

The Balkans

Albania remained a completely isolated Stalinist dictatorship in the 1980s. Insecurity and poverty explain this situation. The long-ruling leader of Albania, Enver Hoxha, died in April 1985. His successor, Ramiz Alia, whose daughter was married to Hoxha's son, reiterated the Albanian communists' commitment to Stalinist policies. The Albanian communists resisted change of any kind and continued to maintain their strong grip over the country.

Probably the only significant change in Albania came in the area of foreign affairs. Since Ramiz Alia assumed power, something of a foreign relations thaw set in. Diplomatic relations were established with Spain in September 1986 and with Canada and West Germany in September 1987. The state of war with Greece, which had officially existed since the Italian invasion of Greece in 1940, was lifted in August 1987. Two accords were signed with Turkey and Albania took part in the Balkan Conference of Foreign Ministers in February 1988 [131; 133; 136].

Bulgaria's repressive authoritarianism continued under its communist leader, Todor Zhivkov. There was virtually no effort at reform in the political sphere. Zhivkov was not interested in liberalising the political environment, nor introducing political reforms. The Bulgarian Communist Party rejected out of hand any form of political pluralism and continued to dominate most aspects of Bulgarian life.

Only towards the end of the decade did there appear to be changes in the field of domestic politics. In 1987, Zhivkov issued a new policy statement, endorsing Gorbachev's approach in the Soviet Union. There were campaigns against corruption, bureaucracy and inefficiency. During the Party Congress in January 1988, 'decentralisation' was mentioned as a central theme of the Party. Furthermore, in February 1988, parliamentary elections allowed voters, for the first time, a choice of candidates. In July the same year, however, came signs of a retreat, with the dismissal from the party leadership of two prominent reformists.

Bulgarian dissident groups slowly emerged only towards the end of the decade. In January 1988, the dissident Independent Society for Human Rights was formed. *Podkrepa* (Support), the first independent trade union, was established in February 1989 and in April 1989, *Ecoglasnost*, a grassroots social movement, was formed. The major goals of *Ecoglasnost* were free access to environmental information, the protection of people's health and safety, reform of the old system and the construction of democracy. In October 1989, an international environmental conference in Sofia provided opposition human rights campaigners and *Ecoglasnost* access to international publicity.

In 1984, after thirty years of increasing pressure on Bulgaria's Turkish-speaking Muslims, the Bulgarian authorities initiated a broad campaign to complete the assimilation of ethnic Turks, forcing them to change their Turkish and Arabic names to Bulgarian-sounding ones. The anti-Turkish campaign resulted in violent confrontations and many deaths. As a result, 300,000 Turkish-speaking Muslims of Bulgaria were forced to migrate to Turkey. When Todor Zhivkov was forced to resign and Bulgaria began a serious effort to change in late 1989, the then head of the parliament, Stanko Todorov, tried to appease Bulgarian Muslims by announcing that ethnic freedom would be introduced immediately [152; 156; 165].

Romania entered the 1980s under the firm grip of Ceausesçu and his family. The excesses, abuses and irrationalities of communist leadership were causing great suffering and hardship for the Romanian people. Ceausesçu's regime was based on a Stalinist-type leadership cult. He personally controlled appointments to important Party and state positions, and used the *Securitate* to feed his cult and protect his position against any would-be critics and opposition. He had a deep mistrust of anyone not in his immediate family, which created a vicious nepotism. This prompted some experts to describe the Romanian model as 'dynastic communism' [239].

The Ceauşescu regime's extreme abuse of human rights gave Romania one of the worst human rights records in Europe. During the decade relations with the West, especially with the United States, deteriorated. Washington realised that Ceauşescu's independence of the Soviet Union was superficial and self-serving, and that his regime's internal repressiveness could not be overlooked. Romania lost the United States' 'most favoured nation' status in 1983, in part as a result of its introduction of a decree obliging all *émigrés* to repay the costs of their education, a law making abortion illegal for women under the age of forty-two, and increasing attacks on religion.

In the area of foreign policy, Romania retained independence from Moscow by maintaining relations with China, refusing to support the invasion of Afghanistan and signing a treaty with the Khmer Rouge of Cambodia.

Ceauşescu's leadership continued unchallenged and he was duly re-elected General Secretary at the thirteenth Party Congress in November 1984. Even in the mid-1980s, the Stalinist nature of his regime did not diminish.

In Romania's Stalinist climate it is not surprising that no serious opposition movement emerged. This can mainly be explained by the degree of political repression and control of everyday life and the absence of an intellectual elite to challenge the regime. The overwhelming majority of the population were originally peasants and had yet to shake off their sub-missive attitude to authority. Despite heavy oppression, they enjoyed a higher standard of living in the new urban environment than they had in their villages. In ideological terms, nationalism provided Ceauşescu with a certain degree of legitimacy; he tapped into the xenophobia that had always played an important role in Romanian cultural life. He pushed the use of nationalism further than any other leader in the region. The only *samizdat* that emerged in the period was ethnic Hungarian, which was a reaction to the policy of *de facto* Romanianisation that was taking place in Transylvania. The only dissident who gained international renown was Paul Goma who, after expressing solidarity with the Charter 77 movement in Czechoslovakia, was arrested and obliged to emigrate to Paris [228; 233; 238].

Economic frustrations and political unrest in **Yugoslavia** led to a recrudescence of nationalism in the 1980s. After the death of the system's principal architects (Kardelj died in 1979, Tito in 1980), the contradictions intensified. The possibility of conflict and disintegration, which Tito had done everything to prevent, gradually became a serious problem for the country. Without a charismatic, unifying leader the republics divided over a variety of issues, including how much influence the central government in Belgrade should have on social and economic matters in the republics. Centrifugal forces operating through powerful republics started seriously challenging the cohesion and unity of the Federal Republic of Yugoslavia.

The semblance of autonomy and freedom that the Kosovo Albanians enjoyed in the 1970s was brought to an abrupt end in 1981 when the ethnic issue boiled over in Kosovo. In March, student demonstrations over the seemingly trivial issue of hostel living conditions escalated into demonstrations for the release of students and full republican status and equality with the other peoples of the Yugoslav Federation. The demonstrations were met with tanks and automatic rifles. Martial Law was declared in April. The violent suppression of the 1981 uprising signalled the end of peaceful coexistence in Kosovo and, at the same time, the beginning of the fragmentation of Yugoslavia [267; 273].

The most serious inter-ethnic disagreement was the enormous influence over Yugoslav politics enjoyed by the Republic of Serbia. The situation worsened when Slobodan Milosevic, the head of the Serbian branch of the Yugoslav League of Communists, was elected President of Serbia in 1987. Milosevic recognised that the legitimacy of the communist system was declining fast and that the federal administration system was becoming increasingly fragile. He made Serb nationalism his tool in the search for a new identity and to secure his power base. He governed Serbia in a very authoritarian manner, harassed political critics and opponents and skilfully manipulated Serbia's mass media and the general populist sentiments that existed among the Serbian minority populations elsewhere in the rest of the Yugoslav Federation [269].

The 'national question' was probably the most open manifestation of the weakness of the Yugoslav regime. The unclearly defined concept of the 'Yugoslav idea' aggravated national and federal problems in the post-Tito period. Because the Communist Party apparatuses in the individual republics constituted relatively independent power centres, a centralist conception of the Party could not prevail over them. Tito had relied on a heavy-handed policy, that is, purges in Croatia, Serbia, Slovenia and Macedonia. Not only did these purges cause the Yugoslav Party to lose many outstanding personalities, Tito's actions also precipitated a general decline in the authority and prestige of the Party as an institution [258; 260]. The further strengthening of the republics and the decline of the Party's importance in the spectrum of Yugoslav institutions reached a high point in the second half of the 1980s. Both developments were closely linked to growing economic difficulties.

CHAPTER FOUR

EAST EUROPEAN ECONOMIES

The aim of this chapter is to survey the main economic developments of the 1970s and 1980s in the East European countries, and to assess the implications of the pull of COMECON economic integration on the one hand and the attraction of trade with the West on the other.

The East European countries vary with respect to size, resource capacity, historical experience, culture, nationality, language, political orientation, level of economic development and economic performance. There were different initial conditions under which central economic planning was introduced in the eight East European countries. Furthermore, important postwar events and circumstances highlighted diversity among these economies. In terms of population and land area, the East European economies ranged from tiny Albania to medium-sized countries like Poland, Romania and the GDR. In terms of level of development, the region consisted of industrialised nations (the GDR and Czechoslovakia), countries at the beginning of their industrialisation (Hungary and Poland), and poor and mainly agricultural societies (Romania, Bulgaria, Yugoslavia and Albania). In terms of possession and exploitation of natural resources, East European countries ranked from the relatively well-endowed Poland (black and brown coal, copper, sulphur, lead, zinc, iron ore, aluminium, natural gas) to relatively poor Bulgaria (low-grade coal, lead, zinc, copper, chromium, manganese ore, asbestos). As for the suitability of the country's soil and climate for agriculture, the economies in the region ranged from quite well-endowed Hungary, Romania, Bulgaria (reasonably self-sufficient in food and some net exports) to less-endowed Poland and Yugoslavia [22].

At the beginning of the communist era, all of the countries of the region, except Czechoslovakia, were relatively backward, with the majority of people working in the agricultural sector. During the first two decades of the socialist experience, many of these countries achieved a breakthrough in industrialisation. By the late 1960s, all East European countries, with the exception of Albania, had become industrialised. Roughly half of the gross national product (GNP) was produced by industry, and only 20 per cent by agriculture. Industrialisation was built on free or very cheap energy and raw material deliveries from the Soviet Union. Industrialisation was generally successful in creating new branches of industry and increasing significantly the industrial output [23; 70].

Another important area of development was agriculture. The countries of Eastern Europe undertook a complex process of mechanisation in the agricultural sector and dramatically increased the use of artificial fertilisers in farming. Indeed, the use of artificial fertilisers in Eastern Europe soon surpassed the world average. By the late 1980s, the number of tractors per hectare of land increased by six times in Poland, more than 20 times in Yugoslavia, and three to four times in Albania and Romania. The mechanisation of the region's agriculture reached nearly 62 per cent of West European levels. As a result, production of wheat, corn, potatoes and sugar beets doubled. Animal stock increased significantly as well. For example, the pig stock in the region trebled, and poultry production expanded by three to five times. In general, agricultural methods overcame their traditional backwardness in Eastern Europe [77].

THE KEY COMPONENTS OF THE COMMUNIST ECONOMIC SYSTEM

There is no single, comprehensive theory of the functioning of Soviet-style centrally planned economies. The approach to economic systems in Eastern Europe, as discussed here, is based primarily on the works of Kornai [63; 64], Kalecki [61] and Zloch-Christi [130]. Of course, such a broad generalisation needs to be treated, and applied, with caution and the peculiarities of the economic situation in a given country must always be borne in mind.

The first and major institutional component of the Soviet model was the sacred principle of collective ownership of virtually all property rights on physical and human capital. Collective (state) ownership was extended to practically every aspect of East European life.

The second pillar of the communist economic system was the supremacy of heavy industrial development. The leaders of communist Eastern Europe, having inherited largely agrarian economies, held the firm conviction that their first priority was to develop heavy industrial production everywhere in the region. The plans set out to expand vastly the energy-producing and the metallurgical sectors of the economy. Steel was accorded a special significance. A great propaganda effort was devoted to steel production. Over the course of forty years, the Eastern European economies had developed labour-intensive heavy industrial production on a largely agricultural base. Eastern Europe became the land of steel and coal. The process of industrialisation succeeded in transforming the largely peasant societies of Eastern Europe into urban societies.

A third pillar of the communist economic system was the establishment of large-scale, mechanised agriculture. The socialisation of agriculture was a vital step in building socialism. It would eliminate bourgeois elements in the countryside and release vast quantities of surplus labour for work in the rapidly expanding industrial centres. Giant farms, both collective and state, were established in the countryside, with huge farm machinery and cheap labour.

The fourth pillar of the communist economy was the replacement of the market as the coordinating mechanism by state planning. Marx held that capitalism manages to establish a high degree of organisation within the firm, but produces anarchy in society. Socialism, by contrast, avoids the anarchy which results if individual decisions are not coordinated, by granting power to the state to organise the economy centrally on a national scale. Everything was planned, from production targets to the allocation of resources, and nearly everything had an artificial value. The process of planning the economy began soon after the Second World War in most East European states with the introduction of reconstruction plans. The plans shifted investment and labour into heavy industry at the cost of the agricultural sector and consumer goods. The plans, even if implemented, were not always beneficial. Too many heavy metallurgical plants were built and it would have been far better to invest more in chemicals and plastics. Furthermore, central bureaucracies, with their rigidly imposed production quotas, enforced a concentration on the quantity rather than the quality of production.

A fifth characteristic of the system was the denial of infrastructural development. Socialist theory insisted on the distinction between 'productive' and 'non-productive' activities, with the latter comprising most services. As a result, infrastructure and the service sector were not regarded as a part of the value of a product, as they did not directly involve either productive labour or material. In practice, the infrastructure received very low ranking in the scale of investment priorities, and remained largely underdeveloped.

A sixth pillar of the communist economy was the concept of full employment. The irrational arrangement of the labour market created an artificial and unproductive system. A huge under-qualified labour force emerged. A heightened sense of the relationship between politics and economics was created as a result of the state-controlled economy's obsession with full employment. Rapid industrialisation did not create an entrepreneurial class comparable to the ones that were the backbone of Western industries. The organiser and builder of industry in Eastern Europe was the state. The only role individuals played was that of servants of the state. Economic difficulties were therefore seen and understood not as the responsibility of a firm or its management but as the fault of the state. Individual gains and losses came to be seen as the product of the government's bad policies rather than as results of individuals' work or failures [44; 130].

COUNCIL OF MUTUAL ECONOMIC AID (COMECON)

As far as the economic structures were concerned, the first few years of the communist period in Eastern Europe were a period of violent political and social upheaval involving a complete change in the system of property relations and the emergence of the state as the main agent of economic activity. By 1945, all countries made rapid strides in the transition to socialism. Land reform was first on the agenda, followed by the expropriation of industry, banking and financial institutions, and domestic and foreign trade and distribution. During this initial phase, 1946–49, the countries of Eastern Europe were encouraged by the Soviet Union to draw closer together economically, to the exclusion of contacts with the capitalist countries in the West.

The Council of Mutual Economic Aid (CMEA) or COMECON, the economic organisation which combined the socialist economies under its umbrella, was founded on 18 January 1949 by the Soviet Union, Bulgaria, Poland, Romania, Czechoslovakia and Hungary for the purpose of fostering closer economic relationships and more integrated development among the countries of the socialist camp. Albanià became a member in February of the same year and the GDR did so in September 1950. Mongolia followed in 1962, Cuba in 1972 and Vietnam in 1978. Albania resigned in 1962. Cooperation agreements existed between COMECON on the one hand, and Finland, Iraq and Mexico on the other. Other socialist countries (Afghanistan, Angola, Ethiopia, the People's Republic of China, Laos, Mozambique, North Korea, South Yemen and Nicaragua) had observer status at sessions of the Council and in other COMECON organs. Yugoslavia had partial associate status. The establishment of COMECON, on the initiative of the Soviet Union under the leadership of Stalin, can be attributed in essence to political rather than, in the first place, economic reasons. At first, the economic importance of COMECON as a whole remained rather limited. This, however, changed in the 1960s [101; 113].

The official aims of COMECON were several, and were laid down in the COMECON Statute which was adopted in December 1959. They included raising the level of economic integration between the member states, accelerating economic and technical progress, bringing the economic development of the less developed states up to that of the most advanced, and creating the conditions for a virtually simultaneous transition to communism by all the member states.

Stalin's death in 1953 and Khrushchev's denunciation of Stalinist methods had combined to produce a reassessment of the Soviet Union's trading links with its East European partners. This shift gradually led, in the 1960s, to the COMECON assuming greater prominence in the economic relations between socialist states. Khrushchev tried to develop multilateral economic links and encourage the socialist division of labour through looking to persuade each member to specialise in its strongest field of economic activity. For instance, East Germany and Czechoslovakia were asked to develop their heavy industries while Romania was required to concentrate on agriculture and food processing.

The Soviet Union was the dominant economic and military power, and therefore unquestionably the moving force within the COMECON. All long-term and decisive proposals were initiated by Moscow. Over time, however, the role of the Soviet Union within the COMECON was transformed from that of an exploiter (paying below world market prices for East European exports) to that of being willingly exploited (that is, the Soviet Union was prepared for political reasons to sacrifice and run down its raw materials' reservoir, and stoically to accept second-rate, shoddy goods in return). The leaders of the East European states, who relied heavily on the backing of Moscow to remain in power, were more than eager to make a series of long-term agreements with Moscow to ensure the delivery of raw materials, especially oil, from the Soviet Union [7; 64; 94].

1970s: PRESSURE FOR REFORM

In the long decade between the defeat of the last great attempt at 'socialism with a human face' in Czechoslovakia in 1968 and the accession to power in the Soviet Union of Mikhail Gorbachev in 1985, neo-Stalinism ruled triumphant in Eastern Europe. The socialist regimes were politically stable under the Soviet umbrella. The East European economies appeared to be sound, at least in the official statistics. Growth rates had been good in the 1966–70 plan period. The following period, 1971–75, witnessed even better economic performance.

In all East European countries, economic reforms started in the mid-1960s. In some of them they went on until the 1980s without interruption. In others they were interrupted and taken up again. All of them were undermined by the large rise in oil prices in 1973–74, coupled with the burden of hard-currency debt. After 1975, however, things started to go wrong. From the end of the 1970s, the economies entered a period of decline. Growth slowed, living standards stagnated or fell. In the same period, most of the East European countries rapidly increased their hard-currency trade and current account deficits, as well as their debt to the Western commercial banks and government agencies. Most of the increase in debt to the West resulted from commercial borrowing, principally from Western banks. By the end of 1979, commercial bank borrowing by the

East European countries was roughly fifteen times greater than its level in 1971 [77].

Despite common tendencies, the decade was also one of increasing diversification along fissures that began to open in the 1960s. As the fissures widened, they began to take on a Balkans–East-Central Europe dimension. Economic failure was openly acknowledged and addressed in Poland and Hungary, and as the socialist economy declined in these countries, some private and mixed sectors emerged, offering new models of economic organisation.

East Central Europe

East Germany (GDR) was traditionally agricultural, the homeland of the old Prussian Junker class. The communist regime industrialised the country at the expense of severe austerity. Wages were kept low and the production of basic consumer goods was neglected. Living standards were far below those in West Germany and the rest of Western Europe. The GDR economy was dependent on commercial and financial concessions from West Germany. This fact helped mask the weaknesses of the East German economy.

Mainly as a result of the uncertain future of the country until the mid-1950s, the GDR had uniquely preserved a large private sector outside agriculture. There had been no general nationalisation in the Stalinist period. The official view had been that the superiority of national ownership would be revealed through competition. Between 1958 and 1960 many private factories had become semi-state-owned (the state participated in company capital but the private owner remained managing director). In 1971 private and semi-state-owned enterprises employed only 15 per cent of the industrial work force. The 1970s witnessed the nationalisation of much of the private and all of the semi-private sectors of the economy. Such measures reduced the significance of the market. Honecker's 1971 programme specified the main task of domestic policy as economic progress through state planning. A new emphasis was placed on modernisation and experts were brought into the economic system.

The East German economy was widely regarded as having been the most successful in Eastern Europe. By the end of the 1960s East Germany had been listed among the top ten nations of the world in terms of gross national product. By the mid-1970s, per capita national income exceeded that of the United Kingdom and New Zealand. In 1965, a UNESCO study gave the GDR's child-care facilities as the best in the world. East Germany's education and health facilities were also agreed to be excellent.

Behind the official output figures, however, the economy was ailing and becoming increasingly dependent on its special relationship with the Federal

Republic. The rise in world market prices for energy and raw materials was a serious problem for poorly-endowed industrial countries like the GDR. At the beginning of the 1970s rising imports could be financed by exports. By the mid-1970s, however, as a delayed consequence of the 1973–74 oil shock, the foreign trade and payments situation and the GDR's trade in basic commodities deteriorated markedly. The GDR resorted to credits from Western countries, but the interest rate burden subsequently became apparent. In addition, GDR exports were adversely affected by recession in the West. New indebtedness with the West increased at an annual rate of more than 20 per cent during the second half of the 1970s. The second oil shock of 1979 made the situation even worse. The increased foreign trade and payments burden exacerbated the already serious domestic problems that resulted from inefficiency [184; 187].

Hungary's economy had traditionally been underdeveloped owing to a number of historical and socio-economic reasons, and to its lack of natural resources. After two decades of the harsh application of the Soviet model of a centrally planned economy, marked by heavy industrialisation and collectivisation, the political elite realised that the centrally planned economy was not doing for Hungary what it was intended to do. In 1968, the 'New Economic Mechanism' was introduced. This was a plan aimed at decentralising economic decision-making by transferring much of it from the large ministries in Budapest to the managers of enterprises throughout the country. Trading with the outside world was decentralised and measures to encourage greater efficiency and productivity were introduced. It also opened the door to a limited amount of private initiative. Firms were encouraged to make profits rather than solely to meet production targets. Within a couple of years, this economic reform programme was paying solid dividends. It brought greater efficiency with lower costs and improved the standard of living of the working people of Hungary.

In the 1970s, the industrial labour force reached its peak in Hungary. More than 45 per cent of those who were actively employed worked in industry. During the same period, the distribution of wealth became progressively more unequal. The opportunities for career advancement increasingly favoured members of the political, intellectual and social elites. The industrial proletariat was left behind with fixed incomes. The heavy industrialisation campaign of the 1970s led to large-scale urbanisation. Buildings grew in size, frequently rising to twelve to fifteen stories, to accommodate the urbanised work force and individual dwellings were now more spacious.

Until the 1970s, the communist regime paid relatively little attention to the environmental deterioration that resulted from heavy industrialisation and the extensive use of fertilisers in agriculture. However, large sums were now spent on the prevention of environmental pollution and guidelines were established to reduce industrial pollution. Nevertheless, the protection of urban environments remained a low priority.

It had always been intended that there would be a second stage to the 'New Economic Mechanism' which would aim at creating some sort of capital market, breaking up monopolies and making enterprises more sensitive to world market prices. But such plans were shelved and the 'New Economic Mechanism' itself came under attack. All prominent pro-reformers were removed from positions of influence. The Eleventh Party Congress of March 1975 marked the culmination of re-centralisation. Three years later, hard-liners in the Central Committee fell from power and the economic policy changed again. In 1978 macro-economic policies, which aimed at reducing domestic consumption, were initiated.

Hungary was highly dependent on foreign trade, exporting about 50 per cent of its net material product. Hungary had the most liberal foreign trade system within COMECON. When the 1973–74 oil price shock increased energy and raw material prices and recession in the industrialised West, the Hungarian response was to accelerate the growth of total output, investment and consumption, financed by foreign credits. As a result, the Hungarian economy became dependent on heavy foreign borrowing to sustain the illusion of prosperity [195; 205].

Czechoslovakia had a more favourable start than other socialist countries at the outset of the communist period. Among the countries that became communist after the Second World War, Czechoslovakia was the most developed and the only industrialised nation. Czechoslovakia continued to industrialise in the 1970s. Its standard of living was higher than in other East European countries. Ownership of consumer durables, including household appliances, and of automobiles increased markedly throughout the 1970s.

Yet despite these positive aspects, the Czechoslovak economy suffered from many of the systemic problems that beset other centrally planned economies. Some of the economic problems had already been evident before the events of 1968, with the result that Czech and Slovak leaders had already attempted to implement some economic reforms as well as the political ones. Relative technological backwardness, the distorted production structure, the wasteful utilisation of material inputs and the decelerating growth of labour productivity combined to produce a decline in the rate of growth of national income in the 1960s. Labour productivity and morale were low, the production of quality goods poor, and there were few incentives for both workers and managers. The mounting crisis culminated in a sharp decline in Czechoslovak national income and in the real wages of the Czechoslovak workers in the 1960s.

When the 1968 reforms were stopped by force, those reformers with experience in, and contacts with, the West were purged, with the result that

Czech and Slovak expertise stagnated for nearly twenty years. Like everything else, the economy changed after the fall of Dubček. In May 1969, retail prices were increased and then frozen. The direct planning of foreign trade was re-introduced and re-centralisation became the core theme of the Czechoslovak economy. The severe impact of the 1973–74 oil crisis was evident in Czechoslovakia and throughout the winter of 1974–75 heating oil was in short supply. However, the problem which caused most difficulty in the mid-1970s was economic stagnation. The overall picture of the Czechoslovak economy was one of slow and steady decline throughout the 1970s, accelerating towards the end of the decade [173; 178].

In **Poland,** a centrally controlled and inefficient heavy industry dominated the economy. Bureaucratically minded managers of the economy opposed all demands for economic liberalisation, fearing that this would diminish their privileges. Polish agriculture, however, never totally succumbed to Soviet-style management. A large section of the agricultural sector resisted attempts at collectivisation and remained in private hands. The government had little support for private agricultural production but the private sector still supplied most of the food for Polish consumption.

In the 1970s, Poland tried to modernise its industrial base with the help of generous Western credits. The metallurgical industry, especially iron and copper manufacturing, the coal and lignite industry and the chemical industry all underwent considerable expansion in the 1970s. Such expansion, however, had serious repercussions for the environment and there were significant levels of environmental damage. The metallurgical industry became the major source of air pollution and toxic waste while the main water and soil polluter was the chemical industry. The country's planners and enterprise managers had originally tended to ignore ecological damage, instead concentrating on achieving maximum output regardless of cost, but in the 1970s, concern for the environment grew and eventually more rational economic calculations were introduced in the 1980s.

Polish agriculture remained locked in small-scale peasant production. Polish peasants could be persuaded to increase production only by increasing the prices they received for agricultural products. This required raising either state subsidies or consumer prices. Economic reform dictated cutting subsidies but every time this was done, industrial workers went on strike and price increases were withdrawn.

On 12 December 1970 the government announced food price increases averaging about 30 per cent. Demonstrations broke out in the Gdansk Lenin Shipyard, which were soon followed by further demonstrations and clashes with the police in other Baltic cities. On 19–20 December, the Central Committee met and decided to remove Gomułka from power and replace him with Edward Gierek. Gierek announced concessions and promised not to raise prices further for the next two years. This was not enough, however, and the strikers demanded that the increases were withdrawn. Strikes in the Baltic and many other parts of industrial Poland continued until mid-February. After securing a special loan from the Soviet Union, Gierek announced, on 15 February, that prices would be fixed at the pre-December levels and would be frozen for two years.

A Committee for Modernising the Economic System and the State was appointed in 1971, and the reforms it initiated came into effect on 1 January 1973. It was, however, a half-hearted attempt to solve the economic crisis. Investment decisions for all but replacement and modernisation costs remained wholly under the control of the central authorities. The reform faded away between 1978 and 1980.

Still, in general, developments seemed positive in the first half of the 1970s. In the field of agriculture, Gierek abolished the system of compulsory purchases and undertook other measures to help the peasants, including the lifting of the ban on the sale of agricultural machinery to private farmers, the lifting of the ban on the sale of state land to private farmers and, in 1977, the granting of pension and national insurance rights to all private farmers.

Gierek had a predictable plan for the economy: more trade with the West; more imports of capital goods; a bid to industrialise the countryside and improve the industries in the urban areas; and borrowing large amounts of credit from the West. The success of such large borrowing depended on the availability of cheap credits. Competition among the Western commercial banks to recycle the oil-exporting countries' deposits after 1974 made 'cheap credits' available to Poland and other East European countries and these funds were used to finance their expansion drive. Real interest rate levels in the international financial markets during the 1970s were negative, which made borrowing economically justified. Especially in the period of 1975–80, bankers and business people from the West were thrusting financial and technological resources at Polish (and other East European) officials who all too often had a strong self-interest in taking them, regardless of the fact that they might be used unproductively [126].

In the first half of the 1970s, there were some developments in the industrial sector. With the help of the foreign loans, Polish factories were modernised and productivity increased. Standards of living rose markedly, substantially more than anywhere else in Eastern Europe. This policy of industrial investment might have succeeded had it not been for the burden of rising interest rates, the high cost of raw materials (particularly oil), and increasing Western protectionism. From 1975 onwards, problems started to appear. Due to continuing trade deficits with Western countries, foreign indebtedness rose sharply, amounting to US $10 billion. By 1979 external debt had risen to US $20.5 billion, putting Poland at the top of the table of

COMECON countries owing money to the West. A more than five-fold increase in imports from the West was matched by a less than four-fold increase in exports, leading to consistently negative balances. The burden of debt service grew by twenty times by the end of the decade. Inflation rose dramatically while the relative stability of food prices demanded large and rising subsidies from the central state budget. In agriculture, despite the new measures to increase the level of production, production did not meet consumer demand and agricultural imports increased.

The aftermath of the oil crisis produced several important revolts on a scale which was unusual even in Poland. The problems were relative to the amount of debt: the higher the debt, the worse the problems. The attempt to divert foodstuffs to exports and the associated rise in domestic prices led to the popular demonstrations. On 24 June 1976, price increases of 60 per cent were announced. The next day, mass demonstrations and strikes took place in almost all industrial parts of the country. Gierek gave in at once, although in the days that followed the leading militant workers were arrested and dismissed.

It is clear that international factors played a major role in Poland's economic crisis. Despite being a major fuel producer and exporter, the industrial growth policies left Poland unprepared for the 1973–74 oil crisis, the following world recession, inflation and rising interest rates. The effect of the crisis was felt more keenly because the managers of the economy were not used to the import-led growth policy. In practice, the general incompetence, negligence and corruption of individual managers, combined with the disillusionment of the population, made the economy unworkable. All these, basically economic, troubles gave rise to a serious political crisis, which, in turn, led to a complete collapse of the economy in 1980 [214; 217].

The Balkans

Albania, Europe's least developed country, is located along the central west coast of the Balkan Peninsula. Despite attempts by its communist rulers to improve living conditions in the 1960s, Albania remained the least economically developed country in Europe, with the majority of the population living in impoverished conditions. Albania is also one of the most isolated countries in the world, predominantly because it is self-sufficient in most of its basic raw material needs. Chromite (chromium ore), copper, nickel and coal are mined. The country also has some crude oil. Chromite makes the largest contribution to Albania's total exports as it is used in manufacturing chromium and stainless steel, which are used for armour plating, bank vaults, safes, cutting tools and automobile parts. Since the late 1970s Albania has been the world's third largest producer of chrome.

However, in the 1960s and 1970s Albania was not self-sufficient in food production even though almost 90 per cent of the population made their living off the land. Agriculture lacked the basic machinery and technological advances of the twentieth century. During the 1960s and the first half of the 1970s, people were moved from the cities to the countryside – a mini version of Mao Zedong's Cultural Revolution – and exaggerated Maoism informed the economic policies throughout this period. Anti-peasant measures continued: the maximum size of agricultural household plots was reduced to 300 square metres in 1971; then, in 1981, the marketing of private produce was forbidden altogether. The constitution of 1976 forbade all types of foreign investment, including the acceptance of foreign credits. In September 1977, a number of decrees gave ministries rather than local authorities greater control over supply. In July 1978, following the increasing tension between China and Albania after the death of Mao in 1976, China suspended its foreign aid. The Albanian economy went into decline. Per capita output had grown 4.2 per cent per year in 1971–75. It plummeted to 0.5 per cent per year in 1976–80. The combination of agricultural neglect and ideological conflict with the Soviet Union proved fatal to Albania's fragile economy [131; 145].

At the beginning of the communist era in **Bulgaria**, the economy was also underdeveloped and primarily agricultural. The communist leaders developed an industrial base, mainly in the area of heavy industry, and by the 1970s Bulgaria had a Soviet-style, highly centralised command economy involving the extension of state control over almost every aspect of economic life. The 1970s witnessed attempts by the regime to improve output and raise living standards. A modest reform programme, called the 'New Economic Mechanism' (NEM), was introduced. The implementation of this programme was intended to be gradual and the Party's central guiding role in the economy was not questioned in any way. The NEM, however, provided for the decentralisation of decision-making in the industrial sector and encouraged foreign investment.

In the field of agricultural production, the NEM allowed farmers to farm plots set aside for private use and to sell what they produced in public markets at prices decided by supply and demand. In addition, Agri-Industrial complexes, which integrated the agricultural sector with the industrial sector relating to it, were created. Traditional collective farms were abolished by 1977. Despite re-centralisation, Bulgaria encouraged the household-plot production of agricultural labourers.

Bulgaria managed to avoid the worst consequences of the oil price shocks in 1973–74 and 1979 by getting oil from the Soviet Union at lower prices. Indeed, over two-thirds of Bulgaria's total energy demand was met by the Soviet Union in this period [152; 160].

At the beginning of the communist era **Romania** was predominantly agricultural and underdeveloped. The aim of the communist leadership was to transform Romania into an industrialised state as rapidly as possible. As in other East European states, there was an overemphasis on heavy industry at the expense of agriculture. The Romanian leadership was of the opinion that increasing trade links with the West were the key to rapid industrialisation. It thought that Romania could export some of its agricultural produce in return for high-tech machinery from the West. Throughout the 1970s, therefore, Romania exported the best of its agricultural output, yet the result was not rapid industrialisation. Heavy industry was increasingly uneconomical, but still possessed tremendous symbolic power. The 1970s witnessed the creation of monsters like the oil refineries which operated at 10 per cent of capacity and the aluminium complex which used as much energy as the whole of Bucharest.

Romania's more independent foreign policy also cost it dear during the 1973–74 and 1979 oil crises when it could not count on access to cheap Soviet oil to stave off economic difficulties. The cost was especially high in view of the massive expansion of the petrochemical industry that Romania had undertaken with exports to the West in mind. Romania became a net oil importer in the mid-1970s. The energy-intensive strategy of expanding the petrochemical and engineering industries, and Romania's oil-refining capacity, was based on the expectation that exports of machinery and equipment would pay for oil imports and for other raw materials, and that these would be processed with the aid of Western capital goods bought with borrowed funds to provide hard currency exports.

By the mid-1970s it was becoming clear that economic performance was slowing. Annual growth of 3.9 per cent between 1975 and 1980 was lower than in the previous five-year period, and in 1980 it went into the negative. By the end of the decade, living conditions in Romania were extremely poor. There were chronic shortages of all basic items. The scarcity of food was mainly the result of Ceausescu's policy of exporting most of the agricultural output. In the 1970s, 90 per cent of the food produce was being exported. By 1980, Romania had a large deficit in trade, fuel and raw materials. Ceausescu's determination to industrialise the country rapidly led to serious distortions in the economy. His policies victimised almost everyone – peasants, industrial workers and the intelligentsia. Life for ordinary people became progressively more miserable throughout the 1970s [229; 253].

Yugoslavia is made up of large and small Slavic and non-Slavic ethnocultural groups that have diverse historical backgrounds and cultural traditions. The economic structure of the country in the 1970s was one of the main sources of unity for this 'patchwork-quilt' society. The different ethnic groups of Yugoslavia were united by an economic interdependence. Each republic and autonomous region of the country had resources and markets essential to the material well-being of other republics and regions. There existed a dense network of inter-republican trade which was the basis of the national Yugoslav economy.

During the 1970s, the Yugoslav economy expanded enormously. Unique aspects of Tito's economic policies provided Yugoslavia with a higher standard of living than that in neighbouring Balkan countries. The private sector dominance of the agricultural sector meant that Yugoslavia was one of the few socialist countries without a serious food problem. Similarly, the increasing autonomy of plant-level managers, as opposed to central administrators, and the large degree of worker participation in the management of factories resulted in greater efficiency and expanded output. Foreign backing also played an important role in Yugoslavia's rapid economic growth. Crucial assistance came from the International Monetary Fund (IMF). There was also help from the governments of Britain, Italy, France and the United States. By 1980 Yugoslavia had become the seventh largest industrialised nation in Europe.

Despite this optimistic picture, important problems were brewing in the Yugoslav economy. The most serious problem was that Yugoslavia was prone to inflationary pressures. Enterprise indebtedness grew dramatically and at the beginning of the 1970s the bulk of enterprise net income went on servicing debt. More than half the enterprises in Yugoslavia were unable to meet their financial commitments. By September 1975 businesses held unpaid bills totalling 273 billion dinars but themselves owed 262 billion dinars to the banks. The fragmentation and inner disintegration of the Yugoslav economy found its corollary in its growing subordination to foreign capital. To make matters worse, the large sums devoted to investment were put into projects of questionable worth. In 1972, the World Bank rejected 85 per cent of projects proposed by the Yugoslavs because of poor costing or grossly over-optimistic assessments of sales prospects on world markets. The money supply increased by 28 per cent in 1972 and by 36 per cent in 1973. In addition, unemployment was rising and inequalities were widening.

The problem of an international debt crisis in Yugoslavia was related to the basic strategy of the regime since the end of the Second World War. The aim was to industrialise Yugoslavia as quickly as possible; the cost was the relative neglect of traditional exports. During the 1970s, rapid rates of growth of gross material product were achieved, as well as growth in consumption, investment and imports, all of which led to rising trade deficits which encouraged external borrowing. The freedom to borrow abroad at what was a negative rate of interest proved irresistible at first. This fuelled a huge investment boom, but no thought was given as to how those debts would be repaid. Heavy borrowing from the West during the 1970s, as well as the recessionary effects following the 1973–74 and 1979 oil shocks, brought about severe foreign trade and payments difficulties for the Yugoslav economy. Eventually, the state needed to print ever more money to support an increasingly inefficient economy with its hordes of parasitic bureaucrats [281; 283].

1980s: CRISIS IN THE EAST EUROPEAN ECONOMIES

Towards the end of the 1970s, the growth rates of all the East European countries had decelerated significantly. At the beginning of the 1980s, production declines were experienced in Poland, Hungary, Czechoslovakia, Bulgaria and Romania. It was unmistakably clear that Eastern Europe had entered a primarily new economic era. Most of the economic problems were not merely cyclical or temporary, but were fundamental. Since the late 1970s, the East European countries had drastically reduced the absolute level of investment. In many cases, this went hand in hand with a cut in real consumption. During the same period, living standards declined substantially. Increased economic problems were mainly caused by the low and declining growth rates, the fall in productivity rates, further increases in the cost of energy, sluggish agriculture, and declining world prices of raw materials. One major cause of this crisis was related to the foreign indebtedness of East European countries. When faced with problems, almost all East European regimes found an 'easy' remedy in borrowing capital from the West. Communist elites saw Western capital as a means of buying off public opinion and delaying the harsh impact of structural change. The transnational financial markets which emerged in the 1970s, awash with petrodollars, saw Eastern Europe as a neglected area for investment. The East European countries were regarded as responsible borrowers by the Western commercial banks. They convinced themselves that the Soviet guarantee over Eastern Europe ruled out any chance of default. They assumed that the Soviet Union would not allow any Eastern bloc country to default or even re-schedule – the so-called Soviet umbrella. But during that period the Soviet Union allowed its allies to run high trade deficits, and when they experienced serious debt-servicing difficulties, the Soviet Union did not provide direct financial assistance. Thus, the 'Soviet umbrella' did not work as expected.

At the end of 1982, the net hard-currency debt of six East European countries was estimated at slightly over US $53 billion. Viewed in aggregate, this debt represented about 8 per cent of combined East European GNP and amounted to roughly US $480 on a per capita basis. These vast debts did not help to modernise the economy. The rigid structure of command economies made it easier to use foreign credits for food and consumer goods rather than installing foreign technology and modernising their technical base. The debts simply bought the regimes a breathing space [77].

By the 1980s, pollution had become a frightening reminder of state socialism's failed attempt to master nature. The planning system treated all natural resources (land, water, mineral deposits and forests) as state property, virtually as a free good, the cost of which to the user was either minimal or nil [30]. The whole of Eastern Europe had become an ecological disaster zone of dying rivers and barren forests. It pumped out roughly double the amount of sulphur dioxide emitted by the European Community [*Doc. 8*].

East-Central Europe

The 1980s saw **East Germany** coping with trade and payments difficulties more severe than ever before. Indebtedness to the West rose from US $6.7 billion in 1977 to $11.67 billion in 1981, and then fell to $6.83 billion in 1985. In the early 1980s, Western banks introduced restrictions on credit which affected the GDR like all other East European countries. Such foreign trade and payments problems enhanced the need for an all-around increase of the domestic output of energy and raw materials and a reduction in imports. The 1981–85 five-year plan targets were unrealistically high. Given the regime's unwillingness to reduce consumption seriously, it was investment that suffered. 1982, 1983 and 1984 were years of negative growth.

In 1980, about 30 per cent of national income was exported. The GDR was a major supplier of relatively high-quality, high-technology capital goods to COMECON, and was heavily dependent on imports of fuels and raw materials, especially from the Soviet Union. In this decade the GDR simultaneously suffered a cut-back in Soviet crude oil deliveries of more than 10 per cent and an abrupt increase in the price of Soviet oil of nearly 50 per cent. The economic planners of the GDR tried to increase exports and, at the same time, drastically reduce imports from the West, in order to achieve large surpluses. The GDR also made extensive use of its opportunities in inner-German economic relations to moderate the foreign trade and payments burden. European Community tariff restrictions did not apply to the GDR's exports to West Germany.

At the start of the second half of the 1980s the GDR, compared to its COMECON partners, was able to overcome the turbulence and appeared to be in a position to move on from its economic problems, by means of short-term crisis management, to maintain a stable economic life. The GDR also still enjoyed the highest standard of living in the socialist world. This was mainly due to the continuing substantial economic concessions granted by West Germany. Especially following the liquidity crisis of 1981–82, inner-German trade became a stabilising factor in the surmounting of the GDR's economic problems [182; 193].

Hungarian history between 'normalisation' after 1956 and the Gorbachev era continued to be dominated by economic matters. At the beginning of the 1980s, growing inflation and budget deficits emerged as serious problems. A severe liquidity crisis in 1981–82 resulted in Hungary joining the IMF and the World Bank. In 1982–83 enterprises were allowed to issue bonds, creating the beginning of a capital market. In 1983 enterprise directorships were opened to competitive tender, and in 1985 enterprises gained almost total autonomy from the centre. Despite all these measures, problems increased in the economy throughout the 1980s.

One of the major elements of the deepening economic crisis was related to the accumulation of foreign debt. As a result of the rapid increase of foreign debt in the 1980s, the debt-service ratio (i.e. the ratio between interest payments on debt plus annual amortisation and exports) was 60 per cent in 1986, compared to 20 per cent in 1975. In 1982, Hungary came close to re-scheduling its debt burden, having been subjected to rising interest rates and declining markets because of the restrictive monetary policies adopted by the advanced Western countries. It was avoided by a combination of intensified austerity measures and further credits provided by the IMF and the World Bank. By 1987–88, Hungary experienced the highest foreign debt per capita in Eastern Europe. In 1988 the more severe of two austerity programmes was introduced. The intention was to increase productivity and profit margin by limiting the number of employees and the level of salaries as well as increasing the price of basic commodities [130; 195].

At the outset, **Czechoslovakia's** standard of living continued to be higher in the 1980s. Continued industrialisation and modernisation policies increased the proportion of the population working in industry and living in urban areas. The impact of this shift from the countryside to urban areas was most noticeable in Slovakia because development levels there had been significantly lower than those in the Czech lands. Educational levels increased substantially too. There was especially a sizable increase in the number of people with higher technical training.

However, certain problems and difficulties became more explicit in this decade as well. External factors, including the delayed impact of the energy crisis and changes in Soviet willingness to supply cheap energy to Eastern Europe, deepened the structural problems of the Czechoslovak economy. There was a drying-up of markets in the West because of a global recession and the labour force remained concentrated in large, inefficient industries, particularly in heavy industry.

In the face of these economic difficulties, but only towards the end of the 1980s, the Czechoslovak leaders adopted a new approach to economic reform: they acknowledged the need to decentralise and to introduce new parameters and specific factors of a market-based economic system. In this, they were not burdened with large foreign debt, which was the case for other East European countries. Czechoslovakia had not borrowed heavily from the West, and therefore its economy was not strained by servicing its debt [173; 178].

Poland remained the Achilles' heel of the Soviet bloc in the 1980s. The private trading sector continued to grow in this period and tens of thousands of Poles regularly travelled abroad in search of Western consumer goods that could be resold for hefty profits at home. Poles not only ended up controlling flea markets in Istanbul, Vienna and West Berlin, but also accumulated huge amounts of capital that were waiting for investment opportunities. In this way, at the end of the 1980s, although the state sector still occupied a dominant position in the economy, there was next to it an embryonic capitalist class that had no counterpart elsewhere in Eastern Europe.

Like many other East European states, Poland's net hard-currency debt mounted steadily during the decade. Austerity measures brought serious price increases in essential commodities. Following these increases, in July 1980, strikes broke out everywhere. Although initially settled piecemeal in the form of higher salary awards, this was not the end of it. On 14 August, the workers at the Lenin Shipyards at Gdansk, under the leadership of Lech Walesa, a former worker who had been sacked, went on strike. Following the breakdown of initial negotiations, strike committees and inter-factory strike committees were organised. Soon the delegates of the Gdansk committee produced a twenty-one point charter. The first two points were the right to independent trade unions and the right to strike. On 24 August, First Secretary Gierek announced a government reshuffle and promised economic reforms. During the negotiations between the government and Solidarity, concessions were offered by each side. Solidarity accepted 'independent and self-governing' trade unions, instead of 'free' ones, and the government acknowledged the central role and importance of Solidarity for the Polish workers. The final agreement, signed on 31 August 1980, was a radical and serious challenge to the system although it did fall within the accepted parameters of the socialist system – the leading role of the Party was still in place.

Debt to Western commercial banks and government agencies grew rapidly in this decade. The debt-service ratio of 67 per cent in 1986 was the highest in Eastern Europe. There was regular re-scheduling of debt, and austerity policies were heavily oriented towards increasing exports. Poland rejoined the IMF in 1986, having withdrawn in 1950, even though a founding member, and rejoined the World Bank in the same year.

The Tenth Party Congress in 1986, which was attended by President Gorbachev personally, witnessed the acceptance of the 1986–90 five-year plan. The principal aim of the plan was to improve the implementation of reform. This meant eliminating the balance of payments deficit, which necessitated reducing subsidies. Reducing subsidies would mean steep rises in the price of fuel and energy, bringing them into line with world levels, and a 40 per cent increase in the prices of consumer goods and services. In the November 1987 referendum, the government failed to get the required 51 per cent of the vote necessary to secure approval of its economic and political reform programme. As a result, the government planned to implement parts of the economic programme slowly. In February 1988, there was an average increase in prices of 27 per cent. In March 1988, there were increases in the cost of bus and tram fares, and newspapers and nursery school charges. In April, coal prices were raised by 200 per cent, and gas, heating fuel and electricity by 100 per cent. This was followed by the start of significant labour unrest [217; 221; 222].

The Balkans

Hoxha's successor in **Albania**, Ramiz Alia, continued his predecessor's policy of cautiously opening up contacts with a wide range of countries. Albania increased its trade with a number of West European countries. It also strengthened its trade links with the rest of Eastern Europe. Tourism was an important source of hard-currency earnings, yet only a very small number of tourists visited Albania. Industrial plants remained extremely inefficient and were under-invested. A 1990 United Nations report, commissioned by the Albanian government, suggested that since most of the industrial plants were completely outdated they should be closed down.

Agriculture still employed about 60 per cent of the labour force. It was here that the regime's economic policy suffered its most spectacular failure. As a result of a combination of primitive farming methods, bad planning, inefficient management of labour and resources, and lack of investment, the 1980s witnessed a full-scale crisis that engulfed agricultural production. By the end of the decade, stagnating agricultural production, failure to reach export targets, a decline in the output of oil, and a population explosion on a scale that was bound to lead to increased social tensions, combined to create economic misery [145; 147].

In **Bulgaria**, within the wider programme of the 'New Economic Mechanism', a number of measures were introduced in 1982–83 to reform certain aspects of the economy. The main objective was to create financial incentives and better pricing policies. In December 1986, the first direct elections of their factory managers were held by workers. Measures were taken to increase bank credits based on the criterion of economic effectiveness. In June 1987, a two-tier banking system was established with the Bulgarian National Bank supervising eight commercial banks. These were sector-oriented banks which were able to compete for customers and face the threat of bankruptcy.

The Thirteenth Party Congress in April 1986 saw an attack on the defects of the current system: corruption, bureaucracy, incompetence, inertia, irresponsibility, inefficiency, alcoholism and absenteeism. In June 1987, the Central Committee approved the 'Principles of the Concept of the Further Construction of Socialism in Bulgaria'. The basic idea was to leave general, strategic matters to the centre, while, on the whole, allowing a substantial measure of autonomy to constituent organisations. The state would still control the prices of basic commodities, subsidising them if necessary, but, as a rule, domestic prices must match those that could be obtained for the commodities on the world market. Despite this continuous streak of reforms all through the 1980s, the nature of the Bulgarian command economy was not radically altered.

Misdirected investment had often gone on unproductive and bulky industrial enterprises, while safety and pollution standards were continuously neglected. The environmental and health damage was so apparent that ecologists would be in the forefront of the slow-to-emerge Bulgarian dissident groups towards the end of the decade.

In 1989, Zhivkov's intensified campaign of assimilation and repression of Bulgaria's Turkish-speaking minority contributed to an already deteriorated economic situation. The mass exodus of over 300,000 ethnic Turks from May 1989 had a profound impact on food production and led to serious labour shortages. One result was the 4 July Decree, which proclaimed that women aged seventeen to fifty-five and men aged eighteen to sixty were subject to conscription into work battalions [152; 160].

In the early 1980s, **Romania's** trade with West Germany, the United States and Israel grew significantly. The expected large boost to hard-currency earnings from sales to Western markets, however, failed to materialise. As a result, Romania, like many other East European states, had accumulated a hard-currency debt of nearly US $10 billion. In late 1981, Romania followed Poland to become the second COMECON country to request a re-scheduling of its hard-currency foreign debt. The IMF demanded further austerity measures in Romania as a condition for re-scheduling the debt. The increasing dependency on Western financial support clearly alarmed Ceausesçu, and in 1982 he announced the goal of not only meeting the interest repayments but paying off the principal debt entirely by the end of the decade (he succeeded in doing so by March 1989, six months before his demise). In order to achieve this, bread rationing was introduced and the use of refrigerators, vacuum cleaners and other household appliances was banned. With chronic food shortages plaguing the country, Ceausesçu introduced the 'Rational Eating Programme', which he justified by claiming that Romanians were eating too much (see Table 1).

Table 1   The Romanian 'Scientific' Diet (based on the 'Rational Eating Programme'), 1985–86

Commodity	Permitted consumption per year per person
Meat and fish	54.88 kg
Margarine	1.10 kg
Edible oil	9.60 kg
Sugar	14.80 kg
Wheat and flour	114.50 kg
Potatoes	45.30 kg
Fruits and grapes	20.00 kg
Eggs	114 pieces

Note: Announced by Nicolae Ceausescu, in *Scinteia*, 17 November, 1985. Ceausescu also announced that every Romanian was 'entitled' to 1.1 kg of soap and 3.5 kg of detergent.

Source: From Gilberg, T. (1990) *Nationalism and Communism in Romania: The Rise and Fall of Ceausescu's Personal Dictatorship*, Westview Press, page 128.

Arms sales were regarded by Ceausescu as a means of paying off Romania's foreign debt. His best customer was Egypt. Romania also supplied reconditioned equipment to Iraq during the Iran–Iraq war. This strategy made Romania the second largest exporter of arms in the Warsaw Pact after the Soviet Union.

In November 1987, there were serious protests against economic conditions, especially against pay reductions linked to the non-fulfilment of performance targets, redundancies, price increases, serious food shortages and fuel restrictions. Towards the end of the decade, the economy remained highly centralised, with very little prospect of change in the foreseeable future. Of all the countries of Eastern Europe, Romania's prospects seemed the most bleak [228; 229; 253].

In **Yugoslavia**, the 1980s was a time of deepening economic crisis in the country as a whole. The main reason was the debt crisis which was exacerbated by Yugoslavia's impenetrable banking system. Foreign loans were contracted not only by the Yugoslav National bank but also by the republican banks so that Yugoslavia's indebtedness was invariably higher than official figures admitted. At the end of 1982 Yugoslavia was no longer able to honour its debt obligations.

During the 1980s, standby agreements with the IMF were replaced by 'enhanced monitoring'. This involved twice yearly checks on performance for the benefit of creditors and was conceded after Western banks agreed to multi-year re-scheduling. A new agreement over interest rates was concluded in 1985, which involved both interest rate rises based on the average of the rise in producers' prices over the previous quarter and estimated inflation over the next quarter. Fresh standby financing was agreed with the IMF in April 1988 and in the middle of May a programme was put into operation that involved deflationary reductions in the money supply and in public expenditure. In May 1988 ceilings were imposed on wage increases. In December 1988, the government resigned, the first time this had happened since 1945. Failure to win approval for the federal budget was the immediate cause. Towards the end of the decade it was obvious that the Yugoslav economy had severe problems – a high unemployment rate, rapid inflation and especially a massive foreign debt. In 1989, inflation reached an annual rate of 2,500 per cent. By the end of the decade, earlier enthusiasm in the West was replaced by a strong reluctance to undertake unconditional financial rescues in Yugoslavia [269; 280; 283].

REASONS FOR ECONOMIC FAILURE

All East European economies evolved some form of the highly centralised and authoritarian economic model developed by Stalin in the 1930s in the Soviet Union. Although such an economic system seemed no longer valid in the later twentieth century, the communist economies in many East European countries must be given credit for some important achievements: the redistribution of wealth, modernisation of the infrastructure, the development and expansion of industrial sectors and the modernisation of agriculture. In the 1950s and 1960s, growth was spectacular. But Soviet-style communist economies never accomplished a level of individual well-being that was commensurate with each country's resources and capabilities. From the 1970s, the gap with Western Europe widened. By the late 1980s, despite their compulsive micro-management of economic life, managers of the communist economic system had clearly failed to provide people with a level of material well-being comparable to the living standards in the West. Inflation was marked by growing shortages, deteriorating quality and lengthening queues.

Most of the problems experienced by communist economies can be attributed to misguided investment priorities, to managerial mediocrity and incompetence, to limits on the kind of reform that could have expanded output, and to the perverse behaviour patterns of the vast majority of ruling elites. East European communist leaders set misguided priorities without properly considering the real economic consequences of their decisions. They were obsessed with providing full employment, which required keeping unprofitable enterprises working. They also spent heavily on defence and far too little on the production of consumer goods. Heavy industry was favoured at the expense of other sectors, such as housing, welfare and agriculture. There was no real incentive for the individual, and productivity remained extremely low by Western standards. The communist parties of Eastern Europe emphasised conformity, loyalty and obedience to the party line in recruitment to managerial positions. This resulted in the elevation of unimaginative and administratively unsuitable people to positions of responsibility. Real economic reform in the form of a major curtailment of state control over economic life, which could have provided individuals with a strong incentive to work harder, was ruled out by communist leaders because state control over the economy was considered a source of power and prestige. Out of this mismanagement and chaos, a black market, which benefited only a small percentage of people, flourished almost everywhere in Eastern Europe. The results were empty shelves in shops, people wasting increasing amounts of time in queues and, at the extreme, food riots which threatened the bureaucratic-hierarchical and highly centralised state structures in Eastern Europe [26].

Eastern Europe generally followed a strategy of import-led (debt-led) growth during the 1970s to stem the fall in growth rates experienced towards the end of the 1960s. Both investment and consumption growth targets were raised. To sustain high rates of economic growth and investment the managers of the socialist economies turned to borrowing in the Western capital markets. Western credits were freely offered by the banks. The Western commercial banks and government agencies were reacting to the growing profitability crisis in the advanced Western economies by scouring the world for areas where investment could receive a higher return. Eastern Europe appealed to them in this respect. They were confident of Soviet backing and anxious to recycle OPEC surpluses, after the 1973–74 quadrupling of oil prices, to hitherto good repayers.

These credits were sought in the hope of using imported capital goods, embodying the latest technology, to stimulate the hard-currency exports needed to repay debt. Foreign technology was generally seen as a substitute for radical economic reform rather than being a necessary element in the process of economic restructuring and development. Floating interest rates were the norm and they rose considerably during the second half of the 1970s. The East European economies were, in this way, tied into the world economy through their extensive debts to Western banks. They were no longer protected from cyclical economic disturbances such as the energy recessions of the 1970s and early 1980s. This factor, plus recession in the West, which restricted its importing and investment potential, and unwarranted optimism about the prospects for exporting manufactured goods of sufficient quality to the West, led to enormous repayments difficulties which at the end of the 1980s became the major economic reason for the severe crisis of the socialist economies of Eastern Europe (see Table 2) [33; 44; 77].

Table 2   The estimated hard-currency debt of the Soviet Union and East European states, 1990 (billions of US dollars)

	1975	1980	1984	1985	1986	1987	1988	1989
Bulgaria								
gross	2.6	3.5	2.8	3.2	4.7	6.1	8.2	9.2
net	2.3	2.7	1.4	1.2	3.3	5.1	6.4	8.0
Czechoslovakia								
gross	1.1	6.9	4.7	4.6	5.6	6.7	7.3	7.9
net	0.8	5.6	3.7	3.6	4.4	5.1	5.6	5.7
The GDR								
gross	5.2	13.8	11.7	13.2	15.6	18.6	19.8	20.6
net	3.5	11.8	7.2	6.9	8.2	9.7	10.3	11.1
Hungary								
gross	3.9	9.1	11.0	14.0	16.9	19.6	19.6	20.6
net	2.0	7.7	9.4	11.7	14.8	18.1	18.2	19.4
Poland								
gross	8.4	24.1	26.5	29.3	33.5	39.2	39.2	40.8
net	7.7	23.5	24.9	27.7	31.8	36.2	35.6	36.9
Romania								
gross	2.9	9.6	7.2	6.6	6.4	5.7	2.9	0.6
net	2.4	9.3	6.6	6.2	5.8	4.4	2.1	−1.2
Eastern Europe								
gross	24.2	67.0	63.9	71.0	82.7	96.0	97.0	99.7
net	18.8	60.5	53.2	57.4	68.1	78.4	78.2	79.9
The Soviet Union								
gross	10.6	23.5	21.4	25.2	30.5	40.2	46.8	52.4
net	7.5	14.9	10.1	12.1	15.6	26.1	31.4	37.7
COMECON								
gross	34.8	90.5	85.3	96.1	113.1	136.2	143.7	152.1
net	26.3	75.5	63.3	69.5	83.8	104.5	109.7	117.6

Note: These figures are Western estimates based on officially reported data. In the case of the GDR, in particular, internal figures that became available after unification indicate that these estimates understated the net debt. The table nevertheless gives a sense of orders of magnitude.

Source: *Comecon Data 1990*, Macmillan Ltd (Vienna Institute for Comparative Economic Studies), 1991.

CHAPTER FIVE

THE COLLAPSE

Despite the warning signs in all spheres of economic and political life, very few outside observers predicted the collapse of communist rule in the 1980s. It was not just the academics who were taken by surprise; so were policy-makers and intellectuals. Signs of decline were abundant in Eastern Europe, but not of imminent collapse. In 1989 the police and the army seemed reliable enough. The economies of the socialist countries, despite all their weaknesses and problems, continued to function. They provided increases in real wages and in exports, in some cases. There was no obvious reason to expect the imminent fall of the regimes at the end of the 1980s. What is puzzling is that the regimes collapsed so quickly and that they collapsed when they did, in 1989, and not in 1956, 1968 or at any other particular point in time. Not only was the collapse of the Soviet Bloc fast and unexpected, however. It was also largely peaceful and it swept across the region as a whole, in a kind of snow-balling effect.

The reasons for the fall of communism have attracted the interest of historians and political scientists alike. No single explanation is possible. We are dealing here with the most complex kind of problem, one that involves numerous factors of variable importance working in changing combinations. This chapter serves simply to map out some ways of understanding the relative significance of the different origins of this historic change in European history. Economic factors played an important and probably decisive role. But it is certain that other factors, without being essential causes, also contributed significantly to the ultimate collapse, in particular to its timing.

THE RESULTS OF ECONOMIC FAILURE

In the chain of events leading to the collapse of the socialist regimes of Eastern Europe, the role of the economic problems facing these countries is the first factor that requires consideration. Warning signs were plentiful in the economic sphere. The period beginning in the mid-1970s came to be

called 'the period of stagnation' in the Soviet Bloc and generated an accelerated economic crisis and an absolute deterioration of living standards in
most of Eastern Europe. This period also witnessed significant deterioration
and retrogression in its competitive standing compared to Western Europe:
the gap with the West, which had been closing since the war, widened
again. Only in terms of alcohol consumption was the East surpassing the
West.

A chronic feature of the 1980s was the emergence of a multiplicity of
private enterprises, legal as well as illegal, which existed side by side with
the official, state-controlled economy. Towards the end of the decade, this
'second economy' had become an important element of the national
economies of many Eastern European countries, absorbing a considerable
amount of resources and labour. This situation eroded the communist
economic system from within and contributed to its gradual disintegration.

Domestic economic organisation and ineffective policies were, however,
not the only, or even the dominant, reason for economic failure. To explore
the general nature and long-term causes of the collapse of communism in
Eastern Europe, the key factor lies in the changing pattern of the balance of
global socio-economic and political forces: the process of the progressive
integration of Eastern Europe into the world capitalist economic system.
This took two forms: trade and debt. Eastern Europe was always in a weak
position in the development of its international trade, and the direction of
trade was increasingly towards the West. The relative weakness of the
socialist economies in the world capitalist system became the dominant
aspect governing East European trade and left these countries permanently
vulnerable to global forces beyond their control.

The socialist economies stepped up their involvement with the capitalist
world economy in the late 1960s. In many Eastern European countries
central planning was reformed to allow imports of high-tech machinery and
goods produced in insufficient qualities at home. This process of integration
into the world economy was made necessary, in effect, by the shortages and
contradictions of the Soviet model of economic development. As a result, in
the 1970s, the Eastern European countries (and the Soviet Union) decided
vastly to increase their trade with the West. They sought to fuel their
growth by importing technology and capital from the West. The communist
leaders of the Soviet Bloc countries came to see imports from the West as a
way of achieving the economic goals of modernisation under a general
policy of balanced trade. They would import technology from the West and
use it to produce industrial commodities.

The Eastern European governments intended to pay for Western technology in part with the export of raw materials and in part with the export
of the derivative manufactures that would be produced with the imported
technology. This, however, did not materialise. There were domestic reasons

for this failure, but the main reason was related to the ups and downs of the world economy. Instead, the 'solution' everywhere was to run up debts. The debts of the socialist countries increased dramatically. The Western commercial banks and financial institutions, awash with investible money, loaned and loaned. The willingness to borrow, however, depended on the internal policy choices of the East European countries. Some countries (Poland, Romania, Hungary, GDR, Yugoslavia, as well as the Soviet Union) borrowed heavily, while others (especially Czechoslovakia) were more cautious.

The 1973–74 and 1979 oil crises, and the deep 1979–82 recession in the world economy created a global economic downturn and limited possibilities of trade. Because of the military style conformity of state socialism and lack of flexible organisational and political procedures, the downturn affected the economies of Eastern Europe much more seriously than the advanced capitalist economies of the West. The East European economies were unable to pay for their imports by exporting more because of ferocious competition from the low-wage and low-cost newly industrialising countries such as South Korea and Taiwan. Even securing the basic commodities and simple technological products involved a mounting burden of foreign debt. By the end of the 1980s the burden of debt remained heavy for the six Eastern European members of the COMECON (except Romania, which wiped out its debt completely by 1989). The strain of servicing debt had far-reaching economic and political consequences, the most important of which was the fact that Western creditors such as the IMF could demand austerity measures as pre-conditions for re-scheduling debt payments. The communist rulers themselves were held responsible for such measures. The economic strategies that relied on foreign debt then generated social and political crises within the economic crisis. Because the economy, the government and the Party were inseparable in the minds of the citizens of the socialist countries, it effectively meant that the economic crisis automatically became a magnified political crisis. It fatally undermined the Party's sense of its own governing mission.

Centralisation of power inevitably led to a centralisation of blame. When the gap between the declared aims of socialism and the results achieved widened, the conflict deepened. The abandonment by the early 1980s of any convincing hope of surpassing the West economically left the Party with little general purpose. It degenerated into an increasingly ineffective instrument of crisis management. The ruling Party was stripped of purpose and legitimacy and the ideological justification of the regimes was lost as a result [44; 130].

The overall structural determinants of the collapse of communism were set a long time ago in the specific route that the Soviet Bloc countries pursued in the world economy. However, the particular timing of the collapse can be seen as a result of the political responses of the leaders, especially those in the Kremlin, to the general crisis. In retrospect, one can claim that the Cold War could not have been brought to an end, nor Communist Party rule in Moscow terminated and the Soviet Bloc countries set on a path towards liberal democracy and market-based economies, had it not been for Gorbachev's vision, courage and commitment to engineering these system-transforming changes.

GORBACHEV AND THE IMPACT OF THE CHANGE IN THE SOVIET UNION

Throughout the 1970s and the first half of the 1980s, Soviet policy towards the region confronted an inevitable dilemma: either to enforce ideological orthodoxy and political cohesion or to promote the development of more viable, legitimate and stable regimes in Eastern Europe. The latter would necessitate tolerating or even encouraging a process of economic and political reform. This dilemma was never adequately resolved in the pre-Gorbachev years, but the catalytic impact of Gorbachev's reforms was to change all this.

The evolution of Gorbachev's thinking is an important element of the dramatic changes that took place in Eastern Europe in the 1980s. Without Gorbachev, change would have been slower and more violent. His efforts to democratise his country's political system and decentralise its economy led to the collapse of the communist system and the break-up of the Soviet Union. Believing in socialism and in the legitimacy of the rule of the Communist Party, Gorbachev aimed at reforming communism rather than replacing it. He did not envisage the break-up of the Soviet Union. Indeed, he had two primary and interrelated goals: to increase the authority of the Communist Party by opening channels for greater popular participation and to reform the economic system and thus improve the living standards of the Soviet people [3].

Mikhail Gorbachev was born in 1931, the son of Russian peasants in Privolnoye, a village of 3,300 people about 100 miles north of Stavropol District in south-western Russia. He was the first General Secretary of the Party to have started his career after Stalin's death. His career, unlike Brezhnev's, Andropov's and Chernenko's, did not benefit from Stalin's purges. Trained in law and appointed to a Party position in the Stavropol District, Gorbachev heard Khrushchev's 1956 speech criticising Stalin's extremism when it was read to him and other Party workers by the Chairman of the Stavropol District. Khrushchev's speech had a great impact on the young Gorbachev. The speech and the project of reform communism it launched became the guiding vision of the rest of Gorbachev's political life. Bright, articulate, intellectually curious and hard-working, loyal and well-liked, he worked his way up the Soviet political hierarchy. Gorbachev became a member of the Central Committee of the Communist Party in 1971 and was appointed Party Secretary of Agriculture in 1978. He became a candidate member of the Politburo in 1979 and a full member in 1980. Over the course of Yury Andropov's fifteen-month tenure (1982–84) as General Secretary of the CPSU, Gorbachev became one of the Politburo's most highly active and noticeable members. After Andropov died and Konstantin Chernenko became General Secretary in February 1984, Gorbachev became a likely successor to the latter. Chernenko died on 10 March 1985, and the following day the Politburo elected Gorbachev General Secretary of the CPSU. Upon his accession, he was still the youngest member of the Politburo.

When Gorbachev was elected General Secretary, he inherited, by his own admission, an enormous backlog of problems. The emphasis on military strength throughout the Cold War had drained Soviet resources and irrevocably damaged its domestic economy. The Soviet economy was stagnant and unable to react to the challenge of 'Star Wars'. In addition there were numerous and intractable external difficulties, ranging from the collapse of *détente* to stalemate in the war against Afghanistan [19].

Gorbachev's basic goal was to arrest this decline. First, he set about consolidating his power base in the Soviet leadership. His short-term domestic goal was to revitalise the stagnant Soviet economy after its years of drift and low growth during Brezhnev's tenure in power (1964–82). To this end, he called for rapid technological modernisation and increased productivity. When these initial steps failed to yield tangible results, Gorbachev, in 1987–88, proceeded to initiate deeper reforms of the Soviet economy and political system. His policy of *glasnost* ('openness'), allowed greater freedom of expression and access to information. The press and broadcasting authorities were now allowed unprecedented openness in their coverage of political events and criticism of the Soviet leadership. Daniel Gros and Alfred Steinherr describe *glasnost* as 'rendering public what was hidden' [44 *pp*. 30–1]. Gorbachev's policy of *perestroika* ('restructuring') represented the first modest attempt to democratise the Soviet political system [*Doc. 10*]. Multi-candidate contests and the secret ballot were introduced in some elections to Party and state posts.

In foreign affairs, from the beginning Gorbachev encouraged warmer relations and trade with the developed nations of the West. In December 1987, he signed an agreement with the United States President, Ronald Reagan, by which both countries agreed to destroy all existing stocks of intermediate-range nuclear missiles, and in 1988–89, he oversaw the withdrawal of Soviet troops from Afghanistan after their nine-year occupation of that country [25].

The election of Mikhail Gorbachev to the leadership of the Soviet Communist Party in March 1985 at first did not bring any significant change to the situation in Eastern Europe. During his first two years in power, there was no immediate change in the overall Soviet policy with regard to the Eastern Bloc. The foreign policy implications of Gorbachev's programme for Eastern Europe took time to emerge. Within the Soviet Union, however, a programme of far-reaching domestic reforms had already been instigated. This programme of domestic restructuring necessitated a benign international environment. Gorbachev argued that cooperation with the West was now a realistic possibility and that the West was not irredeemably hostile to the Soviet Union. This profound reassessment of the international security concerns of the Soviet state and the domestic imperatives of restructuring had fundamental implications for Eastern Europe.

Gorbachev's reforms in the Soviet Union paved the way for a serious leadership challenge to the East European old guards. Gorbachev and his political allies persuaded, manoeuvred and bullied their more orthodox allies into accepting a redefinition of basic Soviet goals and objectives in Eastern Europe. They had realised that the Soviet Union was now in too weak a position domestically to maintain its iron grip on Eastern Europe. In December 1986, Gorbachev talked about the rights of countries to choose their 'different paths' to socialism. By mid-1988 Gorbachev expressed the view that Soviet control in Eastern Europe violated the principle of genuine communist internationalism, and therefore that the East European governments should be left to govern as they wished, without outside interference. This was a clear repudiation of everything that earlier Soviet leaders had espoused. Gorbachev's rejection of his predecessors' commitment to the socialist bloc ensured that the military option was no longer possible. In this way, Gorbachev foreswore any legitimate resort to force to maintain communism in Eastern Europe. The so-called 'Sinatra doctrine' (that they could 'do it their way') reversed the earlier 'Brezhnev Doctrine' [*Doc. 9*] [118]. As a result, Eastern Europe was no longer regarded as an irreplaceable buffer zone. The Soviet Union willingly relieved its military control over the developments in Eastern Europe.

Throughout 1989, Gorbachev seized every opportunity to voice his support for reformist communists in the East European countries. Many of the East European leaders, who were installed and protected by Moscow, felt threatened and vulnerable as a result of Gorbachev's 'openness'. As democratically elected non-communist governments came to power in East Germany, Poland, Hungary and Czechoslovakia in 1989–90, Gorbachev agreed to the phased withdrawal of Soviet troops from those countries. By the summer of 1990, he agreed to the reunification of East Germany and the Federal Republic of Germany [*Doc. 10*] [33; 66].

In short, Gorbachev, with his reforms, allowed the political and economic worlds to drift. He undermined the authority and role of the

Communist Party without offering a replacement and, most importantly for Eastern Europe, as part of a global *perestroika*, he willingly abandoned the 'Brezhnev Doctrine'. Gorbachev's role in the collapse of the communist system can hardly be exaggerated. A different Soviet leader most likely would have acted differently. The choices Gorbachev made in the late 1980s were by no means regarded as the only ones available. Still, it would be wrong to assume that it was Gorbachev who brought the communist system to an end. The actions taken by individuals, however honest and coherent their expressed intentions may be, are influenced by external factors which determine what alternatives are open to them. More importantly, the actions of individuals usually have unintended consequences. One of the main reasons why this is so is that they cannot possibly have a full grasp of the structural constraints under which they are operating, nor can they know how those who are actually affected by their actions will respond.

POLITICAL CHALLENGE: THE SNOWBALL EFFECT, 1989–91

The rapid disintegration of communism in Eastern Europe began in Poland, the weakest link in the chain. The rest of the East European countries followed in rapid succession. There was a kind of domino effect.

In the late 1980s, **Poland** was the country where communist rule was visibly closest to collapse. The economic situation was worsening and there was a continuing problem with political reform. Although the imposition of martial law in 1981 brought an end to the strike movement, it failed to stop the crisis: Poland's economic situation continued to deteriorate and resentment among workers remained strong. There was a fresh upsurge of strikes in 1988. The deterioration of the economy was largely because its structural problems could not be tackled effectively without a serious long-term reform programme. The capability of the government to manoeuvre between the urgent demands of the workers and the requirements for a sound economy was severely limited by the pressure of ever-increasing foreign debt. The foreign debt was US $39 billion in 1988, real wages were 20 per cent lower in 1988 than in 1980, national product per head was 13 per cent lower in 1988 than in 1978 [33].

The crisis of 1988 was set off by an attempt to stimulate agricultural production with incentives. Farm procurement prices were raised by an average of 48 per cent. To pay for this, retail prices were also raised by an average of 48 per cent. These steps were followed by a wave of strikes in May and August 1988. At first the strikers wanted compensatory wage increases, but they soon broadened their objectives to the re-legalisation of Solidarity (which was formally banned in October 1982), the release of political prisoners and the reappointment of people sacked for political reasons. The opposition, led by Solidarity, was getting more vocal and daring in its demands. The seriousness of the 1988 strikes prompted the communist government of General Jaruzelski to offer to negotiate with the still banned Solidarity movement. Solidarity and Jaruzelski agreed to round table talks to discuss a possible way out of the conflict. In the end a compromise programme was agreed: free elections would be held to a resurrected Polish Senate, or upper house, and to 35 per cent of the seats in the *Sejm*. In return, the opposition agreed to the creation of a new office, the Presidency, whose occupant would have power over the army and foreign policy [210].

In the elections of June 1989, Solidarity candidates swept the board, standing as representatives of 'Citizens' Committees': all of the open seats in the *Sejm* went to Solidarity candidates, and 99 out of the 100 seats in the Senate went the same way. This opened the way to the formation of a coalition government under the leadership of Tadeusz Mazowiecki. Twelve of the cabinet seats were given to Solidarity, making a majority. Poland thus became the only Warsaw Pact country with a non-communist government.

The importance of what had happened in Poland was not lost in the other countries of Eastern Europe, especially in **Hungary**. Indeed, the process of compromise had long been ripening in Hungary, while in Poland it started rather suddenly and unexpectedly. János Kádár's decision to consolidate his regime by a partial compromise set a policy framework which lasted, despite ups and downs, until the late 1980s.

Multiple candidatures were introduced for the Hungarian elections of June 1985. In the field of the economy, certain restrictions on private agriculture had already been removed in 1980. In industry, there were a number of relatively minor liberalising moves in the early 1980s. Meanwhile, disturbances were felt within the ruling Communist Party, the Hungarian Socialist Workers' Party (HSWP). Gorbachev's accession to power in the Soviet Union and his espousal of the policies of *perestroika* encouraged reformist communists in Hungary, the most prominent of whom was Imre Pozsgay. In 1986 a major study by thirty-five leading Hungarian economists, entitled 'Turning Point and Reform', called for political, organisational, institutional and social reform. It stopped short of demanding a multi-party system, but avoided mentioning the leading role of the Party. In the economic sphere, the report recommended that the government's task was the constant and conscious elimination of constraints on the market [202].

Faced by a strong challenge from the faction around Pozsgay, it was obvious that Kádár's position was in decline. The moderate opposition and reformist section of the Party joined forces in September 1987, establishing the Hungarian Democratic Forum (HDF), which adopted a Christian Democratic and nationalist orientation. The founding conference of the HDF was opened by a speech by Pozsgay. On 22 May 1988, Kádár and many of his Politburo colleagues were removed from their positions. The following month, on 16 June, a demonstration commemorating Imre Nagy, the liberal Party leader hanged for treason in 1956, and the Hungarian Revolution of 1956 was suppressed by force. Nagy had been buried in an unmarked grave in a cemetery outside Budapest. In 1988 a citizens' committee was formed to campaign for Nagy's rehabilitation and reburial. In early 1989 the Hungarian government announced that it would allow a funeral to be held for Imre Nagy. As a result of the pressure from below and also the news from Poland that Solidarity was to take part in discussions with the regime as an equal partner, the reformers were able to tip the balance within the Party in their direction. On 10 February 1989, at a decisive Central Committee meeting, the conservative, anti-reformist wing of the Party was decisively defeated. In February 1989 the Party leadership committed itself to a multi-party system. In April it renounced one of the central principles of Communist Party rule – democratic centralism. In May, another principle, the *nomenklatura* system, was abandoned. In June, a funeral ceremony and reburial of Imre Nagy took place in Budapest's Heroes' Square, with a quarter of a million people in attendance. In September, an agreement was signed with the opposition for free parliamentary elections. In October, the parliament banned Communist Party cells in the workplace, abolished the 60,000 strong Workers' Militia and converted Hungary from a People's Republic into a Republic. Finally, on 7 October, the Party dissolved itself, thus ending single-party rule in Hungary. The flexibility of the Party and its involvement in a serious dialogue with the opposition were key factors in the Hungarian experience. The ruling elite in Hungary gave up its power because it realised that it had a good chance of converting the power it had possessed in the old system into a new kind of power.

But it was the change in Hungarian foreign policy that had the greatest external impact. In May 1989, the barbed-wire fence on the Austrian border was removed. It was a great symbolic step, marking the end of the 'iron curtain'. East German holiday-makers in Austria flooded into Hungary to take advantage of this. In August, the West German embassy in Budapest had to close because its grounds were overcrowded with East German refugees seeking a way to the West. On 10 September, the Hungarian government threw open the border with Austria, allowing 12,000 East Germans to leave within seventy-two hours. This was a previously unthinkable breach of a longstanding agreement with the GDR but it brought down no Soviet retribution or condemnation [19; 196; 206].

In **East Germany** itself, people could not be insulated from the events going on around them. Access to West German television constantly reminded them that the GDR was far behind the Federal Republic in material terms. The reforms of Gorbachev in the Soviet Union also had a considerable impact. Censorship of news from the Soviet Union was ineffective because West German radio and television reported Gorbachev's activities in full. An increasing awareness of environmental issues was also contributing to a recently achieved self-confidence among the East German people. They could not remain unaware of the level of pollution which resulted from the one-sided emphasis on heavy industrial production for production's sake [182; 189].

Compared with Poland, Hungary or Czechoslovakia, there was very little open dissidence in the GDR. The main reason for this was repression by the ever-present and massive network of the *Stasi* intelligence service. However, 1987 saw the emergence of two major unofficial journals, *Ecology News* and *Borderline Case*. The former concentrated on environmental issues, the latter on developing an understanding of peace and human rights. Later, in the spring of 1989, the Evangelical Lutheran Church and peace groups raised their sights to the more political arena of the local elections. In April, forty-eight prominent clergy called on people to boycott them. It was this movement that gave birth, in the tense and emotional circumstances of September 1989, to the 'New Forum', a body initially intended to promote a dialogue on change between the dissidents and the authorities. From the middle of September hundreds of thousands of ordinary East Germans attempted to escape to the West. There was a marked absence of decisive action from Berlin to stop the departures. Larger numbers took part in the marches and demonstrations mounted under the auspices of New Forum in Leipzig, Dresden, East Berlin and other cities. When Gorbachev visited East Germany in early October 1989, at the fortieth anniversary of the establishment of the socialist system there, he warned Honecker that it was time to change and that 'dangers only exist for those who don't grasp the situation, who don't react to life' [33 *p. 186*; 186].

Within the party leadership, Honecker's position had been weakened both by his chronic ill health and by the pressure for reform which was coming from Gorbachev. Ultimately, convinced of the need for change by the attitude of the Soviet leader, the exodus of asylum-seekers and the size and tenacity of the demonstrations, the Politburo engineered the ousting of Honecker. On 18 October he was forced to resign. He was replaced as First Secretary by Egon Krenz. The whole of the government and the party Politburo resigned on 8 November. Finally, on 9 November 1989, twenty-eight years after it built the Berlin Wall to stop an earlier flood of refugees, the East German government announced the end of all travel restrictions to the West, including those via Berlin. The fall of the Berlin Wall was surely one of the most emotional and symbolically important European events of the postwar era. After that, it was too late to salvage even the existence of the GDR itself. The collapse of the regime was spectacularly rapid and, within a year, quite unexpectedly complete [188].

Czechoslovakia was next on the list. The collapse of the communist system was precipitated by events outside the country. The negotiated end of communist rule in Poland and Hungary and the fall of the hardline communist regime of Honecker in the GDR were important catalysts in bringing about the collapse of communism in Czechoslovakia.

The end of the Communist Party's dominance was also conditioned by important changes that occurred at the level of politics/policy making and participation between 1987 and 1989. The process of change began in December 1987 when Jakeš replaced Husák as General Secretary of the Party. Jakeš's elevation was followed by the removal of more conservative members of the Presidium in 1988. These changes were accompanied by the promotion of younger and more dynamic members to the Presidium. Several of these newcomers were less personally attached to the policies of the Husák era and were less fearful of reform than their predecessors.

The change in the political climate was also evident in the new willingness of the population to challenge the regime by organising independent groups and taking part in unauthorised demonstrations. There was a sharp increase both in the formation of independent associations and in political activism.

In August 1988, 10,000 people marched through the streets of Prague to mark the twentieth anniversary of the Warsaw Pact intervention in Czechoslovakia. In October 1988, the leaders of the official Writers' Union decided to begin rehabilitating some of the many writers whose works were banned after 1968. In January 1989, several thousand people gathered to mark the anniversary of the death of Jan Palach, a student who had set himself on fire in 1969 to protest at the intervention. The demonstration was harshly broken up by the police, which led to several days of further demonstrations. Approximately forty leading dissidents, including Václav Havel, were arrested during the January 1989 demonstrations. In the wake of Havel's trial in February 1989, thousands of letters of support and petitions were circulated in the country. During the summer of 1989, some 30,000 individuals signed the manifesto 'Several Sentences' that called for political freedom and an end to censorship.

On 17 November 1989 a march was organised in Prague in commemoration of the funeral of Jan Opletal, a student killed by the Nazis in 1939. It was permitted because of its apparently 'harmless' theme. The opposition, however, used the opportunity to call for 'freedom', 'justice', the release of political prisoners, the dismissal of the leading communist rulers and even the ending of communist rule. The riot police intervened brutally. The harsh suppression of the 17 November students' demonstration became a key catalyst in the end of the Party's monopoly of power.

On 19 November, Prague students, actors and the veteran dissidents from Charter 77, led by the playwright Václav Havel, set up the Civic

Forum to give direction to the protest movement. There followed a succession of militantly non-violent demonstrations, each one bigger than the one before. As the events unfolded and massive demonstrations followed one after another, so the ruling elite desperately reshuffled one government after another to preserve power. At the end of November 1989, the abolition of Article 4 of the constitution (which referred to the Party's leading role in society) was approved by the Federal Assembly. The final phase of the fall started with the formation of a new government on 10 December 1989. In this government the Communist Party held only eight out of twenty-one ministries. When President Husák resigned, Václav Havel was unanimously elected by the Federal Assembly on 29 December 1989. Alexander Dubček, the tragic hero of the 1968 'Prague Spring', emerged in triumph as chairman of the national parliament. These events marked the end of the communist system in Czechoslovakia. The change in Czechoslovakia was brief, euphoric and quite remarkably thorough in levering the communists from power. The relatively peaceful run of events in Czechoslovakia gave rise to the term 'velvet revolution' [166; 169; 173].

In the Balkans, the ways the regimes collapsed were similar to those in East-Central Europe but they developed slowly and more painfully because of the weakness of the non-communist opposition and the superior ability of the communist elites to stay in power. The change in **Bulgaria** was certainly aided by the sequence of events throughout Eastern Europe in 1989 and 1990, yet the nature of the transition was somewhat different from that in other countries. In Bulgaria the change occurred more cautiously, and in a series of stages.

A number of warning signs had appeared in Bulgaria in the late 1980s. Agricultural output fell by 5.1 per cent in 1987 and by 0.1 per cent in 1988. In 1989 national income fell by 0.4 per cent, the volume of exports to the West by 3.4 per cent. The net debt to the West rose from US $5.9 billion in 1988 to $9.3 billion in 1989. As a consequence, by the end of the decade the economy was saddled with a burden of foreign debt which it could not afford to service. It also became clear, from the mid-1980s, that the Soviet Union was neither willing nor able to go on propping up the Bulgarian economy. A kaleidoscopic spectrum of dissidence and opposition emerged in 1989 – hunger strikes by the Turkish-speaking minority and demonstrations by the ecological pressure group *Ecoglasnost*. There was also an independent trade union, *Podkrepa* (Support), a Club for the Support of *Perestroika* and *Glasnost*, and a Committee for the Defence of Religious Rights. There was an outpouring of pent-up, anti-Zhivkov feeling but an absence of anti-Soviet slogans. Petar Mladenov, Zhivkov's Foreign Minister, and his faction in the Bulgarian Communist Party (BCP), decided to forestall what was coming by introducing some liberalising measures from above. As a result of a kind of 'palace coup', Zhivkov was removed from power on 10 November 1989 by the other members of his communist elite. Petar Mladenov replaced him as president and Party leader. Over the following months a rapid series of concessions followed, including the promise of free elections. In January 1990, at its Fourteenth Party Congress, the BCP adopted the name 'Bulgarian Socialist Party' and committed itself to multi-party democracy and a 'socially oriented market economy'. In November 1990 the BSP government of Andrei Lukanov was forced to resign, following a general strike jointly organised by *Podkrepa* and the former official communist trade union. The opposition Union of Democratic Forces (UDF) was brought into a coalition government. The leader of the opposition, Zhelyu Zhelev, had already been made President in August. Further elections in October 1991 resulted in a defeat for the BSP and its complete removal from office. Thus the transition to post-communist era was made relatively smoothly and peacefully in Bulgaria [10; 33; 161].

The collapse of the regime came with astonishing suddenness in **Romania,** which suffered from a series of special factors that made a violent denouement unavoidable. The regime of Nicolae Ceausescu followed the old-fashioned Stalinist model and was based on an increasingly repressive system of control by the latter part of the 1980s. Ceausescu's tyranny was deaf to any form of dialogue. The regime relied heavily on its huge security police apparatus and Ceausescu's own personal rule aggravated the tensions. The Ceausescu version of communist rule was highly centralist, concentrating power within a narrow circle of family members and close associates. Alone among Eastern European rulers, he took pride in paying off his country's debts, which could only be done with the most extreme austerity measures. Moreover, the earthquake of 1977, centred on the country's oil fields, caused a significant drop in oil production. As a result, Romania became a net importer of oil from the West. Therefore, the 1979 increase in world oil prices severely affected Romania. The attempt to replace oil with coal was a failure. Because of the stagnant condition of electric power generation, the Romanian consumer was continually harassed with power cuts. Moreover, due to south-east Asian competition, the range of Romanian exports was severely reduced in the 1980s. Food alone could be exported, and this meant less food for a rapidly expanding population. Repression took the form of economic deprivation.

The changing Soviet stance towards Eastern Europe, in terms of the influence of *perestroika* and *glasnost*, was not much felt in Romania. The crisis in Romania was in fact sparked off by an attack on the Hungarian minority. Ceausescu's policy of 'systematisation' involved the destruction of half the country's villages and the resettlement of the inhabitants in agro-industrial centres where they could be controlled more easily. The systematisation scheme became synonymous with the worst excesses of the Ceausescu regime. The process was actually started in purely Romanian areas around Bucharest. It was, however, in the Hungarian villages of Transylvania that it met with severe resistance, led by the Hungarian pastor of Timisoara, Laszlo Tökes. It was the authorities' attempt to remove him from his parish that provided the unlikely spark for an uprising on 17 December 1989. Special security units, known as the *Securitate*, fired on the demonstrators in Timisoara, the major town of western Transylvania. According to official figures, seventeen people died.

When the news spread across the country, a feeling of revulsion for the regime grew among the people, including the army. On 21 December, during a stage-managed rally in Bucharest, the *Securitate* again fired on people when Ceausesçu's speech was interrupted by demonstrators. The turning point came when large sections of the army changed sides and supported the protesters. Over the next four days there were pitched battles between the army and the people on one side and the *Securitate* on the other. In the end, the *Securitate* was defeated and, on 22 December, a National Salvation Front led by Ion Iliescu seized power. Iliescu was not a dissident but a communist who had remained in the Politburo until his removal in 1984. He had been sidelined during the period of the burgeoning Ceausesçu personality cult. Ceausesçu and his wife tried to flee. They were subsequently arrested and, after a summary trial on 25 December 1989, were shot by firing squad.

The National Salvation Front (NSF) immediately moved into the power vacuum. The NSF was run by an inner circle of reform-minded communists. They were concerned above all to stabilise the situation and to preserve Party rule under another name. By the judicious use of nationalist and class demagogy, and elections of a semi-fraudulent character, the NSF remained in power but, as with other governments elsewhere in Eastern Europe, was compelled to preside over a process of transition. In its programme of March 1991 the NSF described itself as a social democratic party committed to a market-oriented economy. On 21 November 1991, a new constitution received parliamentary approval, giving substantial powers to an executive presidency and enshrining guarantees of pluralism, respect for human rights, and a free market economic system [20; 233; 243; 244].

Albania was slow in following the same broad trend. The same process took place, but with a delay of two years. The country's international isolation provided a barrier against any spread of the influence of *glasnost* and *perestroika*. 1990, however, was to show that Albania was no exception. Under the pressure from demonstrators and industrial unrest, the first half of 1990 witnessed the lifting of the ban on religion and limited political and economic liberalisation. In December 1990 protests by students and workers in all Albanian cities were defused by concessions. Popular discontent forced Ramiz Alia to loosen control over the economy and to legalise political opposition. The formation of independent political parties was allowed, and it was announced that these parties could take part in elections. Although the ruling Communist Party, the Albanian Party of Labour, won the 1991 elections, the result revealed the extent of support for the opposition's newly-formed Democratic Party in urban areas. In a second set of elections in March 1992, the socialists were defeated, retaining only about a quarter of the parliamentary seats. The rest of the seats were won by the non-communist Democratic Party and other free parties. Ramiz Alia resigned as President a few days later. Meanwhile Albania remained in deep economic poverty and distress [134; 136; 148].

In the case of **Yugoslavia** it was economic failure which weakened the federal structure of the state to the point where its strong centrifugal forces would pull it apart. When the consequences of economic failure could no longer be masked by the high level of foreign borrowing, the main justification for the Federal Republic of Yugoslavia disappeared. The key event for Yugoslavia's eventual fragmentation, however, was the March 1989 change in the Yugoslav Constitution limiting the autonomy of Kosovo and Vojvodina. This measure by Milosevic led to the emergence of separatism in Slovenia, and its re-emergence in Croatia. The intense Serbian nationalist feeling around the status of Kosovo and the domination of Yugoslavia's subsequent political developments by Serbian nationalism escalated the alienation of the other nationalities in Yugoslavia and provoked separatist demands everywhere.

Meanwhile, bitterly divided as they were by the end of the 1980s, Yugoslavia's leading elites had a common interest in finishing off what remained of the two most important unifying factors, the Federal Government and the League of Communists of Yugoslavia (SKJ). The SKJ finally fell apart at its Fourteenth Congress in January 1990. By then, its Slovene and Croatian components had transformed themselves into new political parties to contest the multi-party elections in spring 1990. The victory of non-communists in elections in the other constituent republics of Yugoslavia meant that the national question took on the shape of a relationship between the non-communist periphery and the communist centre.

The Serbian party leader, Slobodan Milosevic, by going on to launch a campaign aimed at unifying the Serbs for the first time since the great migration into the Habsburg Empire at the end of the seventeenth century, made himself the disturber of Yugoslavia's already fragile inter-ethnic balance and became the final liquidator of the 'Yugoslav idea'. The total collapse of the communist political system in Yugoslavia unleashed a series of wars and secessions, particularly in Bosnia and Herzegovina [269; 271; 280].

AN OVERVIEW OF THE COLLAPSE

1.   Certain weaknesses in the structure of the Eastern European communist states were underlined in the course of the 1980s, especially in the economic sphere. The countries of Eastern Europe were characterised as 'shortage economies' throughout the period. All shortages (in investment, labour, imported goods, convertible foreign currency, foreign credit, household consumer goods, household services and private production activities) were linked. Shortage, as a summary description of a large group of phenomena, remained a basic form of persistent imbalance in the centrally planned economies.

2.   The key factor in understanding the origins of the economic collapse was, however, related to the effects of the international debt crisis. When in the late 1970s, the East European economies switched from import-substitution to import-led growth, they sought to fuel their growth by importing technology and capital from the industrialised West. The East European leaders were expecting to pay for this by exporting the derivative manufactures back to the West. When this did not materialise, they ran up debts. The Western financial institutions, awash with investible money, loaned and loaned. When the communist rulers of the East European countries imposed severe austerity measures, demanded by the Western financial institutions as conditions for re-scheduling debt, strikes and protest movements emerged in many places, putting a heavy strain on the already fragile balance of political legitimacy.

3.   The character of the ruling parties had changed dramatically between 1945 and 1989. What had once been revolutionary, vanguard parties evolved into bureaucratic vehicles for career advancement. It is widely accepted that the success or failure of the East European regimes came to depend on the maintenance of sustained economic growth and rising consumption levels. Because the Party controlled and assumed responsibility for all the political, economic and social functions of the state and society, the Party was held accountable when the state did not meet popular expectations.

4.   Most of those who brought the system to an end worked within the system rather than outside it. Without them it is difficult to imagine the dissidents and the popular majority succeeding. Indirectly, the people had indeed played a crucial role. The dissident opposition movements were not strong enough to overthrow the regimes by themselves, but they were growing in strength everywhere towards the end of the decade.

5.   The communist leadership in the East European countries ceded power in exchange for an implicit agreement that they would not face trial, imprisonment or execution for their past crimes. The ruling parties did not go willingly, but only when their own failures could no longer be covered

up. They were crushed when they finally exhausted their reserves of political legitimacy. The transformation was accomplished largely without violence, Romania being the only exception. Indeed, several analysts had already predicted that violent revolution was the only way that Ceausescu could be dislodged from power. The smoothness of the transformation in the other East European states was a reflection of each ruling elite's sense of its own weakness, its abandonment by the Soviet Union and its own historic failure.

6.   The precise mode of the abandonment of power varied from country to country. It was voluntary in some cases, done under tremendous pressure in others. Where it was voluntary, communist elites were able to retain some power in the new post-communist era. Tremendous changes in the political scene and the organisation of the economy masked a fundamental continuity in social structure.

7.   External forces were of great importance in pushing the East European ruling elites towards a surrender of their position. The growing disintegration of the Soviet Union played a major part. Gorbachev's personal role was significant in this. Without Gorbachev, change would have been slower and more violent. Indeed, it is hard to imagine any other leader willingly relinquishing Soviet control over Eastern Europe as smoothly as Gorbachev did.

8.   In many East European states, nationalism came to dominate affairs during the final years of the socialist regimes. As the regimes failed to fulfil their targets of providing higher living standards for their citizens and hence were faced with finding an alternative means of legitimacy, many leaders turned to nationalism. In order to understand the eruption of ethnic hatred in Eastern Europe, one also has to take into account the radical uncertainty caused by the changes in political sovereignty in the wake of the communist collapse. The psychological impact of these changes was considerable.

9.   The historic events of 1989–90 produced a snowball effect rather than a simultaneous cataclysm. The 'demonstration effect' and the availability of more information on events in neighbouring countries, helped to spark off each of the movements.

10.   Finally, what happened in 1989 was the culmination of a lengthy period of change. Yet, the fall of communism may not have been inevitable. The forces that built up over decades became so formidable that the outcome cannot be attributed to chance, but must be understood as the logical consequence of events.

PART THREE ASSESSMENT

CHAPTER SIX

POST-COMMUNIST TRANSITIONS: OLD PATTERNS, NEW TRENDS

After the collapse of the communist regimes in 1989–91, major changes occurred in Eastern Europe. The fall of the Berlin Wall in 1989 unleashed great expectations that the world was entering a new period of peace and stability. Freedom of the press, the right to assemble and to form political parties and other societal interest groups, and the opportunity to travel came into effect for the whole of Eastern Europe. From the borders of Germany to the heartlands of Russia, a profound process of change has been under way (see Map 3 on p. xii). New economic and political systems are being constructed from the ashes of the old structures. As once feared authoritarian regimes crumbled, a mood of euphoria engulfed the region. The fall of the iron curtain and the unification of Germany raised the possibility of a whole Europe integrated and at peace. People began looking forward optimistically to a united Europe [2; 12; 14].

Sadly, this euphoria quickly evaporated as the practical problems of adapting to a new society, built upon radically different values and institutions, have proven much more difficult than could have been imagined a few years earlier. For example, it soon became evident that the collapse of the communist regimes did not lead automatically to the creation of liberal democracy and market economies. The heritage of the past forty years created barriers that could be overcome only with the utmost effort.

The events in Eastern Europe after 1989 comprise the third set of transformations in the modern history of the region. The first was their achievement of independence in the nineteenth century. The second involved their re-subjugation by the Soviet Union after 1945 and their absorption into the Soviet bloc. The present change is already in its second phase. First came the replacement of communist rule, its institutions and procedures. That was the easy part. The second phase involves progress towards a market economy, liberal democratic institutions, and European integration. This is the immensely difficult and slow part [54; 56].

The end of the Cold War has resulted in a recycling of history. The grip of Moscow did not solve the historic problems of national rivalries, economic backwardness and political instability. Events in Eastern Europe seemed to open up a new chapter in European history. The collapse of socialist regimes has transformed the economic and political parameters of the European continent. The cost of German unification was high, there has been bloody fighting in former Yugoslavia, and ethnic animosities have been rekindled throughout Eastern Europe. 'Shock therapy' plunged much of Eastern Europe into severe economic depression. Social inequalities have widened and racism and aggressive nationalism have resurfaced [28; 41].

DILEMMAS OF TRANSITION

Transition, in its broad sense, is an interval between two different political systems. It implies a temporary state between two fixed positions, a movement between the point of departure and that of arrival. It includes the dissolution of the old, authoritarian system as well as the laying down of the institutional foundations of the new one. Transition is a collective concept, a collective concept of systemic change. It can take shape as a revolution, a coup, or as a slow evolution of events over time which accomplishes the objectives of a revolution while avoiding its sacrifices. Therefore, transition can show the features of reform as well as revolution. Yet it is fundamentally different from both. Democratic transition is a controlled transformation from a more illiberal state to a more liberal one. In the context of recent developments in Eastern Europe, the change in state is from a Soviet-type command economy to a form of market-based economic system.

Although the transition from communist to post-communist societies varies from country to country, some general patterns have emerged over the past ten years. Post-communist developments in Eastern Europe went beyond the framework of reform everywhere. Still, they did not take the shape of classical revolutions. Many analysts use the term 'negotiated revolution' or 'peaceful revolution' when speaking of post-communist Eastern Europe. The process of political, social and economic reform in the 1990s has had a dramatic impact on the way the East European countries are governed, their economic development and their integration into wider global structures. The post-communist transition is unique in its speed, and sudden and deep change to a different economic system. Whether implemented gradually or through so-called 'shock therapy', transition has involved a series of important economic reforms together with political, social and cultural restructuring [34; 35; 55; 86].

Eastern Europe is engaged in a transformation that involves, simultaneously, building a sort of liberal democratic political system and a market economy. The problems of transition are related to both the present process and the communist legacy, future tasks and past influences. They constitute the East European agenda. After forty-five years of communist rule, this agenda appears to be a particularly discouraging one. However, it does seem to be the only possible one. Some of the reassuring basics of the socialist state system may be missed. Czech and Polish workers may bemoan the uncertainty and lack of security that the new era has brought. Some Hungarians may criticise their post-communist rulers and make references to the 'good old communist days'. In Romania, those who used to be in the service of Ceausesçu may benefit from new support as people become disaffected and disillusioned with the economic difficulties and political chaos. But it seems that nobody in Eastern Europe seriously wants the old-style communist system back. The communist state system in Eastern Europe has gone for good.

The experience of the communist period, however, is difficult to deal with easily. The communist system in Eastern Europe lasted more than forty years and looked as if it might go on forever. For decades laws and legislations were framed, interpreted and implemented in the service of state socialism. Even good laws often lost their value because of the ends to which they were put. Pressures for compromise and accommodation multiplied and were then followed by cooperation, collaboration and co-option. In the period of normalisation that followed the Soviet intervention of 1968, the regimes in Eastern Europe made sure that, in one way or another, the majority of people were somehow morally discredited, compelled to violate their own moral standards. The regimes relied on and actively condoned the moral bankruptcy of their subjects. Even in Poland, where communist rule was thinnest and most contested, there were more than 3 million Communist Party members in 1980, one in ten of the adult population. Hardly a single Polish family was without some association with the regime [44].

In the field of the economy, initial economic reform programmes destroyed the old forms of economic organisations before, and much faster than, the ones replacing them could be established. Since 1989–91, the break-up of COMECON and the dollarisation of trade (US dollars being the main means of exchange in trade) within and between Eastern Europe and the former Soviet Union has disrupted supply and demand and therefore drastically reduced production and employment. As the countries of Eastern Europe begin the process of transformation from centralised systems to market-oriented economies, their efforts, in principle, are assisted by governments in the advanced capitalist countries. There is, however, no American Marshall Plan for the recovery of Eastern Europe in the 1990s as there was for Western Europe in the late 1940s. Given its own budgetary difficulties and persistent public attitudes against capital-based foreign aid, the US government is substantially constrained in the amount of direct financial assistance it can provide. The US State Department readily admits that 95 per cent of the burden of making economic and political reform in Eastern Europe work will have to be borne by the East Europeans themselves [65; 72].

In post-communist Eastern Europe, elements of continuity are interacting with new components in a complex and multi-level relationship. Traditional political and economic problems are resurfacing in the context of a domestic and international setting which has been profoundly and irreversibly changed by the forces of twentieth-century modernisation. Although the past may provide some clues to the changing pattern of domestic and international relations in the region, the aspects of late twentieth-century modernisation have created a unique historical conjuncture in Eastern Europe. There are huge difficulties associated with the transformation from communism to democracy, and from a command economy to a private market [66].

During the process of transition, following the events of 1989–91, the two countries most often thought of as exceptions to the regional pattern became even more exceptional: East Germany is being absorbed into the neighbouring Federal Republic and Yugoslavia has dissolved into bitter conflict among its constituent nationalities. Three others – Romania, Bulgaria and Albania – are in a state of arrested transformation. Gradual reform measures were introduced without jettisoning the old order decisively. The remaining three countries – Poland, Czechoslovakia and Hungary – are engaged in wholesale reconstruction. They are searching for the distinctive paths that will lead each one to a market economy and a legitimate system of government [181; 269].

The individual states of Eastern Europe have found different paths out of socialism, but they were faced with similar problems when they emerged. Their vast, subsidised and hugely inefficient heavy industrial plants were now useless. Their products were too low in quality and too high in price to survive in a competitive world market. They employed thousands of workers for whom alternative employment was difficult to find. In addition, the old heavy industries left another and more dangerous legacy: environmental pollution on a prodigious scale [44; 71].

Heavy industrialisation, the inefficient use of energy, obsolete technology and a lack of environmental legislations have all contributed to a serious deterioration in the environmental situation in Eastern Europe. Although the situation has improved over the last ten years, mainly due to the decline in industrial output and increased awareness by post-communist governments, pollution nonetheless remains serious and threatens sustainable regional development. In many East European countries, water and air pollution present human health risks and pose a threat to natural resources [6; 23; 24; 30].

Politically, transition to democracy in Eastern Europe is linked to the end of the great projects of modern European history, not only to the end of socialism but also to the end of utopias in general. Other grand constructions are also in deep crisis. The omnipotent and all-protecting state no longer exists. Now there is deep distrust towards the state in post-communist societies and a greater importance is placed on civil society, self-government and democratisation [72; 79].

By and large, democratisation has preceded marketisation in Eastern Europe, but change and reform have not followed a single pattern from country to country, nor have they proceeded in the same timeframe or even at a similar pace. Each country has embarked on a different road of reform and change. However, in nearly all of the countries the supremacy of the Communist Party was abolished, competitive elections were freely organised and fairly held, and a form of political pluralism started to take root. These steps were followed by vigorous bursts of recruitment to the new political elites which replaced (but not yet completely in every country) the old Communist Party elites.

The opening up of the political system revealed tensions and conflicts that had been restrained in the more centralised and rigid communist regimes. With the collapse of the communist regimes, nationalism has re-emerged as the single most powerful political force in the region. The wave of national rivalries that spread quickly across Eastern Europe was one of the most notable consequences of the collapse of the communist regimes. In the context of economic dislocation, social tension and political uncertainty, nationalism is a particularly powerful drive. Yugoslavia provides an extreme-case scenario of this aspect of the post-communist transition [262; 269].

THE TRAGEDY OF YUGOSLAVIA

The violent civil conflicts that have erupted in Yugoslavia since the late 1980s have often been attributed to 'ancient hatreds' and have been depicted in psychological terms. The diagnosis was established as atavistic instincts, stifled during the Cold War, had resurfaced with a vengeance, an illustration of Freud's 'return of the repressed'. If asked to explain the disintegration of Yugoslavia, most informed people would probably name nationalism and take the war-causing character of nationalism for granted. While ethnicity may be invoked to justify aggression, it is neither a sufficient nor necessary precondition for the outbreak of war. In order to understand how and why certain conflicts become ethnicised, it is important to study the chain of events that lead to the outbreak of war itself. It is clear that a variety of agents, including outside powers, international organisations, the media and diaspora communities have all played an important role in the origins, escalation and continuation of ethnic conflicts in the former Yugoslavia in the 1990s. The key to a better understanding of the conflict lies in the interaction between external factors and specific features and dynamics of local conflict.

There is no single explanation of the roots of the Yugoslav conflict. However, it is possible to identify a range of features in the recent history of Yugoslavia that constitutes the roots of this particular conflict and goes some way to explain the rise of nationalism. Yugoslavia's economic problems are analysed in Chapter Four of this volume. An adequate response to the economic crisis was made more difficult by Yugoslavia's political system. The political rigidities prevented Yugoslavia from adapting successfully to its changing economic environment [269; 271]. In addition, one effect of the collapse of the socialist system was the sudden insecurity of finding oneself a citizen of a non-existent state. Taking account of this insecurity is an important dimension of any attempt to understand the ethnic conflict in Eastern Europe. Another can be seen in people's struggles to adapt to the challenges of life in a new, competitive environment. Suddenly, jobs for life are no longer guaranteed. The collapse of heavy industry left thousands of East Europeans without work and lacking the skills to adapt to a different and more flexible labour market. The multiplicity of new political parties in Yugoslavia only compounded the confusion. One way of coping with such a steep learning curve and period of transition is to look for scapegoats within existing borders. In Yugoslavia, nationalism and ethnic conflict have been the tragic results. The events within Yugoslavia would probably not have followed the course they did had it not been for the general disintegration of the Soviet system. The wider failure of 'real socialism' within Europe served to accentuate the lack of legitimacy of the communist leadership of Yugoslavia.

Of all the new states that have emerged from the rubble of the former Yugoslavia, Slovenia has the best chance to integrate itself into the West. The most prosperous and 'Western' of the former republics, it is also highly homogeneous. As a result, ethnic conflict with its neighbours has been minimal. Unlike Croatia and Bosnia and Herzegovina, Slovenia largely escaped the ravages of the civil war. Since 1991, Slovenia has moved rapidly to develop a multi-party political system and a market economy. It has good relations with its immediate neighbours (Austria, Hungary and Italy) and is currently negotiating an association agreement with the European Union [74; 275].

The disintegration of Yugoslavia as an integral state has created an entirely new security situation in the Balkans. It has led to the emergence of a number of new, highly unstable mini-states and groupings, and has generated difficult security concerns in the whole region of Eastern Europe. The main cause of present insecurity comes not from outside powers but from problems internal to the region. The sense of insecurity is heightened by the lack of firmly established regional mechanisms for collective security and conflict prevention. A 'grey zone' of uncertainty has thus appeared in Eastern Europe, which the post-communist states find deeply unsettling [55; 57; 72].

What will the future hold for this part of the world? As most authors tend to agree, transformation is a very complex process. One of the main points that is stressed is the close interconnectedness between what is happening on the global (macro) level and developments on the local (micro) level. The full geopolitical impact of the internal changes which the East European countries are still undergoing cannot as yet be assessed. The most probable impact of the internal transformations on mutual relation-ships between post-communist countries and between these countries and Western Europe and the world in general remains unclear. It seems that the outcome of the transitions will be determined by domestic circumstances and the political traditions prevailing in each country.

PART FOUR | DOCUMENTS

DUBČEK'S 'BLUEPRINT FOR FREEDOM' SPEECH, 21 DECEMBER 1968

The Soviet invasion of Czechoslovakia marks a climactic moment in the history of East European communism. This document is part of a speech by Dubček, the Czechoslovak leader, who intended to reform communism. Dubček speech was delivered at the plenary session of the Slovak Communist Party's Central Committee. Here Dubček was basically optimistic despite the fact that the Soviet army was still in occupation of Czechoslovakia.

People are always asking us the question: What is the sense of their work, what guarantees do they have, what are their prospects? They were convinced that we were proceeding on the correct road and they want to orientate themselves as to whether there are any changes in this policy and what these changes are. The common denominator of these misgivings are meticulous worries, doubts or even distrust as to whether it is truly possible and realistic to preserve the essential characteristics of the post-January policy, and whether room will be preserved for the purposeful solution of the accumulated problems through the socialist initiative and involvement of the Communists, other elements of the national front, people without Party affiliation, and of all the basic strata of our society – features which were the substance of the programme of the Party's policy formulated after January.

These important questions and misgivings we can and we must answer again and again, patiently but in a principled manner and truthfully, and explain the meaning and goals of our actions as expressed by the November resolution and the tasks laid down by the December plenum of the Central Committee of the CPC. We must also greatly improve the level of information. When we explain and give the reasons for the tasks and course of action laid down, words alone will not be enough. There must first of all be deeds. This I want to stress particularly. From our work and its results it must be clear that the whole Party as the leading political force of the country continues to feel fully responsible for the further development of our country, for the solution of the vital questions of our citizens, and that we intend to continue fully to serve these interests and needs also in the future. ...

We do not belittle, play down or distort the complexity of the present situation in which we are working. Everybody sees the difficult political situation we are in. We are trying to see, create and demonstrate a realistic and positive way out of this situation, and in this we are ultimately guided by the interests of our people. Either we manage to win over the people for this solution, and we must first of all win the Communists of our Party, or our society will continue to remain in uncertainty and a waiting situation, and this reduces its strength, its will and creative force for a further positive development.

I am convinced that this is today the main task for our entire CPC. In this the Communists in the press and all other mass information media should give more help in the consistent mission of our socialist society. ...

Our society accepted the post-January course with great hopes. It was accepted by all the workers and working people in general – of this we have convincing evidence. It was accepted by our farmers, by the farming co-operatives and by the workers in the State farms, who were at that very time grouping together as a conspicuous and well-organised social force corresponding to their importance in our socialist society. It is also backed by our socialist intelligentsia as was clearly expressed in numerous statements. It has been accepted as a great hope by our youth who rightly demand scope for their political commitment and their natural entry into public life in our socialist society. Hence to withdraw from this policy, to give up its substance would be a political defeat for the Party and the result would be rigid stagnation of our socialist society.

The post-January political movement, which is clearly socialist in its orientation, did not lack shortcomings, obstacles and difficulties. Forces came to the fore which intended to become parasites of that movement. We realised that and opposed it. Despite all the complexity of the development, the Party always had the movement in its hands and thus guaranteed its continued distinct socialist character. The essence of this movement represented the existing forces, as well as the determination to further the needs of socialist development in our country.

Our policy must systematically follow these sound forces, this determination, and these needs, and at the same time must also more consistently defend them against all abuses and, through self-control of its own work, eliminate shortcomings which could harm a healthy development.

If I were to sum up this problem then, putting it briefly: We wish to and we must return to the consistent implementation of the tasks and ideas of January, but we do not want the repetition of those phenomena which diverted us from their implementation, which carried us away, and finally very much complicated our efforts. The present situation, too, will in the end be successfully mastered only by the implementation of the essence of the post-January policy. Whenever we speak of the post-January policy, what we have foremost in our minds is the official policy of the CPC Central Committee and its Presidium.

On the other hand, this novelty, this flourishing of society and the confrontation finds an outlet in extremities which deviate from the conclusions and the policy of the CPC Central Committee – and this is the chief danger which under certain circumstances can, in the present situation, throw us far back and can destroy our efforts. The uncritical approach to deficiencies which accompanied and obstructed the activities of the CPC Central Committee on the one hand and the very harmful biased view of the post-January development on the other are clear-cut and very serious signs of this. The first opens the scope for trends which continue to exert their effect on the creation of mistrust of the tasks that have been set and chiefly on the solutions and, consequently, cripple the Party's ability to act in implementing an active policy. The second ignores the view of the broadest Party and non-Party masses, driving the Party and its leadership into isolation from the masses, and hence leads to unforeseeable consequences. ...

We must as a permanent positive feature of the post-January policy consistently ensure fundamental civil rights and freedoms, observe socialist legality and fully rehabilitate unjustly wronged citizens. Observance of laws and norms is an urgent task of all Communists, also in intra-Party life. We stand on the principle that no one must be prosecuted, in the courts or otherwise, nor harassed, who supported and endorsed, and who backs the position of Party organs and their decisions, or for support and active carrying out of the position and directions of legal State organs. If this principle were infringed, it would have very grave consequences for our society, which might grow into arbitrariness impairing the principles of legality of intra-Party democracy, and thus into weakening of the foundations of democracy.

Our membership of the socialist community, in the Warsaw Treaty, our alliance with the Soviet Union, our ties to the international Communist movement – these are things which have always been in the policy of the Communist Party and the Government of the Republic beyond any doubt. Czechoslovakia's policy is equally firmly economically orientated to cooperation with the CMEA, with all socialist States. At the same time, we do not rule out an extension of economic cooperation with Western States. Such economic relations are being sought by all socialist countries, especially those who have a great share of external economic relations in their economies. In developing its economy, Czechoslovakia cannot ignore it either. The principles of Czechoslovakia's foreign policy and economic orientation are firm, and cannot be changed even after the August events. We are striving to overcome the consequences which resulted in politics after these events. It is seen in political and economic contacts with the Soviet Union and the other socialist countries. ...

In every organisation it is topical, on the basis of Leninist principles, to enhance the participation of the Communists in the creation and implementation of policy and safeguard their active political work among the people. The interest and the sincere striving of the Party to create the conditions for the development of socialist initiative of all non-Party members must become the hub of concrete measures of our Party's organisations.

It is particularly necessary to ensure and implement greater participation by the workers in the management of public affairs and to cooperate with the trade unions in this respect. Great efforts must be made to remove everything that divides workers and farmers from the intelligentsia and to apply in practice the principle that they have an equal interest in the true progress of our society. Such cooperation is the basis of the active socialist unity of our society. We have realised the strength of this unity and hence we are strengthening and directing it so that we can jointly solve all the problems of our development and carry out the work of our socialist reconstruction. Every Party organ and organisation must devote particular attention to our younger generation; we must endeavour to understand them, give scope for their commitment, contribute to their political development and regard them as heirs to our efforts. Any other attitude would, in my view, be wrong.

Comrades, the setting up of federal and Czech and Slovak national organs is an important and historic task which we are now approaching after having accepted federalisation in the spirit of our Party's Action Programme. In setting up the new federal organs we shall have to carry out basic change not only on the structure but also in the content of their work, so that it is in line with political and administrative tasks in the State and also corresponds to the economic reform.

Comrades, the Slovak Socialist Republic has become a reality. When on various occasions I recall this fact, I try in this joyful mood to grasp the great, vast significance of this fact for the Slovak nation and for its further development, realising all the many things which had to be accomplished in the history of the Slovak nation, as well as how much selfless work was required on the part of national representatives, and also of figures of the revolutionary movement, to ensure that Slovak statehood was created precisely on the basis of the most progressive social principles and that it was created as the result of a popular movement and of a genuine national awareness. When Federation was solemnly declared, we spoke of the days of routine work which lay ahead. We must fully appreciate what a far-reaching impact this constitutes in State power and administration and what a movement and trend in management this will bring about in both parts of the Republic.

The fact that we are able to master all these problems shows that the Party is truly able to lead and guide our society. Naturally, the creation of the Federation, an event made possible by the Party's post-January policy, does not reduce but increases the work of the Party, adds to its importance, to the weight of its decisions, to its leading role and its ability and duty to integrate. We must consistently implement what has been frequently stated on solemn occasions: that the Party is the decisive element of integration, the bearer of the idea of Czechoslovak Statehood, the advocate of the alliance of Czechoslovakia and its revolutionary movement with the revolutionary movements of the world.

In the past year we have made progress in the awareness and understanding, but also in the practical implementation, of the principle that the Party's authority throughout the entire State can only be based on and enhanced by enjoying authority among the workers, farmers, the intelligentsia and the nations and nationalities, and by correctly understanding the complex movement of social and national interests of both nations and of all nationalities. We have based the Party's leading position at the present stage on the effort to achieve a correct scientific Marxist-Leninist expression of the present status and movement of society. In the past few years – even though it is impossible to underrate the positive results – nationality problems in particular have ranked among the most sensitive issues. ...

For the future we all wish to take a further step next year on the basis of our work this year, towards an improved social system and better prospects for our citizens, towards the better fulfilment of the material and cultural needs of our people and towards the expansion of scope for social and political involvement, for the participation of the people in the administration and direction of our social questions. These are aims which we are persistently pursuing in the interest of a better life for the people and to which we want to devote our strength also in the coming period as well. Our Czech and Slovak nations, combining their forces, gifts and industriousness, together with their socialist convictions and loyalty to socialism, will be able to build a fine home in their fatherland and to strengthen in it those securities about which all of us are concerned. I am convinced that the Slovak Communists and working people will also in the future constitute an active force in the Republic in this effort. The Central Committee and the Party leadership, with Comrade Husák at its head, and the organs of the regions and districts, as well as the State organs, will be the organising and directing force in Slovakia which will continue to deepen the progressive socialist character of the development in Slovakia. Let all of us hope that this work will be fruitful and beneficial to our people. ...

From *Dubček's Blueprint for Freedom: His Original Documents Leading to the Invasion of Czechoslovakia*, Profile by Hugh Lunghi and commentary by Paul Ello. London: William Kimber, 1969, pp. 337–47.

DOCUMENT 2   WILLY BRANDT'S *OSTPOLITIK*, 28 OCTOBER 1969

The relations between the two Germanies were transformed by the so-called Ostpolitik *of Willy Brandt's SPD-led government after 1969. Against strong conservative opposition, Brandt pushed through negotiations which regularised relations between the two Germanies. Here Brandt explains his* Ostpolitik, *soon after he formed a coalition with himself as the West German Chancellor.*

This government works on the assumption that the questions which have arisen for the German people out of the Second World War and from the national treachery committed by the Hitler regime can find their ultimate answers only in a European peace arrangement. However, no one can dissuade us from our conviction that the Germans have a right to self-determination just as has any other nation. The object of our practical political work in the years immediately ahead is to preserve the unity of the nation by ending the present deadlock in the relationship between the two parts of Germany.

The Germans are one not only by reason of their language and their history, with all its splendor and its misery; we are all at home in Germany. And we still have common tasks and a common responsibility: to ensure peace among us and in Europe.

Twenty years after the establishment of the Federal Republic of Germany and of the GDR, we must prevent any further alienation of the two parts of the German nation – that is, arrive at a regular *modus vivendi* and from there proceed to cooperation. This is not just a German interest; it is of importance also for peace in Europe and for East–West relations. ...

The federal government will continue the policy initiated in December 1966, and again offers the Council of Ministers of the GDR negotiations at government level without discrimination on either side, which should lead to contractually agreed cooperation. International recognition of the GDR by the Federal Republic is out of the question. Even if there exist two states in Germany, they are not foreign countries to each other; their relations with each other can only be of a special nature.

Following up the policy of its predecessor, the federal government declares that its readiness for binding agreements on the reciprocal renunciation of the use or threat of force applies equally with regard to the GDR.

The federal government will advise the United States, Britain, and France to continue energetically the talks begun with the Soviet Union on easing and improving the situation in Berlin. The status of the city of Berlin under the special responsibility of the four powers must remain untouched. This must not be a hindrance to seeking facilities for traffic within and to Berlin. We shall continue to ensure the viability of Berlin. West Berlin must be placed in a position to assist in improving the political, economic, and cultural relations between the two parts of Germany. ...

The federal government will promote the development of closer political cooperation in Europe with the aim of evolving step by step a common attitude in international questions. Our country needs cooperation and coordination with the West and understanding with the East. The German people need peace in the full sense of that word also with the peoples of the Soviet Union and of the European East. We are prepared to make an honest attempt at understanding, in order to help overcome the aftermath of the disaster brought on Europe by a criminal clique. ...

In continuation of its predecessor's policy, the federal government aims at equally binding agreements on the mutual renunciation of the use or threat of force. Let me repeat: This readiness also applies as far as the GDR is concerned. And I wish to make it unmistakably clear that we are prepared to arrive with Czechoslovakia – our immediate neighbor – at arrangements which bridge the gulf of the past. ...

Today the federal government deliberately abstains from committing itself to statements or formulae going beyond the framework of this statement, which might complicate the negotiations it desires. It is well aware that there will be no progress unless the governments in the capitals of the Warsaw Pact countries adopt a cooperative attitude.

From Keesing's Research Report, *Germany and Eastern Europe Since 1945*. New York: Scribner, 1973, pp. 230–32.

DOCUMENT 3   CHARTER 77: CZECHOSLOVAKIA, 1 JANUARY 1977

Charter 77, the best-known protest initiative in Czechoslovakia, was signed by some 1,500 Czechs and Slovaks, as well as by many intellectuals from other countries. This document, dated 1 January 1977, forms the keystone of this opposition movement.

In the Czechoslovak Collection of Laws, no. 120 of 13 October 1976, texts were published of the International Covenant on Civil and Political Rights and of the International Covenant on Economic, Social, and Cultural Rights, which were signed on behalf of our Republic in 1968, were confirmed at Helsinki in 1975 and came into force in our country on 23 March 1976. From that date our citizens have the right, and our state the duty, to abide by them.

The human rights and freedoms underwritten by these covenants constitute important assets of civilized life for which many progressive movements have striven throughout history and whose codification could greatly contribute to the development of a humane society.

We accordingly welcome the Czechoslovak Socialist Republic's accession to those agreements.

Their publication, however, serves as an urgent reminder of the extent to which basic human rights in our country exist, regrettably, on paper only.

The right to freedom of expression, for example, guaranteed by Article 19 of the first-mentioned covenant, is in our case purely illusory. Tens of thousands of our citizens are prevented from working in their own fields for the sole reason that they hold views differing from official ones and are discriminated against and harassed in all kinds of ways by the authorities and public organizations. Deprived as they are of any means to defend themselves, they become victims of a virtual apartheid.

Hundreds of thousands of other citizens are denied that 'freedom from fear' mentioned in the preamble to the first covenant, being condemned to live in constant danger of unemployment or other penalties if they voice their own opinions.

In violation of Article 13 of the second-mentioned covenant, guaranteeing everyone the right to education, countless young people are prevented from studying because of their own views or even their parents'. Innumerable citizens live in fear that their own or their children's rights to education may be withdrawn if they should ever speak up in accordance with their convictions. Any exercise of the right to 'seek, receive, and impart information and ideas of all kinds, regardless of frontiers, either orally, in writing or in print' or 'in the form of art', specified in Article 19, paragraph 2 of the first covenant, is punished by extrajudicial or even judicial sanctions, often in the form of criminal charges as in the recent trial of young musicians.

Freedom of public expression is repressed by the centralized control of all the communications media and of publishing and cultural institutions. No philosophical, political or scientific view or artistic expression that departs ever so slightly from the narrow bounds of official ideology or aesthetics is allowed to be published; no open criticism can be made of abnormal social phenomena; no public defence is possible against false and insulting charges made in official propaganda; the legal protection against 'attacks on honour and reputation' clearly guaranteed by Article 17 of the first covenant is in practice non-existent; false accusations cannot be rebutted, and any attempt to secure compensation or correction through the courts is futile; no open debate is allowed in the domain of thought and art. Many scholars, writers, artists, and others are penalised for having legally published or expressed, years ago, opinions which are condemned by those who hold political power today.

Freedom of religious confession, emphatically guaranteed by Article 18 of the first covenant, is systematically curtailed by arbitrary official action; by interference with the activity of churchmen, who are constantly threatened by the refusal of the state to permit them the exercise of their functions or by the withdrawal of such permission; by financial or other measures against those who express their religious faith in word or action; by constraints on religious training; and so forth. ...

Further civic rights, including the explicit prohibition of 'arbitrary interference with privacy, family, home, or correspondence' (Article 17 of the first covenant), are seriously vitiated by the various forms of interference in the private life of citizens exercised by the Ministry of the Interior, for example, by bugging telephones and houses, opening mail, following personal movements, searching homes, setting up networks of neighbourhood informers (often recruited by illicit threats or promises), and in other ways. The ministry frequently interferes in employers' decisions, instigates acts of discrimination by authorities and organizations, brings weight to bear on the organs of justice, and even orchestrates propaganda campaigns in the media. This activity is governed by no law and, being clandestine, affords the citizen no chance to defend himself.

In cases of prosecution on political grounds the investigative and judicial organs violate the rights of those charged and of those defending them, as guaranteed by Article 14 of the first covenant and indeed by Czechoslovak law. The prison treatment of those sentenced in such cases is an affront to human dignity and a menace to their health, being aimed at breaking their morale. ...

Charter 77 is a free, informal, open community of people of different convictions, different faiths and different professions united by the will to strive, individually and collectively, for the respect of civic and human rights in our own country and throughout the world – rights accorded to all men by the two mentioned international covenants, by the Final Act of the Helsinki conference and by numerous other international documents opposing war, violence and social or spiritual oppression, and which are comprehensively laid down in the United Nations Universal Declaration of Human Rights.

Charter 77 springs from a background of friendship and solidarity among people who share our concern for those ideals that have inspired, and continue to inspire, their lives and their work.

Charter 77 is not an organization; it has no rules, permanent bodies, or formal membership. It embraces everyone who agrees with its ideas, participates in its work, and supports it. It does not form the basis for any oppositional political activity. Like many similar citizen initiatives in various countries, West and East, it seeks to promote the general public interest. It does not aim, then, to set out its own programmes for political or social reforms or changes, but within its own sphere of activity it wishes to conduct a constructive dialogue with the political and state authorities, particularly by drawing attention to various individual cases where human and civil rights are violated, by preparing documentation and suggesting solutions, by submitting other proposals of a more general character aimed at reinforcing such rights and their guarantees, and by acting as a mediator in various conflict situations which may lead to injustice and so forth.

By its symbolic name Charter 77 denotes that it has come into being at the start of a year proclaimed as the Year of Political Prisoners – a year in which a conference in Belgrade is due to review the implementation of the obligations assumed at Helsinki.

As signatories, we hereby authorize Professor Dr Jan Patočka, Václav Havel, and Professor Jiří Hájek to act as the spokesmen for the charter. These spokesmen are endowed with full authority to represent it *vis-à-vis* state and other bodies, and the public at home and abroad, and their signatures attest the authenticity of documents issued by the charter. They will have us, and others who join us, as their co-workers, taking part in any needful negotiations, shouldering particular tasks and sharing every responsibility.

We believe that Charter 77 will help to enable all the citizens of Czechoslovakia to work and live as free human beings.

From H. Gordon Skilling, *Charter 77 and Human Rights in Czechoslovakia*. London: Allen & Unwin, 1981, pp. 209–12.

DOCUMENT 4   **KOR'S APPEAL TO SOCIETY: POLAND, 10 OCTOBER 1978**

In June 1976, in response to hard-currency payment difficulties, the communist authorities in Poland raised food prices. When workers protested, the Gierek regime severely repressed the strikes. To provide legal and material assistance to the families of workers imprisoned or unemployed because of the 1976 events, a group of intellectuals formed the Committee for the Defence of Workers (KOR). For the first time in Poland, an organised group of intellectuals reached out directly to the workers. During the next four years, KOR became an effective voice for the frustrations that the Polish people felt under the regime. The following portions of 'KOR's Appeal' provide a summary statement of these feelings.

The workers' protest in June 1976 revealed a deep crisis in the economic and social life of our country. The two years that have elapsed since that time have been sufficiently long to warrant the expectation that the authorities would at least have sketched our directions for resolving the crisis. Unfortunately, during these two years the causes of the explosion have not been removed, and various new sources of tension have been introduced. Growing disorganization and chaos have ravaged the economic, social, and cultural life of the country. In this serious situation, we

1 November 1989. The Berlin Wall covered in people. The Wall was finally opened on 9 November.
Source: Gilles Peress/Magnum Photos

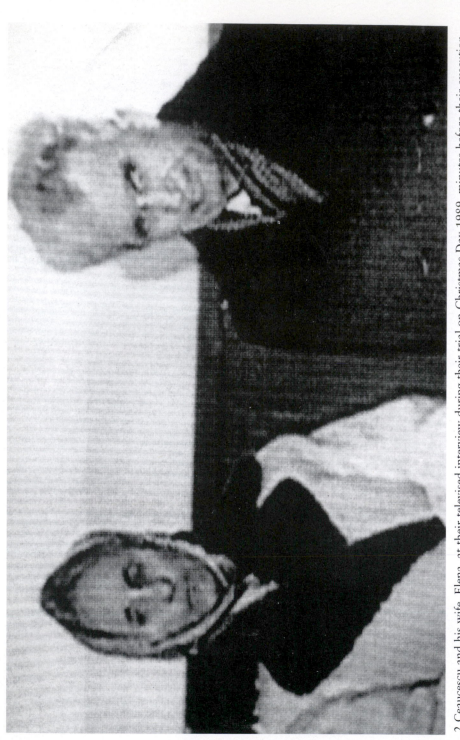

2 Ceaucescu and his wife, Elena, at their televised interview during their trial on Christmas Day 1989, minutes before their execution.
Source: The Associated Press Ltd

3 'We are the people' by Matthias Gubig. This picture addresses the economic problems after German unification. The 'sheep' or 'Ostis' (East Germans) feel consumed by the 'wolves' or 'Westis' (West Germans).

Source: Smithsonian Institution Traveling Exhibition Service, from *Art as Activist: Revolutionary Posters from Central and Eastern Europe*

4 Milosevic and Yeltsin, 1995.
Source: Agence France Presse

consider it our responsibility to present to Polish society an evaluation of the situation, together with an attempt to indicate what possible remedies are available to society. We would also like our statement to serve as a warning to the authorities against continuing their policy of deliberate disregard for genuine social problems and against their evasion of the responsibility for solving these problems. The results of such policies have on many occasions proven tragic for society, and the entire responsibility for this rests with the authorities.

1

1. The increase in prices for foodstuffs that was rejected by the public in 1976 has been replaced by hidden price increases. There exists a widespread practice of introducing more expensive goods labeled with new names onto the market, while eliminating cheaper goods. This tactic has been used with a number of industrial goods and with most foodstuffs, even including bread. The increase of prices in the state trade is also reflected in private trade, causing a severalfold increase in the prices of fruits and vegetables. The scale of this phenomenon is difficult to determine, but there is no doubt that together with the official price changes, inflation is actually much higher than one would conclude on the basis of official data.

Difficulties with supplies are constantly increasing, both in the area of industrial goods and of foodstuffs. It is impossible to purchase many items in the stores without standing in lines, an enormous waste of time, or engaging in bribery or nepotism. ...

2. The state of health services is alarming. Chronic underinvestment over a period of years has recently been reflected in a decrease in the number of hospital beds (in psychiatry and obstetrics: *The Statistical Yearbook 1977*). The overcrowding and the technical conditions in a great many hospitals, which have never been renovated since the prewar period, create sanitary conditions that endanger the health of patients.

Insufficient nutrition and the lack of medications available in the hospitals and on the market are also obstacles to treatment. ...

3. The past several years have also brought about no improvement in the dramatic situation in housing. The number of people waiting for apartments grows larger every year, while the waiting period grows longer. This is coupled with a systematic increase in the cost of housing, which significantly burdens family budgets (monthly rent together with credit payments in housing cooperatives can run as high as three thousand zlotys)

4. The authorities are attempting to make up for the disorganization of the economy through an increased exploitation of the workers. The average working day of many occupational groups has often been lengthened. Drivers, miners, construction workers, many other occupational groups now work ten to twelve hours a day.

The fact that miners were deprived of free days to compensate them for free Saturdays, that work is required on Sundays, and that a single day's absence even for the most valid of reasons (such as death in the family or illness) leads to a loss of approximately 20 percent of a monthly salary – all this can be compared only with early capitalist exploitation.

5. A comparison of the daily earnings of a worker with prices in a commercial store reveals yet another worrisome fact: a growing social inequality. Earnings are overly differentiated (without much regard for qualifications). There are enormous differences in retirement benefits. We have now in Poland families who are struggling under extremely difficult living conditions, and a small number of families who have no financial worries whatsoever. Another factor deepening social inequalities is the extensive system of privileges for groups associated with the authorities: privileged supplies, special health services, allocation of housing and building lots, foreign currency, and special recreational areas. These are only a few of the facilities available to small leadership groups. As a result, we are witnessing the growing social alienation of groups associated with the authorities, and their inability to notice the real social problems. When we learn that funds designated for the development of agriculture are being used to build a government center in Bieszczady and that in connection with this, local residents are being dislodged from the village of Wołosate, we are forced to view this fact as a proof that the authorities have lost all touch with reality.

More and more often, one can observe children inheriting the privileged position of their parents. The principle of equal opportunity for all young people is becoming illusory.

In a situation where the economic crisis threatens all of society, and especially the underprivileged groups, the assurance of special privileges to the governing groups provokes righteous anger and moral indignation.

6. The deepening crisis in agriculture is a fundamental factor in the economic, political, and social situation in the country. The consequences of a policy of discrimination and destruction of family farming, which has been conducted for thirty years, are now becoming visible. In spite of this, the production from one hectare of arable land in private hands is still higher than the production from one hectare of arable land in state agriculture. Still, gigantic investments are directed to the state agricultural farms and to production cooperatives despite the fact that the costs of maintaining state agricultural farms exceeds the value of their production. ...

Disorganization and corruption in the purchasing centers cause wastage of already produced farm goods. ...

7. The violations of the rule of law exhibited during the June events turned out to be a commonly used policy. Beatings of detainees by organs of the police are not isolated cases but constitute a form of police mob rule which is sanctioned by the higher authorities.

The materials gathered by the Intervention Bureau of the Social Self-Defense Committee 'KOR' which have been published in the *Documents of Lawlessness* demonstrate the full impunity of the police and the security services. Even the most dramatic cases of murders of persons who were being detained does not result in any punishment of those functionaries guilty of such crimes. ...

The activities of the sentencing boards for misdemeanors, which have been greatly extended at the expense of the court system, do not respect even the appearances of legality. The Office of the Prosecutor General, in disregard of the law, does not react to complaints that are filed; while the Council of State, the Diet, and the Ministry of Justice remain deaf to all information about the degeneration and anarchy that prevails in the investigative agencies and the justice system.

8. The usurpation by the party of the exclusive and totally arbitrary right to issue and impose judgments and decisions in all areas of life without exception has created a particular threat to Polish science and culture. Drastic limitations of the extent and freedom of scientific research and the publication of its results, especially in the humanities and social sciences such as philosophy, economy, sociology, and history; the stiff demands of the imposed doctrine, which has lost all the characteristics of an ideology and been transformed into a system of dogmas and unrestricted commands dictated by the authorities; the staffing of scientific positions with incompetent people who simply comply with the directives of the rulers – all of this brings harm to Polish culture and not only hinders its development but also the preservation and cultivation of its former achievements. Literature, theater, and film – those branches of culture dominated by language – are especially vulnerable to the arbitrary throttling of the freedom of thought and to the annihilation of creative activities. Under these conditions, culture is being deadened, while literature, an enormously important element in the spiritual life of the nation, though unmeasurable in its effectiveness, is either reduced to the role of an executor of the orders of the authorities or forced to divorce itself completely from expressing the truth about the surrounding reality, or else is simply tolerated as a harmless 'flower on the sheepskin.'

The preservation of culture has been reflected for several years now in initiatives in support of publications beyond the reach of state control and a science independent of official and distorting falsehoods.

The system of preventive censorship harms not only culture and science but the entire social and economic life of the country. Censorship stifles not only all signs of criticism but also all authentic information that could equip society with self-knowledge about its actual situation, which could prove undesirable for the authorities. *The Book of Prohibitions and Directives of the Main Office for Control of the Press, Publications, and Performances* published by KSS 'KOR' demonstrates the extent of the censor's interference in all areas of life. Ever-greater regions of silence, made infertile by the discrimination against living contemporary culture, are invaded by monstrously inflated and omnipresent *ersatz* products privileged by cultural policy: Multifaceted entertainments and numerous pop song festivals are shabby substitutes for culture. This constitutes in fact the main object of such popularization and fulfills its role by blocking the deeper cultural aspirations of society and by systematically debasing its spiritual needs.

The most distinguished representatives of science and culture are subject to prohibitions against publication. The more ambitious films are not allowed to be shown. Entire periods of contemporary history are passed over in silence or falsified. The Polish Episcopate, the highest moral authority in the land, has warned against this phenomenon, seeing in it a threat to the national and cultural identity of society. The threat to culture and art posed by the censorship has been discussed at Congresses of the Polish Writers' Union and the Polish Sociological Association and is the subject of pronouncement by the Polish PEN Club

The system of disinformation constitutes a vicious circle that does not spare even the authorities who created it. According to *Życie Warszawy*, 65 percent of the data supplied by statistical units reporting to the Main Office of Statistics is falsified, and this estimate must be regarded as optimistic. It is impossible to make correct decisions on the basis of false information. Under these circumstances, paralysis must overwhelm the entire life of the country.

The authorities fear society and are therefore unable to provide it with the truth about the current situation. The so-called economic maneuver propounded as a solution to the crisis turned out to be only a set of immediate, arbitrary, and uncoordinated interferences into the economic life of the country. The result of this policy is only an increasing disorganization of the economy.

- The freezing of investments has led to billions in losses because construction that had already started was never completed.
- Drastic limitations in imports have led to weeks of idleness in factories across Poland.
- The plunderous export of foodstuffs has increased shortages on the domestic market.
- The dissolution of the planning system, together with the simultaneous denial of the market economy and the retention of an anachronistic system of directing enterprises by order and commands, has eliminated all regulatory mechanisms from the economy.

The system based on arbitrary and irrevocable decisions by state and party authorities who see themselves as infallible has caused immeasurable damage to the social consciousness of the nation. The persecution of independent views, together with the use of coercion to extort an unconditional compliance with all directives coming from above, has formed attitudes that lack all ideals and has fostered duplicity; the spread of conformism, servility, and careerism has been encouraged throughout society. These characteristics serve as recommendations in the staffing of leadership positions. Competent, enlightened, and independently minded people are deprived of the possibility of advancement, and often even of a job.

The total lack of consideration for public opinion means that an overwhelming majority of the citizens have ceased to identify themselves with the state, and feel no responsibility for it.

Radical economic reform is necessary. But even the most thoroughly developed and most consistent reforms will not be able to change anything if they run up against a barrier of public indifference and despair.

The economy will not be revived by Conferences of Workers' Self-Governments which blindly obey the PUWP. Committees of Social Control selected from among the authorities, and at their service, will not reach down to the sources of inefficiency, corruption, and illegality. The only result of such actions will be to increase the disorganization of life throughout the country.

> From Jan Jozef Lipski, *KOR: A History of the Workers' Defense Committee in Poland.*
> Berkeley and Los Angeles, CA: University of California Press, 1985, pp. 474–9.

DOCUMENT 5	VÁCLAV HAVEL'S *THE POWER OF THE POWERLESS*, 1979

Here Václav Havel, one of the most prominent figures in the Charter 77 movement, deals with an important question: how might it be possible to live a life that is not a lie when all public life is built on lies?

The manager of a fruit and vegetable shop places in his window, among the onions and carrots, the slogan: 'Workers of the World, Unite!' Why does he do it? What is he trying to communicate to the world? Is he genuinely enthusiastic about the idea of unity among the workers of the world? Is his enthusiasm so great that he feels an irrepressible impulse to acquaint the public with his ideals? Has he really given more than a moment's thought to how such a unification might occur and what it would mean?

I think it can safely be assumed that the overwhelming majority of shopkeepers never think about the slogans they put in their windows, nor do they use them to express their real opinions. That poster was delivered to our greengrocer from the enterprise headquarters along with the onions and carrots. He put them all into the window simply because it has been done that way for years, because everyone does it, and because that is the way it has to be. If he were to refuse, there could be trouble. He could be reproached for not having the proper 'decoration' in his window; someone might even accuse him of disloyalty. He does it because these things must be done if one is to get along in life. It is one of the thousands of details that guarantee him a relatively tranquil life ' in harmony with society', as they say.

Obviously the greengrocer is indifferent to the semantic content of the slogan on exhibit; he does not put the slogan in his window from any personal desire to acquaint the public with the ideal it expresses. This, of course, does not mean that his action has no motive or significance at all or that the slogan communicates nothing to anyone. The slogan is really a *sign*, and as such it contains a subliminal but very definite message. Verbally, it might be expressed this way: 'I, the greengrocer XY, live here and I know what I must do. I behave in the manner expected of me. I can be depended upon and am beyond reproach. I am obedient and therefore I have the right to be left in peace.' This message, of course, has an addressee: It is directed above, to the greengrocer's superior, and at the same time it is a shield that protects the greengrocer from potential informers. The slogan's real meaning, therefore, is rooted firmly in the greengrocer's existence. It reflects his vital interests. But what are those vital interests?

Let us take note: If the greengrocer had been instructed to display the slogan, 'I am afraid and therefore unquestioningly obedient', he would not be nearly as indifferent to its semantics, even though the statement would reflect the truth. The greengrocer would be embarrassed and ashamed to put such an unequivocal statement of his own degradation in the shop window, and quite naturally so, for he is a human being and thus has a sense of his own dignity. To overcome this complication, his expression of loyalty must take the form of a sign which, at least on its textual surface, indicates a level of disinterested conviction. It must allow the greengrocer to say, 'What's wrong with the workers of the world uniting?' Thus the sign helps the greengrocer to conceal from himself the low foundations of his obedience, at the same time concealing the low foundations of power. It hides them behind the façade of something high. And that something is *ideology*. ...

The smaller a dictatorship and the less stratified by modernization the society under it, the more directly the will of the dictator can be exercised. In other words, the dictator can employ more or less naked discipline, avoiding the complex processes of relating to the world and of self-justification which ideology involves. But the more complex the mechanisms of power become, the larger and more stratified the society they embrace, and the longer they have operated historically, the more individuals must be connected to them from outside, and the greater the importance attached to the ideological excuse. It acts as a kind of bridge between the regime and the people, across which the regime approaches the people and the people approach the regime. This explains why ideology plays such an important role in the post-totalitarian system: That complex machinery of units, hierarchies, transmission belts, and indirect instruments of manipulation which ensure in countless ways the integrity of the regime, leaving nothing to chance, would be quite simply unthinkable without ideology acting as its all-embracing excuse and as the excuse for each of its parts.

If an entire district town is plastered with slogans that no one reads, it is on the one hand a message from the district secretary to the regional secretary, but it is also something more: a small example of the principle of social *autototality* at work. Part of the essence of the post-totalitarian system is that it draws everyone into its sphere of power, not so they may realize themselves as human beings, but so they may surrender their human identity in favour of the identity of the system, that is, so they may become agents of the system's general automatism and servants of its self-determined goals, so they may participate in the common responsibility for it, so they may be pulled into and ensnared by it, like Faust with Mephistopheles. More than this: so they may create through their involvement a general norm and, thus, bring pressure to bear on their fellow citizens. And further: so they may learn to be comfortable with their involvement, to identify with it as though it were something natural and inevitable and, ultimately, so they may – with no external urging – come to treat any non-involvement as an abnormality, as arrogance, as an attack on themselves, as a form of dropping out of society. By pulling everyone into its power structure, the post-totalitarian system makes everyone instruments of a mutual totality, the autototality of society.

Everyone, however, is in fact involved and enslaved, not only the greengrocers but also the prime ministers. Differing positions in the hierarchy merely establish differing degrees of involvement: The greengrocer is involved only to a minor extent, but he also has very little power. The prime minister, naturally, has greater power, but in return he is far more deeply involved. Both, however, are unfree, each merely in a somewhat different way. The real accomplice in this involvement, therefore, is not another person, but the system itself. ...

The fact that human beings have created, and daily create, this self-directed system through which they divest themselves of their innermost identity is not therefore the result of some incomprehensible misunderstanding of history, nor is it history somehow gone off its rails. Neither is it the product of some diabolical higher will which has decided, for reasons unknown, to torment a portion of humanity in this way. It can happen and did happen only because there is obviously in modern humanity a certain tendency towards the creation, or at least the toleration, of such a system. There is obviously something in human beings which responds to this system, something they reflect and accommodate, something within them which paralyses every effort of their better selves to revolt. Human beings are compelled to live within a lie, but they can be compelled to do so only because they are in fact capable of living in this way.

In highly simplified terms, it could be said that the post-totalitarian system has been built on foundations laid by the historical encounter between dictatorship and the consumer society. Is it not true that the far-reaching adaptability to living a lie and the effortless spread of social autototality have some connection with the general unwillingness of consumption-oriented people to sacrifice some material certainties for the sake of their own spiritual and moral integrity? With their willingness to surrender higher values when faced with the trivializing temptations of modern civilization? With their vulnerability to the attractions of mass indifference? And in the end, is not the grayness and the emptiness of life in the post-totalitarian system only an inflated caricature of modern life in general? And do we not in fact stand (although in the external measures of civilization, we are far behind) as a kind of warning to the West, revealing to it its own latent tendencies?

Let us now imagine that one day something in our greengrocer snaps, and he stops putting up the slogans merely to ingratiate himself. He stops voting in elections he knows are a farce. He begins to say what he really thinks at political meetings. And he even finds the strength in himself to express solidarity with those whom his conscience commands him to support. In this revolt the greengrocer steps out of living within the lie. He rejects the ritual and breaks the rules of the game. He discovers once more his suppressed identity and dignity. He gives his freedom a concrete significance. His revolt is an attempt to *live within the truth*.

The bill is not long in coming. He will be relieved of his post as manager of the shop and transferred to the warehouse. His pay will be reduced. His hopes for a holiday in Bulgaria will evaporate. His children's access to higher education will be threatened. His superiors will harass him, and his fellow workers will wonder about him. Most of those who apply these sanctions, however, will not do so from any authentic inner conviction but simply under pressure from conditions, the same conditions that once pressured the greengrocer to display the official slogans. They will persecute the greengrocer either because it is expected of them, or to demonstrate their loyalty, or simply as part of the general panorama, to which belongs an awareness that this is how situations of this sort are dealt with, that this, in fact, is how things are always done, particularly if one is not to become suspect oneself. The executors, therefore, behave essentially like everyone else, to a greater or lesser degree: as components of the post-totalitarian system, as agents of its automatism. As petty instruments of the social autototality.

Thus the power structure, through the agency of those who carry out the sanctions, those anonymous components of the system, will spew the greengrocer from its mouth. The system, through its alienating presence in people, will punish him for his rebellion. It must do so because the logic of its automatism and self-defence dictates it. The greengrocer has not committed a simple, individual offence, isolated in its own uniqueness, but something incomparably more serious. By breaking the rules of the game, he has disrupted the game as such. He has exposed it as a mere game. He has shattered the world of appearances, the fundamental pillar of the system. He has upset the power structure by tearing apart what holds it together. He has demonstrated that living a lie is living a lie. He has broken through the exalted façade of the system and exposed the real, base foundations of power. He has said that the emperor is naked. And because the emperor is in fact naked, something extremely dangerous has happened: By his action, the greengrocer has addressed the world. He has enabled everyone to peer behind the curtain. He has shown everyone that it *is* possible to live within the truth. Living within the lie can constitute the system only if it is universal. The principle must embrace and permeate everything. There are no terms whatsoever on which it can coexist with living within the truth, and therefore everyone who steps out of line *denies it in principle and threatens it in its entirety*.

Individuals can be alienated from themselves only because there is *something* in them to alienate. The terrain of this violation is their authentic existence. Living the truth is thus woven directly into the texture of living a lie. It is the repressed alternative, the authentic aim to which living a lie is an inauthentic response. Only against this background does living a lie make any sense: It exists *because* of that background. In its excusatory, chimerical rootedness in the human order, it is a response to nothing other than the human predisposition to truth. Under the orderly surface of the life of lies, therefore, there slumbers the hidden sphere of life in its real aims, of its hidden openness to truth. ...

Living within the truth, as humanity's revolt against an enforced position, is, on the contrary, an attempt to regain control over one's own sense of responsibility. In other words, it is clearly a moral act, not only because one must pay so dearly for it, but principally because it is not self-serving: The risk may bring rewards in the form of a general amelioration in the situation, or it may not. In this regard, as I stated previously, it is an all-or-nothing gamble, and it is difficult to imagine a reasonable person embarking on such a course merely because he or she reckons that sacrifice today will bring rewards tomorrow, be it only in the form of general gratitude. (By the way, the representatives of power invariably come to terms with those who live within the truth by persistently ascribing utilitarian motivations to them – a lust for power or fame or wealth – and thus they try, at least, to implicate them in their own world, the world of general demoralization.)

If living within the truth in the post-totalitarian system becomes the chief breeding ground for independent, alternative political ideas, then all considerations about the nature and future prospects of these ideas must necessarily reflect this moral dimension as a political phenomenon. (And if the revolutionary Marxist belief about morality as a product of the 'super-structure' inhibits any of our friends from realizing the full significance of this dimension and, in one way or another, from including it in their view of the world, it is to their own detriment: an anxious fidelity to the postulates of that world view prevents them from properly understanding the mechanisms of their own political influence, thus paradoxically making them precisely what they, as Marxists, so often suspect others of being – victims of 'false consciousness'.) The very special political significance of morality in the post-totalitarian system is a phenomenon that is at the very least unusual in modern political history, a phenomenon that might well have – as I shall soon attempt to show – far-reaching consequences.

There is no way around it: no matter how beautiful an alternative political model may be, it can no longer speak to the 'hidden sphere', inspire people and society, call for real political ferment. The real sphere of potential politics in the post-totalitarian system is elsewhere: in the con-tinuing and cruel tension between the complex demands of that system and the aims of life, that is, the elementary need of human beings to live, to a certain extent at least, in harmony with themselves, that is, to live in a bearable way, not to be humiliated by their superiors and officials, not to be continually watched by the police, to be able to express themselves freely, to find an outlet for their creativity, to enjoy legal security, and so on.

Anything that touches this field concretely, anything that relates to this fundamental, omnipresent and living tension, will inevitably speak to people. Abstract projects for an ideal political or economic order do not interest them to anything like the same extent – and rightly so – not only because everyone knows how little chance they have of succeeding but also because today people feel that the less political policies are derived from a concrete and human 'here and now' and the more they fix their sights on an abstract 'some day', the more easily they can degenerate into new forms of human enslavement. People who live in the post-totalitarian system know only too well that the question of whether one or several political parties are in power, and how these parties define and label themselves, is of far less importance than the question of whether or not it is possible to live like a human being. ...

The point where living within the truth ceases to be a mere negation of living with a lie and becomes articulate in a particular way, is the point at which something is born that might be called 'the independent spiritual, social and political life of society'. This independent life is not separated from the rest of life ('dependent life') by some sharply defined line. Both types frequently coexist in the same people. Nevertheless, its most important focus is marked by a relatively high degree of inner emancipation. It sails upon the vast ocean of the manipulated life like little boats, tossed by the waves but always bobbing back as visible messengers of living within the truth, articulating the suppressed aims of life.

What is this independent life of society? The spectrum of its expressions and activities is naturally very wide. It includes everything from self-education and thinking about the world, through free creative activity and its communication to others, to the most varied free, civic attitudes, including instances of independent social self-organization. In short, it is an area in which living within the truth becomes articulate and materializes in a visible way.

And now I may properly be asked the question: What is to be done, then?

My scepticism towards alternative political models and the ability of systemic reforms or changes to redeem us does not, of course, mean that I am sceptical of political thought altogether. Nor does my emphasis on the importance of focusing concern on real human beings disqualify me from considering the possible structural consequences flowing from it. On the contrary, if A was said, then B should be said as well. Nevertheless, I will offer only a few very general remarks.

Above all, any existential revolution should provide hope of a moral reconstitution of society, which means a radical renewal of the relationship of human beings to what I have called the 'human order', which no political order can replace. A new experience of being, a renewed rootedness in the universe, a newly grasped sense of 'higher responsibility', a newfound inner relationship to other people and to the human community – these factors clearly indicate the direction in which we must go.

From Václav Havel et al., *The Power of the Powerless: Against the State in Central-Eastern Europe*, ed. John Keane and trans. Paul Wilson. London: Hutchinson, 1985, pp. 17–19, 36–41, 45–6, 51–2, 65, 92.

DOCUMENT 6   SOLIDARITY'S 'GDANSK AGREEMENT', 31 AUGUST 1980

Solidarity, the independent trade union movement in Poland, grew from a group of determined strikers in the Gdansk shipyards in August 1980. It was led by an unknown and unemployed electrician, Lech Walesa. It expanded into a nation-wide social protest, millions strong. With the Gdansk Agreement, the government accepted Solidarity as a legitimate political force. This was the first time that a government in the Eastern Bloc recognised the independent existence of another political authority.

The governmental commission and the Interfactory Strike Committee (MKS), after studying the twenty-one demands of the workers of the coast who are on strike, have reached the following conclusions:

On Point No. 1, which reads:

'To accept trade unions as free and independent of the party, as laid down in Convention No. 87 of the ILO [International Labor Organization] and ratified by Poland, which refers to the matter of trade unions rights,' the following decision has been reached:

1. The activity of the trade union of People's Poland has not lived up to the hopes and aspirations of the workers. We thus consider that it will be beneficial to create new union organizations, which will run themselves, and which will be authentic expressions of the working class. Workers will continue to have the right to join the old trade unions, and we are looking at the possibility of the two union structures cooperating.

2. The MKS declares that it will respect the principles laid down in the Polish constitution while creating the new independent and self-governing unions. These new unions are intended to defend the social and material interests of the workers, and not to play the role of a political party. They will be established on the basis of the socialization of the means of production and of the socialist system that exists in Poland today. They will recognize the leading role of the PZPR [Polish United Workers' Party] in the state and will not oppose the existing system of international alliances. Their aim is to ensure for the workers the necessary means for the determination, expression, and defense of their interests. The governmental commission will guarantee full respect for the dependence and self-governing character of the new unions in their organizational structures and their functioning at all levels. The government will ensure that the new unions have every possibility of carrying out their function of defending the interests of the workers and of seeking the satisfaction of their material, social, and cultural needs. Equally it will guarantee that the new unions are not the objects of any discrimination.

3. The creation and the functioning of free and self-governing trade unions is in line with Convention 87 of the ILO relating to trade unions rights and Convention 98, relating to the rights of free association and collective negotiation, both of which conventions have been ratified by Poland. The coming into being of more than one trade union organization requires changes in the law. The government, therefore, will make the necessary legal changes as regards trade unions, workers' councils, and the labor code.

4. The strike committees must be able to turn themselves into institutions representing the workers at the level of the enterprise, whether in the fashion of workers' councils or as preparatory committees of the new trade unions. As a preparatory committee, the MKS is free to adopt the form of a trade union or of an association of the coastal region. The preparatory committees will remain in existence until the new trade unions are able to organize proper elections to leading bodies. The government undertakes to create the conditions necessary for the recognition of unions outside of the existing Central Council of Trade Unions.

5. The new trade unions should be able to participate in decisions affecting the conditions of the workers in such matters as the division of the national assets between consumption and accumulation, the division of the social consumption fund (health, education, culture), the wages policy, in particular with regard to an automatic increase of wages in line with inflation, the economic plan, the direction of investment, and prices policy. The government undertakes to ensure the conditions necessary for the carrying out of these functions.

6. The enterprise committee will set up a research center whose aim will be to engage in an objective analysis of the situation of the workers and employees, and will attempt to determine the correct ways in which their interests can be represented. This center will also provide the information and expertise necessary for dealing with such questions as the prices index and wages index and the forms of compensation required to deal with price rises. The new unions should have their own publications.

7. The government will enforce respect for Article I of the trade union law of 1949, which guarantees the workers the right to freely come together to form trade unions. The new trade union will not join the Central Council of Trade Unions (CRZZ). It is agreed that the new trade union law will respect these principles. The participation of members of the MKS and of the preparatory committees for the new trade unions in the elaboration of the new legislation is also guaranteed.

On Point No. 2, which reads:
'To guarantee the right to strike, and the security of strikers and those who help them,' it has been agreed that
The right to strike will be guaranteed by the new trade union law. The law will have to define the circumstances in which strikes can be called and organized, the ways in which conflicts can be resolved, and the penalties for infringements of the law. Articles 52, 64 and 65 of the labor code (which outlaw strikes) will cease to have effect from now until the new law comes into practice. The government undertakes to protect the personal security of strikers and those who have helped them and to ensure against any deterioration in their conditions of work.

With regard to Point No. 3, which reads:

'*To respect freedom of expression and publication, as upheld by the constitution of People's Poland, and to take no measures against independent publications, as well as to grant access to the mass media to representatives of all religions,*' it has been added that

1. The government will bring before the Sejm (parliament) within three months a proposal for a law on control of the press, of publications, and of other public manifestations, which will be based on the following principles: Censorship must protect the interests of the state. This means the protection of state secrets and of economic secrets in the sense that these will be defined in the new legislation, the protection of state interests and its international interests, the protection of religious convictions, as well as the right of nonbelievers, as well as the suppression of publications which offend against morality.

The proposals will include the right to make a complaint against the press control and similar institutions to a higher administrative tribunal. This law will be incorporated in an amendment to the administrative code.

2. The access to the mass media by religious organizations in the course of their religious activities will be worked out through an agreement between the state institutions and the religious associations on matters of content and of organization. The government will ensure the transmission by radio of the Sunday mass through a specific agreement with the church hierarchy.

3. The radio and television as well as the press and publishing houses must offer expression to different points of view. They must be under the control of society.

4. The press, as well as citizens and their organizations, must have access to public documents and, above all, to administrative instructions and socioeconomic plans, in the form in which they are published by the government and by the administrative bodies that draw them up. Exceptions to the principle of open administration will be legally defined in agreement with Point No. 3, paragraph 1.

On Point No. 10, which reads:

'*To ensure the supply of products on the internal market and to export only the surplus,*'

and Point No. 11, which reads:

'*to suppress commercial prices and the use of foreign currency in sales on the internal market,*'

and Point No. 12, which reads:

'*to introduce ration cards for meat and meat-based products, until the market situation can be brought under control,'* the following agreement has been reached:

The supply of meat will be improved between now and December 31, 1980, through an increase in the profitability of agricultural production and the limitation of the export of meat to what is absolutely indispensable, as well as through the import of extra meat supplies. At the same time, during this period a program for the improvement of the meat supply will be drawn up, which will take into account the possibility of the introduction of a rationing system through the issue of cards.

Products that are scarce on the national market for current consumption will not be sold in the PEWEX shops, and between now and the end of the year, the population will be informed of all decisions that are taken concerning the problems of supply.

The MKS has called for the abolition of the special shops and the leveling out of the price of meat and related products.

After reaching the above agreement, it has also been decided that

The government undertakes

> To ensure personal security and to allow both those who have taken part in the strike and those who have supported it to return to their previous work under the previous conditions.
> To take up at the ministerial level the specific demands raised by the workers of all enterprises represented in the MKS.
> To publish immediately the complete text of this agreement in the press, the radio, the television, and in the national mass media.

The strike committee undertakes to propose the ending of the strike at 5:00 p.m. on August 31, 1980.

From Abraham Brumberg, ed., *Poland: Genesis of a Revolution*. New York: Random House, 1983, from Denis MacShane, *Solidarity – Poland's Independent Trade Union*, trans. Labour Focus on Eastern Europe. Nottingham: Spokesman, 1981.

DOCUMENT 7   **GYORGY KONRAD'S *ANTIPOLITICS*, 1984**

Gyorgy Konrad here develops his criticism of the political sphere in communist Eastern Europe. For him all power is anti-human. His argument is, perhaps, not very practical, but remains a powerful plea for the autonomy of simple human activity in everyday life.

Politics cannot be explained in any context or medium but its own – the rich network of relationships that we call power. Politicians may have to reckon with economic interests, cultural conventions, and religious passions, but politics itself cannot be derived from economics, culture, or religion. Any approach to politics is bound to fail if it strays far from the standpoint of that political genius Machiavelli, who explained power by saying that power wills itself and that the prince wants not only to gain power but also to keep and enlarge it. That's his function – his obligation, if you like. Any philosophy of history will miss its mark if it tries to explain the riddle of political power in terms of economic interest, biological instinct, or religious enthusiasm. ...

I don't believe that a new Central European identity will arise on the wings of emotionally charged movements, even mass movements, with the stormy popular tribunes and revolutionary personalities that typically go with them.

Our deepest feelings cannot be mediated by indignation, or anger, or passionate accusations. That is old stuff, yesterday's game, the style of thinking of the anachronistic left. It is the style of those who appeal melodramatically to others' overheated passions or to the inescapable commands of some historical agenda in order to acquire power for themselves – indeed, an emotionally overblown kind of power.

Nothing would be a bigger mistake for the Eastern European democratic opposition, nothing would hurt our real interests more, than falling captive to the style of thinking, rhetoric, and mythic tendencies of the Jacobin–Leninist tradition. I could only regard as a demagogue anyone who deemed himself a revolutionary today on our political soil.

The reality of Central Europe demands a form of conduct different from that of the communist tradition. In Central Europe, modernity means recognizing the abiding tendencies of our history and applying a sure intuition to extending them; it means recognizing processes that are unfolding and helping them mature, avoiding the clash of ideological and theatrical clichés. Such is the historic enterprise that presents a separate personal challenge to each and every one of us. ...

I ask the authorities not to feel themselves threatened by the independent intelligentsia. I ask the intelligentsia not to alarm the authorities. Grown people should not threaten; they should deal like sensible, well-brought-up Europeans. Bluster, arrogance, and conceit are never civilized behavior. It would be well for my friends – independent intellectuals, oppositionists, people on the fringes, dissidents, critics of the system, protesters, violators of the censorship, people who have been shown the door or banned – if the authorities themselves were to want some of the same things that we want. It doesn't say much for the reputation of our wares if we are unable to sell any of our ideas at all to those in power.

In fact, those who hold the leading positions are not the worst consumers of ideas. In the last analysis they are intellectuals, too: They enjoy reading interesting material – material not written under their control. They hope to find things in it that they too may be able to use sometime without losing their jobs.

In the market where ideas are exchanged, we are at their disposal, too (and also at the disposal of strike organizers, of course). We have to be clear about who is playing what game. If our role is clear, we can tolerate one another more easily. If our self-definition lacks precision, there can be no relative consensus. We can only give the advice we believe in, even if it is unwelcome advice. Everything goes to serve the beauty of the social game.

I am not calling for militant mass pressure against the politicians. It's not becoming for mature men to fear that they will be beaten; how much better if we can instill their superegos with our values. There's no reason why the executive intelligentsia should think exactly the same as the creative intellectuals, but is there any reason why they have to think the exact opposite?

We live in a crabbed society, and what I am most interested in is how we can make it less crabbed. I miss having a worldview adequate to our situation and affording some evidence of real self-knowledge. I take reality for a game and would like to understand the various strategies. I would like to know along what lines we could get in touch more productively.

It is also possible to conclude that we were born in an irredeemably ill-starred corner of the earth and that there is only one way to overcome this misfortune – by leaving it for some happier soil. The other way is to attempt the near impossible: even if our nation and our institutions have no autonomy, to try to work out our own.

I have chosen the latter. I have decided not to take leave of this country permanently. If I can, I will travel for a year or two, familiarizing myself with other cultures so as to view our conditions from a distance. I will cross the Iron Curtain, leaving most of myself here while a part of me sees the West. I am a Central European; here my attitudes are Western European, there they are Eastern European.

Some mad East Central European folly keeps me here; possibly the intoxication of inner freedom compensates for the painful absence of external liberty. At other times I think that this is the only place where there is really something to think about, since even geographically this is the center of Europe.

If Budapest, Bratislava, Prague, Cracow, Warsaw, and Berlin belong to Europe, then why not Leningrad, why not Moscow – indeed, why stop before Vladivostok? It is all part of Eurasia, there is no state frontier between. It is possible to think on a Eurasian scale, too. This is a more fitting perspective for the next millennium than that of little Western Europe, from where the life I live here seems an alien mythology. I would like to think of myself as some utopian son of Europe, able to touch the

Pacific at San Fransisco with one outstretched arm and at Vladivostok with the other, and keeping the peace everywhere within my embrace.

I have the Russians to thank for my life; of all the literatures of the world, that of Russia has affected me the most. Yet I see the role of the Russians in Europe as the biggest question mark for the cause of world peace. It would be foolish for me to pretend that we don't think about them. I know of no way for Eastern Europe to free itself from Russian military occupation except for us to occupy them with our ideas. Think about it: in a free exchange of ideas, who would colonize whom?

What is and what is not allowed in Hungary today? Thinking is allowed. Thinking for yourself seldom entails any unpleasant consequences; if it does, they can be lived through without any serious damage. These unpleasant consequences can even have an incentive effect: They spur one on to freer thinking. Who knows how much more intelligent the country would be if it were free to be intelligent, if there were no political repression at all?

When people cannot express something in one form, they express it in another. To understand a country is to examine what its inhabitants have had to give up and what they have compensated themselves with in return for their sacrifice. What doesn't work for them, and what does work for them instead? What makes them, by and large, just as happy as the inhabitants of other countries? If the values that seem fundamental elsewhere are less powerful here, there must be others that the inhabitants of this country explicitly or implicitly consider primary.

It seems to me that Hungary doesn't excel in the kinds of accomplishments that can be measured by any competitive yardstick. In the global statistics of technical achievements we are seldom near the top. In this area we do better than some Eastern European countries, but in selling our products on the world market we are only average. We do better at those intangibles that one might call the art of living: the cultivation of domestic comfort; an easygoing way of life; the art of getting on with one another; a certain worldly wisdom and a certain distance toward things that others consider vitally important; a healthy, pagan cynicism toward dedicated fanatics. It is as rewarding to sit in a well-kept garden at twilight drinking a quiet glass of wine with friends as it is to tear along a crowded eight-lane highway. ...

In our area the time has come for a kind of politics – or rather antipolitics, as I would call it – which doesn't just mean rising on the ladder of state office. It would not bring a better job, promotion, or jump in income. It would not bring an official car, a bodyguard, and a flock of secretaries. It would mean defending the place, the job, and the work we now have and want to keep. Antipolitics is not a dream of the future; it is respect for the present.

If an architect is an antipolitician, he will try to build better, according to his lights, with fewer constraints, rather than struggle up the official ladder to reach those offices where architects who don't design any more decide on the work of those who still do, generally only to make their work more difficult by burdening them with unnecessary regulations.

When our lives are bleak and we place our hopes in a change of government, we put our own tasks in the hands of a paternal authority; we delude ourselves, accepting the mythology of deputizing others to do our work for us. Why should we hope for more from a different party secretary or a different prime minister than from our friends and relations? I have never met a first secretary or a prime minister; I get along without them. I can find more interesting people among my friends.

If we didn't know what state socialism was like, we could still have hopes for it. As it is, we have no illusions about either capitalism or existing socialism. We cannot expect much good from politicians and political systems. The newpapers puff the chroniclers of the political class and cultivate in their readers the mythology of letting the state do it for them. The newspaper, whose lead story tells of some politician leaving on a trip or issuing a statement, is an accomplice in this self-trivialization of the reader; it is an instrument of the political class. The political discourse of the mass media raises up paternal idols before us and attributes profundity to the vacuities of power.

Autonomy's slow revolution does not culminate in new people sitting down in the paneled offices of authority. I cultivate in myself the illusion that the people who are working for autonomy in Eastern Europe have no desire to lounge in the velvet chairs of ministers, in front of microphones and cameras. I could be wrong: people are capable of strange reactions when an opportunity presents itself. Anyway I still say, let those remain in the government who have a weakness for power. My hope is that, since the dictatorship has already lost its revolutionary sheen, governments in Eastern Europe will learn to wield power more graciously. ...

What occupies our minds above all in Eastern Europe is not whether a policy is good or bad but the overabundance of policies everywhere. The state drags countless matters, questions, and decisions into politics that have no business there – private matters or technical questions with which, in the last analysis, the state has nothing to do.

Because politics has flooded nearly every nook and cranny of our lives, I would like to see the flood recede. We ought to depoliticize our lives, free them from politics as from some contagious infection. We ought to free our simple everyday affairs from considerations of politics. I ask that the state do what it's supposed to do, and do it well. But it should not do things that are society's business, not the state's. So I would describe the democratic opposition as not a political but an antipolitical opposition, since its essential activity is to work for destatification.

The antipoliticians – and in secret there are many of them – want to free biology and religion, rock music and animal husbandry from the pathological bloat of the political state. Wherever the number of informers, provocateurs, and police agents per thousand inhabitants is higher than it is in, say, Iceland, then it's time for the state to slim down. An antipolitician is someone who wants to put the state on a strict diet and doesn't mind being called antistate because of it.

The question is: More state or less? Those who want more state, stand over here; those who want less, over there. Possibly we have reached the point where even those who would like less will say they want more, because they don't trust their own minds any longer. They are state men, they have state minds; in their dreams the state rings the doorbell and takes them away. Yesterday's terror has become tonight's bad dream. We must push the state out of our nightmares, so as to be afraid of it less. That is antipolitics.

From Gyorgy Konrad, *Antipolitics*. New York: Harcourt Brace Jovanovich, 1984, pp. 93–4, 114, 119–21, 128–9, 171–2, 177–8, 184–5, 199–200, 227–30.

DOCUMENT 8   ENVIRONMENTAL CONCERNS IN POLAND, DECEMBER 1988

Communist planners of Eastern Europe emphasised heavy industry and fast modernisation at all costs. An unintended consequence of this policy was the creation of extremely serious levels of environmental pollution. The following excerpt describes the environmental situation in Poland where the levels of pollution and environmental damage are especially high.

The river around which the port city of Gdansk grew is called the Vistula. On its way through the heart of Poland, the Vistula passes through many large and small cities, most of which dump their raw sewage directly into it. Half of the 813 Polish communities that line the banks of the Vistula, including the capital city of Warsaw, have no sewage treatment facilities. Approximately ten thousand industrial polluters also do without waste treatment.

As a result, the Vistula is so polluted that along 81 percent of the river's length, the water is too dirty even for industrial use; it would corrode heavy machinery. The river flushes some ninety thousand tons of nitrogen and five thousand tons of phosphorus into the Baltic, along with eighty tons of mercury, cadmium, zinc, lead, copper, phenol, and chlorinated hydrocarbons.

The filth collects in the bay, where it is further enriched by the sewage from Gdansk, Gdynia, and Sopot. Polish newspapers report that the waters of the Baltic near Gdansk 'exceed bacterial standards for waste water by at least one hundred times, due to sewage dumping.' In 1981, the Polish newspaper *Szpilki* caricatured the Baltic as a gigantic toilet bowl.

This story is being repeated throughout Poland. In 1985, the Sejm, the Polish parliament, recognized four areas of the country, including Gdansk Bay, as 'ecological disaster areas.' The industrial district of Upper Silesia, the Krakow area, and the copper basin of Liegnitz/Glogow shared the distinction. 'Disaster area' is meant literally. By Poland's own environmental standards, the regions are so contaminated with industrial and municipal pollution that the people living there should be evacuated. Evacuation is not an option, however, for these places are home to eleven million people, or 30 percent of Poland's population.

Gdansk's long sandy beaches have been closed for years. The seven nations that border the landlocked Baltic Sea have been poisoning it each year with about fifteen thousand tons of heavy metals, a million tons of nitrogen, seventy thousand tons of phosphorous, fifty thousand tons of oil, and highly toxic PCBs. While the Helsinki Convention of 1974 contains a pledge by these countries to limit damages 'as much as possible, using the best possible methods,' the promise remains unfulfilled. In 1988, 100,000 square kilometers of the seafloor were found to be biologically dead.

Extinction threatens seals, starfish, mussels, crabs, and gray seals. Algal blooms and dead fish float on the brackish waters.

Though Poland has an annual fishing quota of 200,000 tons, in 1984 Polish fishermen caught only 50,000 tons. In 1986, the catch declined to less than 28,000 tons. The last eels that were caught here were corroded by toxic chemicals, says Karola Palka, a resident of Sopot. 'They looked like they were already cooked.'

A few hundred pounds of sick flounder per night is all that the residents of Sopot, with their small boats and nets, can get out of the Baltic. Now they fear that even this will soon be forbidden. How contaminated are the fish? Palka displays her bare feet: Mosquito bites have swelled into purulent sores after contact with the Baltic seawater.

They still call what comes out of most Polish taps 'drinking water,' but only for reasons of nostalgia. According to 1984 official Polish environmental statistics, '71 percent of drinking water samples were disqualified by the national public health authorities for reasons of hygiene.' By the year 2000, say some observers, not a drop of Poland's water will be clean enough to be used for anything.

Despite Eastern Europe's closed political atmosphere, a grass-roots environmental movement is blossoming. The latitude allowed these unofficial organizations varies between countries; Czechoslovakia and Romania tolerate little protest, if any, while independent environmentalists in Hungary and Poland have made surprising progress.

Of the literally hundreds of small regional groups in Poland, Polski Klub Ekologiczny (PKE), the Polish Ecological Club, is the acknowledged leader. Founded in 1980 in Krakow, it today has fifteen regional offices and six thousand members across the country. While it is recognized by the state as a legal opposition group, PKE consistently refuses official support. Government efforts to put Poland's budding environmental movement under one state-sponsored umbrella have been unsuccessful.

In 1981, the PKE and allies in the trade union succeeded in closing down the Skawina Aluminum Works, a plant nine miles south of Krakow whose fluorine emissions had so damaged the environment that cows in neighboring fields were no longer able to walk. In Upper Silesia, the club sees to it that local schoolchildren escape the extremely damaging, poisoned air at least once a year and get out into the country.

In Warsaw, club members have been locked in a hot battle with the local bureaucracy and construction industry over the fate of the last urban green spaces. In Miedzyrzecz, near Poznan, the club organized opposition to a planned nuclear waste site so effectively that the plans were shelved. And in Gdansk, the PKE is currently trying to prevent Poland's first nuclear power plant from being built.

Chernobyl turned Polish environmentalists from moderate supporters of nuclear power (coal is the principal source of Poland's air pollution) into determined anti-nuclear activists. Both PKE and another prominent grass-roots peace and environmental group, Freedom and Peace, have organized opposition to nuclear power plants and radioactive waste disposal plans. AKW Zarnowiec, which is currently being built near Gdansk and is scheduled to go into operation in 1992, has already been dubbed 'Zernobyl' by locals.

'This thing is supposed to cost $5 billion, which is equivalent to the annual income of fifteen million Poles over three years,' groans biophysicist Jerzy Jaskowski. 'It's amazing! We need that money urgently in order to cope with the ecological disasters.' At the beginning of 1988, two hundred scientists wrote an open letter to Prime Minister Zbigniew Mesner calling for a halt to construction at Zarnowiec.

Ministrations to this battered environment are desperately needed. Krakow's air, for example, is so contaminated as to defy description. The west wind blows in tons of toxic dust laden with heavy metals, sulfur, and nitrous oxide from Upper Silesia; when the east wind blows, the filth comes in even greater concentrations from Nowa Huta, the enormous steel complex in the eastern part of the city.

Krakow is enveloped in a stationary cloud of smog 135 days of the year. This causes the façades of the buildings in the medieval city center to crumble even faster; the corroding vapors have even decomposed the gold roof of the Sigismund chapel on the Wawel–Hugel. And in the old part of town, the oxygen content can drop from a normal of 21 percent to 17 percent, making the atmosphere literally fatal for heart patients, asthmatics, and old people.

The life span of Krakow residents is three to four years shorter than that of their fellow countrymen. The chances of developing lung cancer are twice as high here. PKE doctors have determined that the residents of this city suffer in disproportionately high numbers from allergies, chronic bronchitis, degenerative bone diseases, arteriosclerosis, and circulatory illnesses. And the infant mortality rate, at over 2.5 per thousand inhabitants, is more than one-and-one-half times the national average.

For the largest air polluter in Krakow, the Lenin foundry in Nowa Huta, the PKE drafted a plan to reform the production processes. Huta Lenina, as it is called, annually emits 400,000 tons of carbon monoxide, 50,000 tons of sulfur dioxide, and 60,000 tons of particulates. In addition, the antiquated plant uses two and a half times as much energy as modern foundries. In July, Krakow's environmental director, Bronislaw Kaminski, brought together the directors and the PKE experts for roundtable discussions about the PKE proposal. The enterprising Kaminski hoped 'that in one to two years, we can begin to have actual ecological discussion about facilities like Huta Lenina.'

But the conditions in Krakow are surpassed by those of Upper Silesia. This coal-producing and heavily industrialized region holds the uncontested world record for all kinds of pollution. Upper Silesia produces 60 percent of Poland's industrial waste, 40 percent of its gas emissions, and 30 percent of the toxic particulates. According to official statistics, in two-thirds of the region, all the emissions standards for particulates, gases, and heavy metals are continually broken by wide margins.

There is no improvement in sight. Until the year 2000, emissions will continue to rise, according to pessimistic assessments by the PKE. The sulfur dioxide content alone is expected to go from the current total of approximately 5 million tons annually to 9.1 million tons. Today, 60 percent of Polish forests are sick, and hundreds of thousands of hectares of ground are devastated.

'Do you have your gas masks with you?' asks PKE member Dr. Aureliusz Miklaszewski. Trained as a mining engineer and currently a lecturer at the technical high school, Miklaszewski offers this as a greeting before taking us into hell. 'No? Then I advise you to suspend all breathing. We are about to inspect the site of legal murder.' ...

A 1983 report from the government and the World Health Organization about the Glogow region predicts 'emissions from the copper industry will double by 1990. It is therefore likely that public health standards will be seriously and frequently broken and that the health of the surrounding population will worsen.'

Yet everywhere in the disaster area, contaminated fields continue to be farmed. The result: 20 percent of the food products tested were classified as hazardous to public health by the authorities. Among other things, vegetables were found to contain 220 times the limit for cadmium, 165 for zinc, 134 for lead, 34 for fluorine, and 2.5 times for uranium. Green lettuce, grown in the vicinity of the Boleslaw zinc plant near Krakow, contained 230 milligrams of lead per kilo. A kilo of cabbage held 30 milligrams of lead, a kilo of onions, 42. Lead causes brain damage, particularly in children. The 1983 report noted an 'alarming increase' in the number of retarded children in Upper Silesia.

From Sabine Rosenbladt, 'Is Poland Lost?', *Greenpeace* 13 (6), November–December 1988, pp. 14–19.

DOCUMENT 9   THE END OF THE BREZHNEV DOCTRINE, 1989

In this short article, Polish dissident intellectual Adam Michnik points out the clear implications of Gorbachev's abandonment of the Brezhnev doctrine of 'limited sovereignty'.

In Mikhail Gorbachev's television appearance last Saturday, one can detect some important new emphases. Analyzing the current state of relations between nationalities in the USSR, Gorbachev stated, 'Today, we are reaping the fruits of the abuses of power that were committed during previous decades – the expulsion of entire nations from their land, the disregard for the interests of numerous nationalities.' He condemned the use of force and coercion in relations between the peoples of the USSR. He stated clearly that we can 'count on changes for the better only if each nationality, each nation feels secure in its own home, in its own land.' His argument implied the need for far-reaching reform of the federal structure.

What implications does this have for us Poles and our view of the world? We must think seriously and logically about de-Stalinization and about transforming relations between our countries. Now that the Soviet leadership has abandoned the Brezhnev doctrine of 'limited sovereignty', we must try to achieve a new agreement between peoples who are free and equal, an agreement between sovereign states and nations.

It will soon be twenty-one years since the Prague Spring was crushed by force. A wave of new-Stalinism then engulfed Czechoslovakia for many years. We would like to believe that Polish forces will never again be used to offer this kind of 'fraternal assistance', that the Brezhnev doctrine is gone forever. Gorbachev is right when he says that the well-being of one nation can never be achieved at the cost of limiting the rights and freedoms of other nations.

We appreciate the evolution that has taken place and that continues to take place in the relations between our eastern neighbor and the countries of the Warsaw Pact. In contrast with the military interventions in Hungary, Czechoslovakia, and Afghanistan, which aroused helpless anger and moral repugnance, today's policies are characterized by tolerance and imagination.

Further evidence of this evolution is provided by the recent statement by Vadim Zagladin. After all, we can remember the summer of 1981. We can remember the daily fear we experienced when reading the aggressive, lying commentaries in Soviet newspapers. And we can remember our even greater fear of military intervention. Today, Moscow newspapers express friendly interest, which evokes an appropriate Polish response on the pages of our papers.

We must try to think, speak, and write about Polish–Soviet relations that are no longer dominated by tanks, with a realistic sense of the state and national interests of all those involved. We must try to rid ourselves once and for all of our Stalinist inheritance. This should be the essence of our efforts to build a democratic and sovereign Poland.

Adam Michnik, 'Farewell to the Brezhnev Doctrine', *Gazeta Wyborcza*, 4 July 1989, trans. Jane Cave. Also printed in Adam Michnik, *Letters from Freedom: Post-Cold War Realities and Perspectives*, ed. Irena Grudzińska Gross, trans. Jane Cave. Berkeley, CA and London: University of California Press, 1998, pp. 132–3.

DOCUMENT 10 IVAN IVANOV'S '*PERESTROIKA* AND FOREIGN ECONOMIC RELATIONS', 1988

Ivan Ivanov was one of the brains behind Gorbachev's policy of perestroika. *Here he explains the economic justification of the new policy in relation to Soviet foreign economic policy.*

Foreign economic relations, being part of the Soviet economy, are also undergoing radical changes. Their role in the development of the national economy is to be increased to make the country by the beginning of the twenty-first century not only a great industrial nation but a great trading power as well. Restructuring in this sphere is based on the same principles as the general economic reform: it covers the whole range of foreign trade, from central planning agencies right down to the commercial activities of individual enterprises. ...

In the post-war period the Soviet Union has entered the world market on a large scale, and its national economy is now considerably involved in the international division of labour. The turnover of foreign trade has grown faster than national income, and by the mid-1980s the export element already accounted for 6 per cent of the GDP. Now imports provide for 20 per cent of the increment in installed machines and equipment, and up to 15 per cent of consumer goods in retail trade.

But the mid-1980s also marked the time when stagnation phenomena had accumulated. They impeded the growth of foreign economic relations and held in check the integration of the country into the world trade system.

The former centralized directive-laden system of planning regulated contacts with the outside world rigidly, and in the development of the country the inertia of reticence and non-sensitivity to outside influences was kept intact. This resulted in plans being dominated by the principle of 'residual' allocation of goods for export purposes. Exports have become oriented towards energy and raw materials, which does not carry prospects along the lines of expanded demand and is also vulnerable to market fluctuations. Due to these reasons alone, the country received 20,000 million dollars less in export earnings in 1985–8 than was expected. Imports are basically tailored to tackling immediate problems and the consumer goods element has soared unjustifiably, to the detriment of an investment component. ...

In this context, restructuring is aimed at establishing a new model for Soviet foreign economic relations – industrial, technological and competitive. It would link Soviet and world science, and turn foreign economic relations into an important, independent factor in the growth and intensification of the country's economy, reserving the nation a worthy place in the international division of labour.

Introducing new thinking into the management of the Soviet economy, the model proceeds from the premise that, in the modern interdependent world, our economy is a part of the world economy and therefore should develop and be managed as such. It is also understood that attainment of world standards in major technological and economic indices is only possible when the national economy of the country interacts with and competes in the world market.

Finally, plans are being made to use foreign economic relations as a catalyst for domestic economic reform, primarily for promoting money-and-commodity relations and competitiveness in the domestic market.

The model calls for intercomplementation of the Soviet economy with other economies, above all with those of Socialist countries, and for continuous use of foreign economic capabilities and alternatives to resolve the problems of the national economy. In the future, imports will be viewed not only as a means of satisfying domestic demand, but also as a competitive substitute for inefficient home production. Exports will be regarded as an independent channel for expanding the sales of products and, most important of all, as an undistorted indication of their cost, technological level and consumer properties.

This basis would enable the USSR by the year 2000 to increase its turnover of foreign economic activities by 2.4 to 2.5 times as against 1985 (thus doubling national income over the same period), while the proportion of income contributed by exports is planned to reach 9 per cent. Soviet exports are to grow at an overriding rate to enable the country to increase its share in world exports from 4 to 6 per cent. ...

Under the new economic conditions, the foreign economic ties of the country are to be managed at Government level as a unified complex. The State Foreign Economy Commission built up in 1986 as a standing organ of the Council of Ministers is the supreme organ of such management. It guides and coordinates the work of all ministries and departments participating in foreign economic activities, takes part in working out the strategy and the plans for such activities, works out drafts for relevant legislation, and keeps an eye on how these plans and this legislation is effected.

The newly born USSR Ministry for Foreign Economic Relations directly represents the interests of the country in the foreign market. Unlike the previous Ministry of Foreign Trade, it is largely free of operational commercial functions. Instead of the eighty or more foreign-trade associations that worked for the old ministry, the new one retains only twenty-five associations, which carry on trade in fuel, food and other primary commodities.

Instead, the new Ministry is concentrating on the analysis, planning, organization and political functions of trade. It is working out drafts for foreign trade plans, regulating export and import operations, improving its own economic mechanism, and shaping the foreign trade policy of the country and its system of operating controls. The Ministry renders technical and economic assistance to foreign countries, supervising the construction of projects in which foreign companies are participating. It is also responsible for supplying the foreign economy complex with commercial information and for the training of personnel.

Democratization of social and economic life in the Soviet Union has considerably increased the authority and widened the functions of the USSR Chamber of Industry and Commerce. Embracing nearly 5,000 enterprises and having a vast network of representative groups, it now stands out as a 'collective voice' for Soviet business. The Chamber has the right of legislative initiative, it keeps up contacts with foreign enterprise amalgamations and renders all kinds of services to Soviet and foreign clients, giving them consultations and advising them on patents, exhibitions, advertising and arbitration. Since January 1988, an association of exporters, the council of directors of joint ventures, and associations for business and cooperation with a number of foreign countries and regions have been working at the Chamber.

At the same time, the epicentre of the reform of foreign economic relations may be found at the level of enterprises. A stable course has been pursued for their contacts with foreign markets and for working out a mechanism for making them economically interested in such contacts. ...

Direct ties are being established with enterprises and organizations in the Socialist countries on a contract basis. They include cooperation in production, research and training personnel, and the consequent exchange of commodities. The partners themselves determine the scale, nomenclature and prices for the exchange, the Soviet enterprises receiving 100 per cent of the currency earned.

Direct ties that are profitable for the partners are also of great macro-economic importance for the Soviet Union and other CMEA countries. They increase Socialist economic integration, widen its production level and are laying the foundation for a future CMEA common market. But their development has run into its own obstacles. The economic rights of enterprises vary in different Socialist countries. Differences in national prices often also make it difficult to arrive at a unified opinion in evaluating the level of profit in transactions. A further point is that wholesale trade is not yet developed, and USSR enterprises have now only small volumes of free product which can be sold directly. The situation may improve by 1990 when the share of wholesale trade in the domestic economic turnover becomes predominant and the CMEA countries start working on bringing their price system together. ...

The use of foreign capital in the Soviet economy caused much ideological dispute. But it was evident that with the economy being internationalized, economic ties between the two systems, even though they were totally different from one another, could not be brought down to mere trade contacts. Lenin's works of the 1920s and the experience of other Socialist countries proved the exclusion of joint enterprises to be wrong. As a result economic expediency, supported by new political thinking, prevailed. From the very outset, Soviet investment legislation was planned as being balanced, giving due consideration to the interests of both sides.

In building up joint ventures, the Soviet side pursues the policy of better satisfying the country's economic requirements and has, in particular, the following goals: (a) to draw on modern technology and management experience; (b) to replace imports; (c) to attract additional money and materials; and (d) to develop the export basis of the country. These goals are viewed as interconnected and complex, and have for the time being been attained. A number of joint ventures are based on Soviet as well as foreign technology. ...

Being a part of the world trade system, the Soviet Union aims at participating in its main institutions or at closer contacts with them. The USSR is one of the countries that initiated the creation of UNCTAD and UNIDO, and it is ready to fully participate in GATT. In August of 1986 the Soviet Union applied to the GATT Secretariat to participate in the 'Uruguay round' of trade negotiations. It planned to outline its interests there, in order to accumulate some experience in international trade negotiations and to show a readiness to participate that might later help the USSR to join GATT. But the negative position of the USA, and to a lesser extent the European Community and Japan, saw the application rejected. Nevertheless, Soviet economic diplomacy is continuing with preparations to conduct negotiations with GATT and the USSR's reform of foreign economic relations will serve as a foundation for such negotiations, since it makes the mechanism of Soviet trade policy compatible with the rules of GATT.

The establishment of official relations between CMEA and the European Community opened the way for direct negotiations between the USSR and the EC regarding an economic agreement. The Soviet Union would want such an agreement to be as wide-ranging as possible, to cover both the full range of interests of Soviet industry and the full powers of the two communities. Such an approach corresponds to the policy of a 'common European home', and takes into account the tendencies of Soviet economic restructuring plus the reform of the EC. The goal is a 'unified market' by 1992. ...

The USSR is also actively involved in the restructuring of CMEA to advance the economic integration of the Socialist states. The CMEA members are searching for ways of bringing together their price-formulation systems, as well as full reciprocal interchange of each other's currencies and the introduction of a convertible rouble. The ultimate objective is to create a united market of CMEA countries. Specialists think that this way zones of free trade can be created in Eastern Europe and a CMEA customs union arranged.

As the political report of the CPSU Central Committee to the 27th Party Congress stated: 'The approach to mutually profitable economic relations should be on a large scale, it should face the future.' This is the primary aim of restructuring the foreign economic relations of the USSR.

From Ivan D. Ivanov, '*Perestroika* and Foreign Economic Relations', *Perestroika Annual*, ed. Abel Aganbegyan. London: Futura, pp. 145–64.

GLOSSARY

Agitprop   The Agitation and Propaganda Department of the Communist Party's Central Committee.

Albanian Party of Labour   The governing party of Albania that was a communist party in everything except name (which was adopted in 1948) and was more wholeheartedly communist than most.

Balance of payments   A summary statement of a state's financial transactions with the rest of the world, including such items as foreign aid transfers and the income of citizens employed abroad.

Balance of trade   A state's net trade surplus or deficit, based on the difference in the value of its imports and exports.

Black economy   That portion of a nation's output of goods and services which (illegally) escapes taxation.

Brezhnev Doctrine   A real, if undeclared, principle of Soviet foreign policy in the 1960s and 1970s, by which the interests of the socialist community as a whole took precedence over the interests and wishes of any of its individual members.

Bulgarian Communist Party (BCP)   The foundation of the BCP can fairly be dated to 1903. The party adopted this name in 1919 and became affiliated to the Communist International. The BCP gradually emerged as the dominant party in Bulgaria and established an effectively one-party system in the late 1940s.

Candidate member   Before a person can become a full member of the Communist Party he/she has to serve a probationary period during which he/she is called a candidate member.

Central Committee (CC)   A high policy-making and administrative organisation of the Communist Party, nominally elected by and responsible to the Party Congress.

Charter 77   A movement named after a manifesto published in Czechoslovakia on 1 January 1977, in which the 241 initial signatories committed themselves to campaign for human and civil rights. The Charter 77 movement sought to avoid organisational structures and to remain an informal community of people.

Civic Forum   Formed following the student-led demonstrations of November 1989 in Czechoslovakia, Civic Forum was set up by representatives of opposition groups to coordinate the campaign for political reform.

Collective farm   In the socialist countries, the collective farm was commonly organised as an artel in which some possessions were owned by the whole group and some by individual households. In many countries, individual households were allowed to own their own house, a garden plot of about an acre (which was increased steadily in many instances), hand tools and some farm animals.

COMECON   The Council for Mutual Assistance (CMEA) was created in January 1949 as a response to the announcement of the Marshall Plan. Its full members in 1990 were the USSR, Bulgaria, Czechoslovakia, the GDR, Hungary, Poland, Romania, Cuba, Mongolia and, since 1978, Vietnam. Albania was a founder-member but stopped participating in 1961.

Cominform   The Communist Information Bureau, established in 1947 and disbanded in 1956.

Communist Party of the Soviet Union (CPSU)   The ruling party of the Soviet Union. It was the longest-ruling party anywhere in the world.

Croatian Spring   The Croatian Spring is the name given to the upsurge of nationalism in Croatia between 1967 and 1972. It occurred in the context of a wave of nationalism across Yugoslavia, much of it anti-Serbian.

Debt service ratio   The cost to a country of servicing its foreign debts and, in particular, debts owed by the public sector and publicly guaranteed debt. The cost comprises the total of interest payments and repayments of principal as a percentage of export earnings. A level of 20 per cent is normally considered an acceptable maximum, but accurately establishing the exact figure is often difficult.

Democratic Party (of Albania)   The outbreak of student demonstrations in 1990 created the Democratic Party. Led by Sali Berisha, the Democratic Party called for the establishment of a multi-party system, full respect of human rights and the creation of a market economy.

Détente   Soviet–American relations took a dramatic turn with Richard Nixon's election. Coached by his National Security Adviser, Henry Kissinger, Nixon initiated a new approach to relations with the Soviet bloc that, in 1969, he officially labeled *détente*. The Soviets also adopted the term to describe their policies towards the United States.

Ecoglasnost   A Bulgarian group, founded in early 1989 to exert pressure on ecological issues and to insist on openness of information about them.

Evangelical Church (in the GDR)   The traditional Church of the vast majority of the population of the GDR. The Evangelical Church had a relatively privileged position in the years of Ulbricht and Honecker. From 1980 onwards, the Evangelical Church became an umbrella for the emerging peace movement.

Gross National Product (GNP)   The total value of goods and services produced within a period of time by an economy, including government and private spending, fixed capital investment, net inventory change and net exports. Real GNP growth describes the increase in national output after subtracting inflation.

Hungarian Democratic Forum (HDF)   The origins of this important Hungarian opposition movement date back to a meeting which took place on 27 September 1987. About 150 leading reform economists, social scientists, historians and writers gathered for a critical discussion of the state of the nation, the economic crisis and the political system.

Hungarian Socialist Workers' Party HSWP   The name by which the Communist Party in Hungary has been known since 1956.

Import-substitution industrialisation   A strategy that involves encouraging domestic entrepreneurs to manufacture products otherwise imported from abroad.

International Monetary Fund (IMF)   A specialised agency of the United Nations that seeks to maintain monetary stability and assist member states in funding balance of payments deficits.

JNA   The Yugoslav Peoples' Army was the most powerful military force during the Yugoslav wars of the 1990s and formerly one of the power centres within the ruling League of Communists of Yugoslavia.

Junker Class   A name applied to the group of Prussian landowners with great estates east of the Elbe. They provided Prussia with its leading administrators and formed the main component of the Prussian and later German officer corps.

KOR   The Committee for Workers' Defence was set up in Poland in direct response to the repression of worker demonstrations which broke out in June 1976 following the announcement by Gierek's administration of immediate price rises for food products.

Marshall Plan   A programme of grants and loans established by the United States to assist the recovery of Western Europe after the Second World War.

Most Favoured Nation principle   Tariff preferences granted to one nation must be granted to all others exporting the same product.

National Salvation Front (NSF)   This took power after the fall of the Ceausescu regime in Romania. At first declaring itself as solely an interim government, it later stated that it would stand as a political party in elections scheduled for May 1990.

New Economic Mechanism (NEM)   The NEM was introduced in Hungary in January 1968. Among the basic features of the NEM were a softening of central control over industrial and state enterprises, the implementation of indirect methods of state control over the firms and the establishment of market relations and market prices.

New Forum   Founded in the autumn of 1989, New Forum came to be the first major opposition group to make an impact in the GDR. It was not conceived as a political party but literally as a 'forum' for open discussion.

Nomenklatura   This has often been used as a somewhat mysterious and even threatening term for the central governing groups in the Soviet Union and Eastern Europe and the source of their power. In essence, *nomenklatura* consists of two sets of lists: one of all the important posts in the Party and the state bureaucracies and leading socialist organisations, and a second of all those regarded by the authorities as suitably qualified to fill them.

North Atlantic Treaty Organisation (NATO)   An organisation established on 4 April 1949 by Belgium, Canada, Denmark, France, Iceland, Italy, Luxembourg, the Netherlands, Norway, Portugal, the United Kingdom and the United States. Greece and Turkey joined in 1952, the Federal Republic of Germany in 1955.

Orgburo   The Organisational Bureau of the Central Committee which handled all matters of an organisational and administrative nature, except those deemed important enough to be passed over to the Politburo.

Ostpolitik   In 1969, a few days after Willy Brandt's Social Democrats took power on their own for the first time in West Germany, Brandt introduced a new foreign policy initiative, called *Ostpolitik*. In 1970 this led to treaties with the Soviet Union and with Poland, and in 1973 to full mutual recognition between East and West Germany.

Petofi Circle   A movement of university students in Hungary who protested in 1956 against censorship and despotic methods in the cultural field.

Podkrepa   An independent Bulgarian trade union, founded in Plovdiv in late February 1989, *Podkrepa* [support] was subject to official harassment during the first few months of its existence but emerged as a force to be reckoned with after the fall of Todor Zhivkov.

Politburo   The Political Bureau of the Party's Central Committee and its chief policy-making agency.

Prague Spring   The popular name attached to the period of reform in Czechoslovakia which followed the election of Alexander Dubček as First Secretary of the Communist Party of Czechoslovakia in January 1968.

Rescheduling   The renegotiation of terms and conditions of existing borrowings with the objective of obtaining more favourable terms.

Roman Catholic Church   Throughout the years of the communist rule in Eastern Europe, the Roman Catholic Church represented a challenge to those regimes ruling in countries where it was well presented. It played a part in the transformation of some of the East European states in 1989.

Samizdat   The form of action chosen by the opposition in state-socialist countries. *Samizdat* is defined as unofficially circulated writings with a political objective. The essence of *samizdat* is that its authors accept the possible consequences of this circulation.

Second Economy   The 'second economy' is the term which economists use to cover the various types of private economic activity which are a vital component of Soviet-type economic systems. Sometimes the terms 'shadow economy' or 'informal economy' are also used. It was generally defined as including all economic activities which were carried out for direct private gain and, in some significant respects, in knowing contravention of existing law.

Securitate   Under Ceausescu, the well-armed and much feared secret police. When the uprising against Ceausescu occurred, the *Securitate* upheld their oath to him personally by opening fire on the people and by their determined resistance of the regular forces.

Sejm   The *Sejm*, or Polish parliament, is the highest organ of state power in Poland. For most of the postwar period it passed or confirmed all legislation.

'Shock Therapy'   Some post-communist leaders in Eastern Europe rejected a gradual, incremental implementation of change in favour of a shock therapy to be administered at once. The argument was that the state of the economy necessitated an immediate infusion of remedy rather than a slow cure.

SKJ   The League of Communists of Yugoslavia was the ruling party during the period of the Socialist Federal Republic of Yugoslavia from 1952 to 1990.

Solidarity   The independent self-governing trade union Solidarity grew out of the strike movement of August 1980 in Gdansk and the agreement signed there on 31 August by the authorities and the strike committee.

Stalinism   A form of dictatorial, centralised and frequently repressive rule that was characteristic of Soviet politics during the Stalin era but was also encountered in Eastern Europe at other times.

'Star Wars'   In 1983 President Reagan's announcement of the multi-billion-dollar Strategic Defence Initiative, commonly known as 'Star Wars' – a space-based anti-ICBM (Inter Continental Ballistic Missiles) defence system. It openly challenged Moscow to a race that it simply could not run.

Stasi   Stasi is the nickname of the office and personnel of the *Ministerium für Staatssicherheit* (Ministry for State Security) in the GDR. A notorious instrument of repression, it was founded in 1950 and abolished in 1989.

State Farms   The state farms were large mechanised and state-operated units, each of which had a single director (as an industrial enterprise had) and was cultivated by hired labour. The state farms were generally overlarge, overspecialised and lacked trained management. They were subsequently broken up into more manageable units.

Terms of trade   The relationship between export and import price indices. If export prices rise more quickly, or fall at a slower pace than import prices, there is a favourable ratio.

Union of Democratic Forces (UDF)   This was set up as an umbrella organisation in December 1989 to coordinate the activities of the various Bulgarian opposition groups flourishing in the aftermath of Zhivkov's removal from power.

'Velvet Revolution'   The events leading to the collapse of the communist system in Czechoslovakia came to be known as the 'Velvet Revolution' because of their peaceful nature. They ushered in the process of negotiation between the protesters and the communist authorities.

Warsaw Treaty Organization (Warsaw Pact)   The Warsaw Treaty Organisation (WTO) was established by the Treaty of Friendship, Cooperation and Mutual Assistance signed in the Polish capital on 14 May 1955. The signatory states were the Soviet Union, Bulgaria, Czechoslovakia, the German Democratic Republic, Hungary, Romania and Albania.

Yugoslav Idea   The belief that the South Slav peoples share a common identity that should be expressed in their unification in a common state is known as the Yugoslav Idea. The Yugoslav Idea was a creation of the nineteenth century and primarily the work of Croat thinkers.

Znak   A Catholic group in Poland, consisting of intellectuals, writers, journalists and academics, which was set up to represent the Church's interests. *Znak* formed the Clubs of Catholic Intellectuals.

WHO'S WHO

Adamec, Ladislav (1926–) Elected chairman of the Communist Party of Czechoslovakia in 1989, he was head of the Industry Department of the Party's Central Committee from 1963 until his appointment as Deputy Prime Minister in the government of the Czech Socialist Republic in 1969. Adamec always made clear his commitment to economic reform and modernisation o f Czechoslovak industry.

Alia, Ramiz (1925–) Albanian statesman and president (1985–92). In 1955 he was Minister of Education. He was made a candidate member of the Politburo in 1956 and moved to the Central Committee's Agitprop department in 1958. His subsequent career was as a close associate of Hoxha. Alia succeeded Enver Hoxha as chairman of the Albanian Communist Party in 1985.

Andropov, Yuri (1914–84) Soviet politician and General Secretary of the Communist Party of the Soviet Union (1982–84). From 1953 onwards Andropov engaged in diplomatic work, serving from 1954 to 1957 as Soviet Ambassador in Hungary. In May 1967 Andropov became head of the KGB (Committee of State Security) and later the same year a candidate member of the ruling Politburo, becoming a full member in 1973. Andropov's security background tended to obscure his earlier exposure to the Eastern European reform experience while he was Soviet Ambassador to Hungary.

Bahro, Rudolf (1935–) An intellectual and disillusioned member of East German Communist Party. Working quietly in East German industrial bureaucracy, he secretly wrote a major analysis of the shortcomings of East German socialism, entitled *The Alternative in Eastern Europe*, parts of which were published in *Der Spiegel* in 1977. Bahro was sentenced to eight years in prison in 1978, but left for West Germany after a deal arranging this in 1979. In West Germany he became a prominent member of the Greens in the early 1980s.

Beria, Lavrentiy Pavlovich (1899–1953) Head of the Soviet Security Service (1938–53). He was a plotter of ruthless ambition and a notoriously skilled organiser of terror and espionage. On Stalin's death in March 1953, he attempted to seize power, but was foiled by fearful military and party leaders. Following his arrest, he was tried for treason and was executed in December 1953.

Brezhnev, Leonid Il'ich (1906–82) Soviet politician and General Secretary of the Communist Party of the Soviet Union (1964–82). Khrushchev's successor as party leader, Brezhnev eventually became the longest-ruling General Secretary apart from Joseph Stalin.

Ceausescu, Elena (1919–89) The Romanian president's wife came to assume a growing role in the affairs of Romania during the 1970s and 1980s. She was widely disliked in Romania, seen by many as wielding excessive influence over her husband.

Ceausesçu, Nicolae (1918–89)   The Romanian party leader from 1965 and head of state. He joined the illegal Communist Youth Movement in 1933 and the party in 1936. He was mostly in prison until 1944, when he was released. After 1960 he emerged as the heir to party leader Gheorghe Gheorghiu-Dej, whom he succeeded in 1965. His personality cult broke all precedents. He was overthrown in 1989 and executed.

Dubček, Alexander (1921–)   A Slovak, Dubček was First Secretary of the Communist Party of Czechoslovakia from January 1968 until April 1969. His identification with 'socialism with a human face' during the 1968 Prague Spring quickly won him widespread popularity. At Soviet insistence, he resigned in April 1969, and soon after was expelled from the Communist Party. Dubček never abandoned his commitment to reform communism and his continuing popularity was made apparent when he addressed the demonstrators in Bratislava and Prague in 1989 under the auspices of the Civic Forum. In December 1989 he returned to active politics as Chairman of the Federal Assembly.

Gheorghiu-Dej, Gheorghe (1901–65)   Romanian Prime Minister (1952–59) and President (1961–65). Having spent the war in prison, he led the Romanian Communist Party from 1944 to 1965. Gheorghiu-Dej pursued a 'Romania first' policy in industrialisation.

Gierek, Edward (1913–)   Polish statesman. In 1954 he was elected to the Central Committee of Polish United Workers' Party. In 1956 he became a Central Committee secretary and joined the Politburo. He was First Secretary of the party between 1970 and 1980.

Gomułka, Wladyslaw (1905–82)   Polish communist leader. From 1923 he held various posts in the union of chemical industry in Poland. He became secretary of the newly founded Polish Workers' Party in 1942, and became First Secretary in 1943. In 1948 Gomułka fell victim to the intensification of Stalinism in Eastern Europe and was accused of right-wing tendencies and nationalist deviation. Re-elected to the party leadership after Stalin's death, Gomułka soon restored control over party leadership. As a result of extensive worker unrest in 1970 he was removed from office.

Gorbachev, Mikhail Sergeevich (1931–)   General Secretary of the Communist Party of the Soviet Union Central Committee from March 1985; Chairman of the USSR Supreme Soviet Presidium (1988–89); Chairman of the USSR Supreme Soviet from May 1989; President of the USSR from March 1990 to December 1991.

Grosz, Karoly (1932–)   General Secretary of the Hungarian Socialist Workers' Party from May 1988 to October 1989. His career was made entirely in the Hungarian party administration. In 1984 he was promoted to head the Budapest party organisation. He was regarded as a spokesman for heavy-industrial workers and was no friend of market-oriented reform.

Havel, Václav (1936–)   Playwright, President of Czechoslovakia (1989–92) and President of the Czech Republic (1993–). Havel sprang to prominence in the early 1960s as the leading playwright at the Theatre on the Balustrade in Prague with the political satires 'The Garden Party' (1963) and 'The Memorandum' (1965). In 1968 he played a prominent part in debates over political reform.

After 1969 Havel's work was banned in Czechoslovakia. Havel was imprisoned on a number of occasions. He led the Civic Forum negotiators who forced the Communist Party to agree to the formation of a government with minority communist participation in December 1989. On 29 December 1989 he succeeded Gustáv Husák as President of Czechoslovakia.

Honecker, Erich (1912–94)   East German statesman and head of state (1976–89). He became a member of the German Communist party (KPD) in 1929 and was arrested under Hitler in 1935, sentenced to ten years in prison in 1937 and was released only at the end of the war. He succeeded Walter Ulbricht as party leader in 1971. In October 1989 he was dismissed 'on health grounds' and replaced by Egon Krenz.

Hoxha, Enver (1908–85)   Albanian Prime Minister (1946–54) and First Secretary of the Party of Labour of Albania (Albanian Communist Party) (1954–85). Hoxha ensured a smooth transfer of power to Ramiz Alia by eliminating the strongest candidates in the struggle for power. The 1981 purges included Mehmet Shehu, the long-serving Prime Minister.

Husák, Gustáv (1913–91)   Czechoslovakian politician and president (1975–89). A Slovak, party leader after 1969 and President from 1975. A member of the Communist Party before the war, he was one of the leaders of the Slovak national uprising against the Nazis in 1944. In the early 1970s he presided over a massive purge of real and alleged supporters of the 1968 reforms. Thereafter he achieved his greatest success maintaining the same system, intact and unchanging, for a decade and a half. He showed little evidence of sympathy with reformist policies. His resignation as party leader in December 1987 seems likely to have been the result of personal rivalries and his declining health. He remained President until December 1989.

Iliescu, Ion   Former Communist Party Politburo member and the first chairman of the National Salvation Front in Romania. Iliescu had been an established member of the Romanian Communist Party (RCP) elite during the early Ceausescu period, rising from leadership of the Communist Youth League to the position of RCP secretary for ideological affairs in 1970. He became the first President of the post-communist Romania as a result of May 1990 elections.

Jakeš, Milos (1922–)   General Secretary of the Communist Party of Czechoslovakia from December 1987 until November 1989. In the 1960s he served in the Ministry of Interior, and at the moment of the Soviet-led invasion lined up with the handful of those supporting the Soviet action. In 1977 he was made a candidate member of the Communist Party Presidium and the Central Committee secretary in charge of agriculture. In 1981 he was promoted to full membership of the Presidium and the secretary responsible for economic policy. He succeeded Gustáv Husák as party General Secretary in December 1987. He resigned from that post in November 1989 after a series of public demonstrations demanding political reform.

Jaruzelski, General Wojciech (1923–)   Polish general, Prime Minister (1981–85), head of state (1985–90) and President (1989–90). He was born to a landowning family. In 1939, having been deported to the Soviet Union, he worked as a manual labourer, then received military training and took part in the fighting both during the war and afterward in the anti-guerilla campaign in Poland. In 1956 he was promoted to general, the youngest in the Polish army at the time. He was appointed Prime Minister in the midst of the Solidarity crisis in February 1981 and became First Secretary of the party in October the same year. In December he masterminded the *coup d'état* that led to the suppression of Solidarity.

Kádár, János (1912–89)   Hungarian statesman, premier (1956–58, 1961–65) and the leader of the Hungarian Socialist Workers' Party (1956–88). Kádár was a pragmatic realist rather than a fanatical communist. During the early 1960s Kádár launched his alliance policy, accepting that non-members of the party had a useful role to play. While no Stalinist, Kádár's conception of reform was cautious and minimal. His tenure of office was one of the longest in modern Hungarian history. He was finally removed from power at the special party conference in May 1988. He was shifted to the newly created, ceremonial post of party President, but was excluded from the Politburo. One year later he was relieved of this post and his Central Committee membership, officially for health reasons.

Kardelj, Edward (1910–79)   Tito's closest colleague who was credited with the development of the ideological basis of the Yugoslav economic experience. He joined the Central Committee of Yugoslav Communist Party in 1937 when Tito became its Secretary-General, and remained a member of the Committee until his death.

Khrushchev, Nikita Sergeevich (1894–1971)   Soviet politician and party leader (1953–64). He became the First Secretary of the party after Stalin's death. Under Khrushchev's leadership an attempt was made to decentralise economic management.

Kosygin, Aleksei Nikolaevich(1904–80)   A Soviet politician and Prime Minister during the Brezhnev era. A member of the Communist Party from 1927, Kosygin joined the Central Committee in 1939.

Krenz, Egon (1937–)   Krenz was briefly the third leader of the GDR. He rose steadily in the East German hierarchy and by 1984 he was regarded as one of the leading contenders for the succession to Honecker. Between 1964 and 1967 he was in Moscow at the Soviet party's Central Committee College. On his return to East Germany, he took over as head of the Agitprop department of the party's Youth Movement (FDJ). He became chairman of the FDJ in 1974 and candidate member of the Politburo in 1976. Krenz succeeded Honecker in October 1989 and resigned in December the same year.

Malenkov, Georgiy Maksimilianowich (1902–88)   Soviet statesman and Prime Minister (1953–55). He became a member of the Politburo and Deputy Prime Minister in 1946, succeeding Stalin as party First Secretary and Prime Minister in 1953. He resigned in 1955, admitting responsibility for the failure of Soviet agricultural policy.

Mazowiecki, Tadeusz (1927–)   Polish dissident activist and politician. He was an activist in the independent Catholic group *Znak* and represented it as a deputy in the *Sejm* between 1961 and 1972. Mazowiecki acted as spokesman for the KOR in 1977 and as adviser to Solidarity from 1980. Following the events in 1989 he became Poland's first non-communist Prime Minister for over forty years.

Milosevic, Slobodan (1941–) He studied law at university, worked with Tehnogas and was appointed Director of Belgrade banking combine Beobank. From there he was elected to the Belgrade city party committee and the Serbian party presidency. He was elected leader of the Serbian League of Communists in April 1987. He became President of Serbia in November 1989. He was indicted for war crimes in The Hague by the International Criminal Tribunal for the former Yugoslavia in May 1999. In October 2000 Milosevic was ousted (after twelve years in power) following his election defeat in September.

Mladenov, Petur Toshev (1936–2000) Bulgarian communist politician; Secretary of Bulgarian Komsomol (1966–69); First Secretary of Vidin Province committee of the Bulgarian Communist Party (1969–71); Minister of Foreign Affairs (1971–89); Politburo member from 1977; General Secretary of the Communist Party from November 1989 to February 1990; Chairman of State Council from November 1989.

Molotov, Vyacheslav Mikhailovich (1890–1986) Soviet statesman and Prime Minister (1930–34). He became foreign minister (1939–49, 1953–56) and was Stalin's chief adviser at Tehran and Yalta. His name is preserved in the term 'Molotov cocktail' – a bottle of inflammable liquid used as a weapon – which he put into production during the Second World War.

Nagy, Imre (1896–1958) Communist leader in Hungary at the time of the 1956 uprising. He stayed in the Soviet Union from the late 1920s until after the Second World War. During this time he became a close associate of the leading Soviet communist George Malenkov. In 1953 Nagy was promoted to Prime Minister of Hungary. This appointment was clearly due to direct intervention by Malenkov, who at this time was Soviet Prime Minister. In 1956 after the defeat of the Hungarian revolution he was seized by Soviet troops, tried and executed for conspiracy to overthrow the Hungarian socialist regime. His execution was announced on 17 June 1958.

Novotny, Antonin (1904–75) Czech politician and President (1957–68). First Secretary of the Communist Party of Czechoslovakia from September 1953 until January 1968 and President from November 1957 until March 1968. He was succeeded as First Secretary by Alexander Dubček.

Pozsgay, Imre Leading reform communist in the Hungarian Socialist Workers' Party (HSWP). In June 1989 Pozsgay was elevated to membership of the newly created four-man Presidium of the HSWP.

Tito, Josip Broz (1892–1980) Yugoslav statesman and President (1953–80). From 1948 to 1953, when he became President of Yugoslavia, he served as Prime Minister and Minister of Defence. He became Life President of the republic in 1971 and Life President of the League of Communists of Yugoslavia until his death in 1980.

Tökes, Laszlo Hungarian pastor of the provincial city of Timisoara in Romania. Tökes, who had emerged in the late 1980s as a local spokesman for anti-Ceausesçu forces, came under increasing pressure from the regime as a consequence of his activities. Finally, Ceausesçu's secret police demanded and obtained his agreement to leave his parish. But the local supporters attempted to shield Tökes. On 15 December 1989 they came into conflict with the security police. This confrontation rapidly escalated, bringing the entire city into a state of revolt.

Tudjman, Franjo (1922–99)   Founding leader of the Croatian Democratic Union (HDZ), which has been the ruling party in Croatia since 1990. He was the first President of Croatia since its independence from Yugoslavia in 1992.

Ulbricht, Walter (1893–1973)   The first political leader of the GDR, he dominated its development until his dismissal as First Secretary of the Socialist Unity Party of Germany (SED) in 1971.

Walesa, Lech (1943–)   A former shipyard worker who was elected chairman of the workshop strike committee following the worker demonstrations in 1970. When representatives of the new independent labour groups were established, in September 1980, the National Coordinating Commission of Solidarity (free trade union) elected Walesa as chairman. He was awarded the Nobel Prize for Peace in 1983.

Wyszynski, Stefan Cardinal (1901–81)   Roman Catholic clergyman, Archbishop of Warsaw and Gniezno (1948), and a cardinal (1952). Following his indictment of the communist campaign against the Church, he was imprisoned in 1953. Freed in 1956, he agreed to a reconciliation between Church and the state under the Gomułka regime.

Zhelev, Zhelyu   Bulgaria's first post-communist President.

Zhivkov, Todor (1911–98)   Bulgarian party leader since 1954 and the longest-serving party boss in the Warsaw Pact. Zhivkov presided over the gradual development of Bulgaria from a predominantly agrarian economy to a mixed agrarian-industrial structure with a corresponding increase in prosperity.

BIBLIOGRAPHY

The works listed here are those which I found most useful in writing this book. They will help readers who wish to study particular topics more deeply. It is, necessarily, a selective list and concentrates on books written in English. Articles in scholarly journals have been excluded on the grounds that their inclusion would expand the list beyond reasonable limits. The bibliography is arranged, after a section on general works, on a country-by-country basis for ease of reference.

Unless otherwise stated, the place of publication is London.

GENERAL WORKS

1 Abel, E., *The Shattered Bloc*, Boston, 1990.
2 Abrahams, R. (ed.), *After Socialism: Land Reform and Rural Social Change in Eastern Europe*, Berghahn, Oxford, 1996.
3 Aganbegyan, A. (ed.), *Perestroika Annual*, Futura, 1988.
4 Agh, A., *The Politics of Central Europe*, Sage, 1998.
5 Aldcroft, D. H. and Morewood, S., *Economic Change in Eastern Europe since 1918*, Gower, Aldershot, 1995.
6 Batt, J., *East Central Europe from Reform to Transformation*, Pinter, 1991.
7 Bender, P., *East Europe in Search of Security*, Johns Hopkins University Press, Baltimore, MD, 1972.
8 Berglund, S. and Dellenbrant, J. (eds), *The New Democracies in Eastern Europe*, 2nd edn, Edward Elgar, Aldershot, 1994.
9 Berglund, S., Hellen, T. and Aarebrot, F. H., *The Handbook of Political Change in Eastern Europe*, Edward Elgar, Aldershot, 1998.
10 Bideleux, R. and Jeffries, I., *A History of Eastern Europe: Crisis and Change*, Routledge, 1998.
11 Blackburn, R. (ed.), *After the Fall: The Failure of Communism and the Future of Socialism*, Verso, 1991.
12 Bridger, S. and Pine, F. (eds), *Surviving Post-socialism: Local Strategies and Regional Responses in Eastern Europe and the Former Soviet Union*, Routledge, 1997.
13 Brown, J. F., *Eastern Europe and Communist Rule*, Durham, NC, 1988.
14 Brown, J. F., *Hopes and Shadows: Eastern Europe After Communism*, Longman, 1994.
15 Brzezinski, Z., *The Grand Failure. The Birth and Death of Communism in the Twentieth Century*, Macdonald, 1990.
16 Bugajski, J., *Nations in Turmoil: Conflict and Cooperation in Eastern Europe*, Westview Press, Boulder, CO, 1995.
17 Calvocoressi, P., *World Politics since 1945*, 7th edn, Longman, 1996.

18   Carlton, D. and Schaerf, C. (eds), *South-Eastern Europe after Tito. A Powder-keg for the 1980s*, Macmillan, Basingstoke, 1983.
19   Chafetz, G. R., *Gorbachev, Reform and the Brezhnev Doctrine*, Praeger, New York, 1995.
20   Cipkowski, P., *Revolution in Eastern Europe: Understanding the Collapse of Communism in Poland, Hungary, East Germany, Czechoslovakia, Romania, and the Soviet Union*, Wiley, New York, 1991.
21   Colton, T. J. and Tucker, R. C., *Patterns in Post-Soviet Leadership*, Westview Press, Boulder, CO, 1995.
22   Connor, W. D., *Socialism, Politics, and Equality: Hierarchy and Change in Eastern Europe and the USSR*, Columbia University Press, New York, 1979.
23   Crampton, R. and Crampton, B., *Atlas of Eastern Europe in the Twentieth Century*, Routledge, 1996.
24   Davies, N., *Europe: A History*, Pimlico, 1997.
25   Dawisha, K., *Eastern Europe, Gorbachev and Reform*, Cambridge University Press, Cambridge, 1988.
26   Drewnowski, J. (ed.), *Crisis in the East European Economy*, Croom Helm, 1982.
27   East, R., *Revolutions in Eastern Europe*, Pinter, 1992.
28   Feffer, J., *Shock Waves: Eastern Europe after the Revolutions*, Black Rose Books, Boston, MA, 1993.
29   Fejto, F., *A History of the People's Democracies*, 2nd edn, Pelican Books, 1974.
30   Feshbach, M. and Friendly, A., *Ecocide in the USSR*, Basic Books, 1992.
31   Fischer-Galati, S. (ed.), *Eastern Europe in the 1980s*, Croom Helm, 1981.
32   Fleron, F. J. Jr. and Hoffmann, E. P. (eds), *Post-Communist Studies and Political Science. Methodology and Empirical Theory in Sovietology*, Westview Press, Boulder, CO, 1993.
33   Fowkes, B., *The Rise and Fall of Communism in Eastern Europe*, 2nd edn, Macmillan, Basingstoke, 1995.
34   Garton Ash, T., *The Magic Lantern: The Revolutions of 1989 Witnessed in Berlin, Prague, Budapest and Warsaw*, Random House, 1990.
35   Garton Ash, T., *The Uses of Adversity. Essays on the Fate of Central Europe*, Random House, 1990.
36   Gati, C. (ed.), *The International Politics of Eastern Europe*, Praeger, New York, 1976.
37   Gati, C., *The Bloc That Failed. Soviet–East European Relations in Transition*, I. B. Tauris, 1990.
38   Gellner, E., *Conditions of Liberty: Civil Society and Its Rivals*, Penguin, Harmondsworth, 1996.
39   Glenny, M., *The Rebirth of History. Eastern Europe in the Age of Democracy*, Harmondsworth, Penguin, 1990.
40   Goldman, M. F., *Revolution and Change in Central and Eastern Europe*, M. E. Sharpe, Armont, NY, 1997.
41   Grancelli, B. (ed.), *Social Change and Modernisation, Lessons from Eastern Europe*, de Gruyter, Berlin/New York, 1995.
42   Grant, N., *Society, Schools and Progress in Eastern Europe*, Oxford, 1969.
43   *Granta* [magazine], New Europe, Winter 1990.

44 Gros, D. and Steinherr, A., *Minds of Change. Economic Transition in Central and Eastern Europe*, Longman, 1995.
45 Halliday, F., *Revolution and World Politics*, Macmillan, Basingstoke, 1999.
46 Hammond, T. (ed.), *The Anatomy of Communist Takeovers*, Yale University Press, New Haven, CT, 1975.
47 Harman, C., *Class Struggles in Eastern Europe 1945–83*, Bookmarks, 1988.
48 Hawkes, N. (ed.), *Tearing Down the Curtain*, Hodder and Stoughton, 1990.
49 Hersh, J. and Schmidt, J. D. (eds), *The Aftermath of 'Real Existing Socialism' in Eastern Europe*, Vol. 1: *Between Western Europe and East Asia*, Macmillan and St Martin's Press, 1996.
50 Hobsbawm, E., *Nations and Nationalism Since 1780*, 2nd edn, Cambridge University Press, Cambridge, 1992.
51 Holden, G., *The Warsaw Pact, Soviet Security and Bloc Politics*, Basil Blackwell, Oxford, 1989.
52 Holmes, L., *The End of Communist Power: Anti-Corruption Campaigns and Legitimation Crisis*, Polity Press, Cambridge, 1993.
53 Holmes, L., *Post-Communism: An Introduction*, Polity Press, Cambridge, 1997.
54 Huntington, S., *The Third Wave*, University of Oklahoma Press, 1991.
55 Hupchick, D., *Conflict and Chaos in Eastern Europe*, Macmillan, Basingstoke, 1994.
56 Hyde-Price, A., *European Security Beyond the Cold War: Four Scenarios for the Year 2010*, Sage, 1991.
57 Hyde-Price, A., *The International Politics of East Central Europe*, Manchester University Press, Manchester, 1996.
58 Kagarlitsky, B., *Restoration in Russia*, Verso, 1995.
59 Kaldor, M., *The Imaginary War: Understanding the East-West Conflict*, Basil Blackwell, Oxford, 1990.
60 Kaldor, M. (ed.), *Europe from Below: An East–West Dialogue*, Verso, 1991.
61 Kalecki, M., *Selected Essays on the Economic Growth of the Socialist and Mixed Economy*, Cambridge University Press, Cambridge, 1972.
62 Konrad, G. and Szelenyi, I., *The Intellectuals on the Road to Class Power*, New York, 1979.
63 Kornai, J., *Growth, Shortage and Efficiency*, University of California Press, Berkeley, CA, 1982.
64 Kornai, J., *The Socialist System: The Political Economy of Communism*, Princeton University Press, Princeton, NJ, 1992.
65 Köves, A., *Central and East European Economies in Transition. The International Dimension*, Westview Press, Boulder, CO, 1992.
66 Lane, D., *The Rise and Fall of State Socialism. Industrial Society and the Socialist State*, Polity Press, Cambridge, 1996.
67 Lane, J. and Ersson, S. O., *European Politics*, Sage, 1996.
68 Laqueur, W., *The Dream that Failed: Reflections on the Soviet Union*, Oxford University Press, Oxford, 1994.
69 Lewis, P., *Central Europe since 1945*, Longman, 1994.
70 Longworth, P., *The Making of Eastern Europe from Prehistory to Postcommunism*, 2nd edn, Macmillan, Basingstoke, 1997.
71 Lorentzen, A. and Rostgaard, M. (eds), *The Aftermath of 'Real Existing*

Socialism' in Eastern Europe, Vol. 2: *People and Technology in the Process of Transition*, Macmillan and St Martin's Press, 1997.

72   Mandelbaum M. (ed.), *Postcommunism. Four Perspectives*, Council on Foreign Relations, New York, 1996.

73   Marcuse, H., 'Repressive Tolerance', in P. Connerton (ed.), *Critical Sociology. Selected Readings*, Penguin Books, Harmondsworth, 1976, pp. 301–29.

74   Mayhew, A., *Recreating Europe, The European Union's Policy towards Central and Eastern Europe*, Cambridge University Press, Cambridge, 1998.

75   Miliband, R. and Panitch, L. (eds), *Communist Regimes: The Aftermath*, Merlin Press, 1991.

76   Morris, L. P., *Eastern Europe since 1945*, Heinemann, 1984.

77   Narkiewicz, O. A., *Eastern Europe*, Croom Helm, 1986.

78   Okey, R., *Eastern Europe 1740–1980. Feudalism to Communism*, Hutchinson, 1982.

79   O'Loughlin, J. and van der Wusten, H. (eds), *The Political Geography of Eastern Europe*, Belhaven Press, 1993.

80   Partos, G., *The World that Came in from the Cold*, Royal Institute of International Affairs, 1993.

81   Pearson, R., *The Rise and Fall of the Soviet Empire*, Macmillan, Basingstoke, 1998.

82   Pinder, J., *The European Community and Eastern Europe*, Pinter for the Royal Institute of International Affairs, 1991.

83   Pipes, R., *Communism: The Vanished Specter*, Oxford University Press, Oxford, 1994.

84   Poznanski, K. (ed.), *Constructing Capitalism: The Reemergence of Civil Society and Liberal Economy*, Westview Press, Boulder, CO, 1992.

85   Pravda, A. (ed.), *The End of the Outer Empire. Soviet–East European Relations in Transition, 1985–90*, Sage for the Royal Institute of International Affairs, 1992.

86   Pridham, G. (ed.), *Transition to Democracy*, Gower, Aldershot, 1995.

87   Pridham, G., Herring, E. and Sandford, S. (eds), *Building Democracy? Democratisation in Eastern Europe*, Leicester University Press, 1994.

88   Pridham, G. and Vanhanen, T. (eds), *Democratisation in Eastern Europe: Domestic and International Perspectives*, Routledge, 1994.

89   Prins, G. (ed.), *Spring in Winter: The 1989 Revolutions*, Manchester University Press, Manchester, 1990.

90   Pryce-Jones, D., *The War That Never Was: The Fall of the Soviet Empire, 1985–1991*, Weidenfeld & Nicolson, 1995.

91   Ramet, S. P. (ed.), *Eastern Europe. Politics, Culture, and Society since 1939*, Indiana University Press, Bloomington, IN, 1998.

92   Rollo, J. (ed.), *The New Eastern Europe: Western Responses*, Pinter for the Royal Institute of International Affairs, 1990.

93   Roskin, M., *The Rebirth of East Europe*, Prentice-Hall, 1991.

94   Rothschild, J., *Return to Diversity: A Political History of East Central Europe since World War II*, Oxford University Press, Oxford, 1989.

95   Rupnik, J., *The Other Europe*, Weidenfeld & Nicholson, 1989.

96   Schöpflin, G., *Politics in Eastern Europe*, Blackwell, Oxford, 1993.

97 Scott, H., *Does Socialism Liberate Women? Women and Socialism: Experiences from Eastern Europe*, Allison and Busby, 1976.

98 Selucky, R., *Economic Reforms in Eastern Europe*, New York, 1972.

99 Seton-Watson, H., *Eastern Europe between the Wars, 1918–1941*, Harper & Row, New York, 1967.

100 Simons, T., *Eastern Europe in the Postwar World*, 2nd edn, Macmillan, Basingstoke, 1993.

101 Smith, A. H., *The Planned Economies of Eastern Europe*, Croom Helm, 1983.

102 Smith, D. M., *Urban Inequality under Socialism: Case Studies from Eastern Europe and the Soviet Union*, Cambridge University Press, Cambridge, 1989.

103 Staar, R. F., *Communist Regimes in Eastern Europe*, Hoover Institution Press, Stanford, CA, 1977.

104 Staar, R. F. (ed.), *East-Central Europe and the USSR*, Macmillan, Basingstoke, 1991.

105 Steiner, G., *Proofs and Three Parables*, Faber & Faber, 1992.

106 Stojanovic, S., *In Search of Democracy in Socialism*, Buffalo, NY, 1981.

107 Stokes, G., *From Stalinism to Pluralism. A Documentary History of Eastern Europe since 1945*, Oxford University Press, Oxford, 1991.

108 Stokes, G., *The Walls Came Tumbling Down. The Collapse of Communism in Eastern Europe*, Oxford University Press, Oxford, 1993.

109 Sugar, P. F. (ed.), *Ethnic Diversity and Conflict in Eastern Europe*, ABC-Clio, Denver, CO, 1980.

110 Sugar, P. F. and Lederer, I. (eds), *Nationalism in Eastern Europe*, University of Washington Press, Washington, DC, 1969.

111 Summerscale, P., *The East European Predicament*, Royal Institute of International Affairs, 1982.

112 Swain, G. and Swain, N., *Eastern Europe since 1945*, Macmillan, Basingstoke, 1993.

113 Tampke, J., *The People's Republics of Eastern Europe*, Croom Helm, 1983.

114 Thompson, K. W. (ed.), *Revolutions in Eastern Europe and the USSR*, University Press of America, 1995.

115 Todorova, M., *Imagining the Balkans*, Oxford University Press, Oxford, 1997.

116 Tokes, R. L. (ed.), *Opposition in Eastern Europe*, Macmillan, Basingstoke, 1979.

117 Torpey, J. C., *Intellectuals, Socialism and Dissent*, University of Minnesota Press, Minneapolis, MN, 1995.

118 Turnock, D., *The Human Geography of Eastern Europe*, Routledge, 1989.

119 Turnock, D., *Eastern Europe: An Economic and Political Geography*, Routledge, 1989.

120 Van del Doel, T., *Central Europe: The New Allies? The Road from Visegrad to Brussels*, Westview Press, Boulder, CO, 1994.

121 Waller, M., *Peace, Power and Protest. Eastern Europe in the Gorbachev Era*, The Centre for Security and Conflict Studies, 1988.

122 Waller, M., *The End of the Communist Power Monopoly*, Manchester University Press, Manchester, 1994.

123 Wallerstein, I., *After Liberalism*, The New Press, New York, 1995.

124   Wandycz, P., *The Price of Freedom: A History of East Central Europe from the Middle Ages to the Present*, Routledge, 1992.

125   White, S. (ed.), *Political and Economic Encyclopaedia of the Soviet Union and Eastern Europe*, Longman, 1990.

126   White, S., Batt, J. and Lewis, P. (eds), *Developments in East European Politics*, Macmillan, Basingstoke, 1993.

127   Wilczynski, J., *The Economics of Socialism: Principles Governing the Operation of the Centrally Planned Economies in the USSR and Eastern Europe under the New System*, Allen and Unwin, 1977.

128   Williams, A. (ed.), *Reorganising Eastern Europe: European Institutions and the Refashioning of Europe's Security Architecture*, Dartmouth, Aldershot, 1994.

129   Wolff, L., *Inventing Eastern Europe: The Map of Civilization and the Mind of the Enlightenment*, Stanford University Press, Stanford, CA, 1995.

130   Zloch-Christi, I., *Debt Problems of Eastern Europe*, Cambridge University Press, Cambridge, 1987.

ALBANIA

131   Biberaj, E., *Albania between East and West*, Institute for the Study of Conflict, London, 1986.

132   Biberaj, E., *Albania: A Socialist Maverick*, Westview Press, Boulder, CO, 1990.

133   Bland, W. B., *Albania*, Clio, Denver, CO, 1988.

134   Costa, N. J., *Albania: A European Enigma*, Colombia University Press, New York, 1995.

135   Griffith, W. E., *Albania and the Sino-Soviet Rift*, Cambridge University Press, Cambridge, 1963.

136   Hall, D., *Albania and the Albanians*, Pinter, 1994.

137   Hamm, H., *Albania: China's Beachhead in Europe*, 1963.

138   Hutchings, R., *Historical Dictionary of Albania*, Scarecrow Press, 1996.

139   Keefe, E. K., *Area Handbook for Albania*, US Government Printing Office, Washington, DC, 1971.

140   Logoreci, A., *The Albanians: Europe's Forgotten Survivors*, 1977.

141   Marmullaku, R., *Albania and the Albanians*, 1975.

142   Pipa, A., *The Politics of Language in Socialist Albania*, East European Monographs, Westview Press, Boulder, CO, 1989.

143   Pipa, A., *Albanian Stalinism: Ideo-political Aspects*, Westview Press, Boulder, CO, 1990.

144   Prifti, P., *Socialist Albania since 1944: Domestic and Foreign Developments*, MIT Press, Cambridge, MA, 1978.

145   Schnytzer, A., *Stalinist Economic Strategy in Practice: The Case of Albania*, Oxford University Press, Oxford, 1982.

146   Sjöberg, O., *Rural Change and Development in Albania*, Westview Press, Boulder, CO, 1991.

147   Vaughan-Whitehead, D., *Albania in Crisis: The Predictable Fall of the Shining Star*, Edward Elgar, Cheltenham, 1999.

148 Vickers, M. and Pettifer, J., *Albania. From Anarchy to a Balkan Identity*, Hurst, 1996.
149 Winnifrith, T. (ed.), *Perspectives on Albania*, Macmillan, Basingstoke, 1991.

BULGARIA

150 Bell, J. D., *The Bulgarian Communist Party from Blagoev to Zhivkov*, Hoover Institute Press, Stanford, CA, 1986.
151 Bell, J. D. (ed.), *Bulgaria in Transition: Politics, Economics, Society and Culture after Communism*, Westview Press, Boulder, CO, 1998.
152 Bokov, G. (ed.), *Modern Bulgaria: History, Policy, Economy, Culture*, Sofia Press, Sofia, Bulgaria, 1981.
153 Boll, M. M., *Cold War in the Balkans: American Foreign Policy and the Emergence of Communist Bulgaria, 1943–1947*, University Press of Kentucky, Lexington, KY, 1984.
154 Brown, J. F., *Bulgaria under Communist Rule*, 1971.
155 Detrez, R., *Historical Dictionary of Bulgaria*, Scarecrow Press, 1997.
156 Eminov, A., *Turkish and Other Muslim Minorities of Bulgaria*, Hurst, 1997.
157 Genchev, N., *The Bulgarian National Revival Period*, Sofia Press, Sofia, Bulgaria, 1977.
158 Konings, J. and Repkin, A., *How Efficient Are Firms in Transition Countries?: Firm-level Evidence from Bulgaria and Romania*, Centre for Economic Policy Research, 1998.
159 Lang, D. M., *The Bulgarians from Pagan Times to the Ottoman Conquest*, Thames and Hudson, 1976.
160 McIntyre, R. J., *Bulgaria, Politics, Economics and Society*, Pinter, 1988.
161 Melone, A. P., *Creating Parliamentary Government: The Transition to Democracy in Bulgaria*, Ohio State University Press, Columbus, OH, 1998.
162 Oren, N., *Bulgarian Communism*, Columbia University Press, New York, 1971.
163 Todorova, M., *Language in the Construction of Ethnicity and Nationalism: The Case of Bulgaria*, University of California Press, Berkeley, CA, 1992.
164 Wightman, G. (ed.), *Party Formation in East-Central Europe: Post-Communist Politics in Czechoslovakia, Hungary, Poland and Bulgaria*, Edward Elgar, Aldershot, 1995.
165 Zhivkov, T., *Statesman and Builder of New Bulgaria*, Pergamon, Oxford, 1982.

CZECHOSLOVAKIA

166 Adam, J., *Why Did the Socialist System Collapse in Central and Eastern European Countries?: The Case of Poland, the Former Czechoslovakia and Hungary*, Macmillan, Basingstoke, 1996.
167 Allio, R., *White Paper on Czechoslovakia*, International Committee for the Support of Charter 77 in Czechoslovakia, 1977.
168 Burcher, T., *The Sudeten German Question and Czechoslovak–German Relations since 1989*, Royal United Services Institute for Defence Studies, 1996.

169 Dedek, O., *The Break-up of Czechoslovakia: An In-depth Economic Analysis*, Avebury, Aldershot, 1996.
170 Gabal, I. (ed.), *The 1990 Election to the Czechoslovak Federal Assembly*, Sigma, Berlin, 1996.
171 Havel, V., *Living in Truth*, ed. by Jan Vladislav, Faber & Faber, 1968.
172 Kostya, S., *Northern Hungary: A Historical Study of the Czechoslovak Republic*, Association of Hungarian Teachers, Toronto, 1992.
173 Krejci, J., *Czechoslovakia, 1918–92: A Laboratory for Social Change*, Macmillan, Basingstoke, 1996.
174 Mlynar, Z., *Nightfrost in Prague*, Hurst, 1980.
175 Myant, M. R., *Transforming Socialist Economies: The Case of Poland and Czechoslovakia*, Edward Elgar, Aldershot, 1993.
176 Myant, M. R., *Socialism and Democracy in Czechoslovakia, 1945–1948*, Cambridge University Press, Cambridge, 1981.
177 Oxley, A., Pravda, A. and Ritchie, A., *Czechoslovakia: The Party and the People*, Allen Lane, 1973.
178 Teichova, A., *The Czechoslovak Economy, 1918–1988*, Routledge, 1988.
179 Valenta, J., *Soviet Intervention in Czechoslovakia, 1968: Anatomy of a Decision*, Johns Hopkins University Press, Baltimore, MD, 1991.
180 Williams, K., *The Prague Spring and its Aftermath: Czechoslovak Politics, 1968–1970*, Cambridge University Press, Cambridge, 1997.

THE GDR

181 Adler, C., *The GDR in Retrospect*, White and Co., Durham, UK, 1996.
182 Bryson, P. J., *The End of the East German Economy: From Honecker to Reunification*, Macmillan, Basingstoke, 1991.
183 Dennis, M., *Social and Economic Modernisation in Eastern Germany from Honecker to Kohl*, St Martin's Press, 1993.
184 Edwards, G. E., *GDR Society and Social Institutions: Facts and Figures*, Macmillan, Basingstoke, 1985.
185 Fulbrook, M., *Anatomy of a Dictatorship: Inside the GDR 1949–1989*, Oxford University Press, Oxford, 1995.
186 Goeckel, R. F., *The Lutheran Church and the East German State: Political Conflict and Change under Ulbricht and Honecker*, Cornell University Press, Ithaca, NY, 1990.
187 Kaser, M., *The Economic Relationship between the FRG and the GDR*, Oxford University Press, Oxford, 1986.
188 Kupferberg, F., *The Break-up of Communism in East Germany and Eastern Europe*, Macmillan, Basingstoke, 1999.
189 Maier, C. S., *Dissolution. The Crisis of Communism and the End of East Germany*, Princeton University Press, Princeton, NJ, 1997.
190 McKay, J., *The Official Concept of the Nation in the Former GDR*, Ashgate, Aldershot, 1998.
191 Pickel, A., *Radical Transitions: The Survival and Revival of Entrepreneurship in the GDR*, Westview Press, Boulder, CO, 1992.
192 Plock, E. D., *East German–West German Relations and the Fall of the GDR*, Westview Press, Boulder, CO, 1993.

193 Wallace, I. (ed.), *The GDR in the 1980s*, GDR Monitor, Dundee, 1984.
194 Woods, R., *Opposition in the GDR under Honecker, 1971–85: An Introduction and Documentation*, Macmillan, Basingstoke, 1986.

HUNGARY

195 Clark, R. (ed.), *Hungary: The Second Decade of Economic Reform*, Longman, 1989.
196 Cox, T. and Furlong, A. (eds), *Hungary: The Politics of Transition*, Frank Cass, 1995.
197 Csapody, T., *Hungary and the NATO Enlargement*, Institute for Political Science of the Hungarian Academy of Sciences, Budapest, 1999.
198 Feher, F., *Hungary 1956 Revisited: The Message of a Revolution*, Allen and Unwin, 1983.
199 Gero, A., *Modern Hungarian Society in the Making: The Unfinished Experience*, Hungarian Academy of Sciences, Budapest, 1995.
200 Halpern, L. and Wyplosz, C. (eds), *Hungary: Towards a Market Economy*, Cambridge University Press, Cambridge, 1998.
201 Hihnala, P. and Vehvilainen, O. (eds), *Hungary 1956*, Tampereen Yliopisto, Tampere, 1995.
202 Kiraly, B. (ed.), *Lawful Revolution in Hungary, 1989–94*, Atlantic Publications, Boulder, CO, 1995.
203 Molnar, M., *A Short History of the Hungarian Communist Party*, Westview Press, Boulder, CO, 1978.
204 Romsics, I. (ed.), *20th Century Hungary and the Great Powers*, Social Science Monographs, Boulder, CO, 1995.
205 Sugar, P. F., Hanak, P. and Frank, T., *A History of Hungary*, Indiana University Press, Bloomington, IN, 1990.
206 Swain, N., *Hungary: The Rise and Fall of Feasible Socialism*, Verso, 1992.
207 Szekeli, I. and Newbery, D. (eds), *Hungary: An Economy in Transition*, Cambridge University Press, Cambridge, 1993.
208 Tong, Y., *Transitions from State Socialism: Economic and Political Change in Hungary and China*, Rowman and Littlefield, Oxford, 1997.
209 Wight, G. (ed.), *Party Formation in East-Central Europe: Post-Communist Politics in Czechoslovakia, Hungary, Poland and Bulgaria*, Edward Elgar, Aldershot, 1995.

POLAND

210 Cirtautas, A. M., *The Polish Solidarity Movement*, Routledge, 1997.
211 Coenen-Huther, C. and Synak, B. (eds), *Post-Communist Poland: From Totalitarianism to Democracy*, Nova Science Publishers, Commack, NY, 1993.
212 Craig, M., *The Crystal Spirit: Lech Walesa and his Poland*, Hodder and Stoughton, 1986.
213 Dobbs, M., *Poland, Solidarity, Walesa*, Pergamon Press, Oxford, 1981.
214 Halecki, O., *A History of Poland*, Routledge and Kegan Paul, 1978.
215 Hayden, J., *Poles Apart: Solidarity and the New Poland*, Frank Cass, 1994.

216 Kaminski, B., *The Collapse of State Socialism: The Case of Poland*, Princeton University Press, Princeton, NJ, 1991.

217 Kolosi, T. and Wnuk-Lipinski, E. (eds), *Equality and Inequality under Socialism: Poland and Hungary Compared*, Sage, 1983.

218 Kubik, J., *The Power of Symbols Against the Symbols of Power: The Rise of Solidarity and the Fall of State Socialism in Poland*, Pennsylvania State University Press, Philadelphia, PA, 1994.

219 Michnik, A., *Letters from Freedom*, University of California Press, Berkeley, CA, 1998.

220 Millard, F., *The Anatomy of the New Poland: Post-Communist Politics in its First Phase*, Edward Elgar, Aldershot, 1994.

221 Myant, M. R., *Poland: A Crisis for Socialism*, Lawrence and Wishart, 1982.

222 Portes, R., *The Polish Crisis: Western Economic Policy Options*, Royal Institute of International Affairs, 1981.

223 Prizel, I., *National Identity and Foreign Policy: Nationalism and Leadership in Poland*, Cambridge University Press, Cambridge, 1998.

224 Rachwald, A. R., *In Search of Poland: The Superpowers' Response to Solidarity, 1980–1989*, Hoover Institute Press, Stanford, CA, 1990.

225 Simon, M. D. and Kanet, R. E. (eds), *Background to Crisis: Policy and Politics in Gierek's Poland*, Westview Press, Boulder, CO, 1981.

226 Tittenbrun, J., *The Collapse of 'Real Socialism' in Poland*, Janus, 1993.

227 Tworzecki, H., *Parties and Politics in Post-1989 Poland*, Westview Press, Boulder, CO, 1996.

ROMANIA

228 Almond, M., *Decline without Fall: Romania under Ceausesçu*, Alliance for the Institute for European Defence and Strategic Studies, 1988.

229 Bachman, R. D. (ed.), *Romania: A Country Study*, Library of Congress, Washington, DC, 1991.

230 Barnet, T. P. M., *Romanian and East German Policies in the Third World*, Praeger, New York, 1992.

231 Ceausesçu, I. (ed.), *War, Revolution, and Society in Romania*, Columbia University Press, New York, 1983.

232 Ceausesçu, N., *Nicolae Ceausesçu, Speeches and Writings*, Spokesman Books, Bucharest, 1978.

233 Deletant, D., *Ceausesçu and the Securitate: Coercion and Dissent in Romania, 1965–1989*, Hurst, 1995.

234 Deletant, D., *Communist Terror in Romania: Georghiu-Dej and the Police State, 1948–1965*, Hurst, 1998.

235 Fischer, M. E., *Nicolae Ceausesçu: A Study in Political Leadership*, Rienner, London/Boulder, CO, 1989.

236 Gallagher, T., *Romania after Ceausesçu: The Politics of Intolerance*, Edinburgh University Press, Edinburgh , 1995.

237 Georgescu, V., *The Romanians: A History*, Ohio State University Press, Columbus, OH, 1991.

238 Gilberg, T., *Nationalism and Communism in Romania: The Rise and Fall of Ceausesçu's Personal Dictatorship*, Westview Press, Boulder, CO, 1990.

239 Govender, R., *Nicolae Ceausescu and the Romanian Road to Socialism*, Unified Printers and Publishers, 1982.

240 Hale, J., *Ceausescu's Romania: A Political Documentary*, Harrap, 1971.

241 Helsinki Watch, *Since the Revolution: Human Rights in Romania. March 1991*, Human Rights Watch, New York, 1991.

242 Ionescu, S. N., *Who Was Who in Twentieth Century Romania*, Columbia University Press, New York, 1994.

243 Kellog, F., *The Road to Romanian Independence*, Indiana, University Press, Bloomington, IN, 1995.

244 Kirk, R. and Racenau, M., *Romania Versus the United States: Diplomacy of the Absurd, 1985–1989*, St Martin's Press, 1994.

245 Kligman, G., *The Politics of Duplicity: Controlling Reproduction in Ceausescu's Romania*, 1998.

246 Linden, R. H., *Communist States and International Change: Romania and Yugoslavia in Comparative Perspective*, Allen and Unwin, 1987.

247 Nelson, D. N. (ed.), *Romania after Tyranny*, Westview Press, Boulder, CO, 1992.

248 Pacepa, I. M., *Red Horizons*, Coronet Books, 1988.

249 Patterson, W. C., *Rebuilding Romania: Energy, Efficiency and the Economic Transition*, Earthscan, 1994.

250 Popa, O. D. and Horn, M. E., *Ceausescu's Romania: An Annotated Bibliography*, Greenwood Press, Westport, CT, 1994.

251 Rady, M. C., *Romania in Turmoil: A Contemporary History*, I. B. Tauris, 1992.

252 Samelli, A., *Women Behind Bars in Romania*, Frank Cass, 1997.

253 Shafir, M., *Romania: Politics, Economics, and Society*, Pinter, 1985.

254 Stan, L. (ed.), *Romania in Transition*, Dartmouth, Aldershot, 1997.

255 Sweeney, J., *The Life and Evil Times of Nicolae Ceausescu*, Hutchinson, 1991.

256 Tsantis, A. and Pepper, R., *Romania: The Industrialization of an Agrarian Economy under Socialist Planning*, World Bank, Washington, DC, 1979.

257 Verdery, K., *National Ideology under Socialism: Identity and Cultural Politics in Ceausescu's Romania*, California University Press, Berkeley, CA, 1991.

YUGOSLAVIA

258 Allcock, J. B., Milivojevic, M. and Horton, J. (eds), *Conflict in the Former Yugoslavia*, ABC-Clio, Denver, CO, 1998.

259 Auty, P., *Tito: A Biography*, 1970.

260 Banac, I., *The National Question in Yugoslavia: Origins, History, Politics*, Cornell University Press, Ithaca, NY, 1984.

261 Borowiec, A., *Yugoslavia after Tito*, Praeger, New York, 1977.

262 Burg, S. L. and Shoup, P. S., *The War in Bosnia-Herzegovina: Ethnic Conflict and International Intervention*, M. E. Sharpe, New York, 1999.

263 Cuvalo, A., *The Croatian National Movement: 1966–1972*, Columbia University Press, New York, 1990.

264 Djilas, M., *Tito: The Story from Inside*, Weidenfeld & Nicolson, 1981.

265 Djilas, M., *Rise and Fall*, Macmillan, London/New York, 1985.

266   Donia, R. J. and Fine, J. V. A., *Bosnia and Herzegovina: A Tradition Betrayed*, Columbia University Press, New York, 1994.

267   Drezov, K., Kostovicova, D. and Gökay, B. (eds), *Kosovo: Myths, Conflict and War*, Keele European Research Centre, Keele, 1999.

268   Friedman, F., *The Bosnian Muslims: Denial of a Nation*, Westview Press, Boulder, CO, 1996.

269   Glenny, M., *The Fall of Yugoslavia*, Penguin, 1992.

270   Goati, V. (ed.), *Challenges of Parliamentarism: The Case of Serbia in the Early Nineties*, Institute of Social Sciences, Belgrade, 1995.

271   Lampe, J. R., *Yugoslavia as History: Twice There Was a Country*, Cambridge University Press, Cambridge, 1996.

272   Lees, L. M., *Keeping Tito Afloat: The United States, Yugoslavia and the Cold War*, Pennsylvania State University Press, Philadelphia, PA, 1997.

273   Malcolm, N., *Bosnia: A Short History*, Papermac, 1994.

274   Mertus, J., *Kosovo: How Myths and Truths Started a War*, University of California Press, Berkeley, CA, 1999.

275   Mestrovic, S. G., *The Balkanization of the West*, Routledge, 1994.

276   Pervan, R., *Tito and the Students: The University and the University Student in Self-managing Yugoslavia*, University of Western Australia Press, Perth, 1978.

277   Pinson, M. (ed.), *The Muslims of Bosnia-Herzegovina: Their Historic Development from the Middle Ages to the Dissolution of Yugoslavia*, Westview Press, Boulder, CO, 1996.

278   Pipa, A. and Repishti, S. (eds), *Studies on Kosova*, Colombia University Press, New York, 1984.

279   Ra'anan, G. D., *Yugoslavia after Tito: Scenarios and Implications*, Westview Press, Boulder, CO, 1977.

280   Ramet, S. P., *Balkan Babel: The Disintegration of Yugoslavia from the Death of Tito to Ethnic War*, Westview Press, Boulder, CO, 1996.

281   Rusinow, D., *The Yugoslav Experiment, 1948–1974*, 1977.

282   Vucinich, W. S. and Emmert, T. A. (eds), *Kosovo: Legacy of a Medieval Battle*, University of Minnesota Press, Minneapolis, MN, 1991.

283   West, R., *Tito and the Rise and Fall of Yugoslavia*, Sinclair-Stevenson, 1994.

INDEX

SEMINAR STUDIES IN HISTORY

General Editors: Clive Emsley & Gordon Martel

The series was founded by Patrick Richardson in 1966. Between 1980 and 1996 Roger Lockyer edited the series before handing over to Clive Emsley (Professor of History at the Open University) and Gordon Martel (Professor of International History at the University of Northern British Columbia, Canada and Senior Research Fellow at De Montfort University).

MEDIEVAL ENGLAND

The Pre-Reformation Church in England 1400–1530 (Second edition)
Christopher Harper-Bill   0 582 28989 0

Lancastrians and Yorkists: The Wars of the Roses
David R Cook   0 582 35384 X

TUDOR ENGLAND

Henry VII (Third edition)
Roger Lockyer & Andrew Thrush   0 582 20912 9

Henry VIII (Second edition)
M D Palmer   0 582 35437 4

Tudor Rebellions (Fourth edition)
Anthony Fletcher & Diarmaid MacCulloch   0 582 28990 4

The Reign of Mary I (Second edition)
Robert Tittler   0 582 06107 5

Early Tudor Parliaments 1485–1558
Michael A R Graves   0 582 03497 3

The English Reformation 1530–1570
W J Sheils   0 582 35398 X

Elizabethan Parliaments 1559–1601 (Second edition)
Michael A R Graves   0 582 29196 8

England and Europe 1485–1603 (Second edition)
Susan Doran   0 582 28991 2

The Church of England 1570–1640
Andrew Foster   0 582 35574 5

STUART BRITAIN

Social Change and Continuity: England 1550–1750 (Second edition)
Barry Coward   0 582 29442 8

James I (Second edition)
S J Houston   0 582 20911 0

The English Civil War 1640–1649
Martyn Bennett   0 582 35392 0

Charles I, 1625–1640
Brian Quintrell   0 582 00354 7

The English Republic 1649–1660 (Second edition)
Toby Barnard   0 582 08003 7

Radical Puritans in England 1550–1660
R J Acheson   0 582 35515 X

The Restoration and the England of Charles II (Second edition)
John Miller   0 582 29223 9

The Glorious Revolution (Second edition)
John Miller   0 582 29222 0

EARLY MODERN EUROPE

The Renaissance (Second edition)
Alison Brown   0 582 30781 3

The Emperor Charles V
Martyn Rady   0 582 35475 7

French Renaissance Monarchy: Francis I and Henry II (Second edition)
Robert Knecht   0 582 28707 3

The Protestant Reformation in Europe
Andrew Johnston   0 582 07020 1

The French Wars of Religion 1559–1598 (Second edition)
Robert Knecht   0 582 28533 X

Phillip II
Geoffrey Woodward   0 582 07232 8

The Thirty Years' War
Peter Limm   0 582 35373 4

..er Campbell   0 582 01770 X

Spain in the Seventeenth Century
Graham Darby   0 582 07234 4

Peter the Great
William Marshall   0 582 00355 5

EUROPE 1789–1918

Britain and the French Revolution
Clive Emsley   0 582 36961 4

Revolution and Terror in France 1789–1795 (Second edition)
D G Wright   0 582 00379 2

Napoleon and Europe
D G Wright   0 582 35457 9

Nineteenth-Century Russia: Opposition to Autocracy
Derek Offord   0 582 35767 5

The Constitutional Monarchy in France 1814–48
Pamela Pilbeam   0 582 31210 8

The 1848 Revolutions (Second edition)
Peter Jones   0 582 06106 7

The Italian Risorgimento
M Clark   0 582 00353 9

Bismark & Germany 1862–1890 (Second edition)
D G Williamson   0 582 29321 9

Imperial Germany 1890–1918
Ian Porter, Ian Armour and Roger Lockyer   0 582 03496 5

The Dissolution of the Austro-Hungarian Empire 1867–1918 (Second edition)
John W Mason   0 582 29466 5

Second Empire and Commune: France 1848–1871 (Second edition)
William H C Smith   0 582 28705 7

France 1870–1914 (Second edition)
Robert Gildea   0 582 29221 2

The Scramble for Africa (Second edition)
M E Chamberlain   0 582 36881 2

Late Imperial Russia 1890–1917
John F Hutchinson   0 582 32721 0

The First World War
Stuart Robson   0 582 31556 5

EUROPE SINCE 1918

The Russian Revolution (Second edition)
Anthony Wood   0 582 35559 1

Lenin's Revolution: Russia, 1917–1921
David Marples   0 582 31917 X

Stalin and Stalinism (Second edition)
Martin McCauley   0 582 27658 6

The Weimar Republic (Second edition)
John Hiden

0 582 28706 5

The Inter-War Crisis 1919–1939
Richard Overy

0 582 35379 3

Fascism and the Right in Europe, 1919–1945
Martin Blinkhorn

0 582 07021 X

Spain's Civil War (Second edition)
Harry Browne

0 582 28988 2

The Third Reich (Second edition)
D G Williamson

0 582 20914 5

The Origins of the Second World War (Second edition)
R J Overy

0 582 29085 6

The Second World War in Europe
Paul MacKenzie

0 582 32692 3

Anti-Semitism before the Holocaust
Albert S Lindemann

0 582 36964 9

The Holocaust: The Third Reich and the Jews
David Engel

0 582 32720 2

Germany from Defeat to Partition, 1945–1963
D G Williamson

0 582 29218 2

Britain and Europe since 1945
Alex May

0 582 30778 3

Eastern Europe 1945–1969: From Stalinism to Stagnation
Ben Fowkes

0 582 32693 1

Eastern Europe since 1970
Bulent Gökay

0 582 32858 6

The Khrushchev Era, 1953–1964
Martin McCauley

0 582 27776 0

NINETEENTH-CENTURY BRITAIN

Britain before the Reform Acts: Politics and Society 1815–1832
Eric J Evans

0 582 00265 6

Parliamentary Reform in Britain c. 1770–1918
Eric J Evans

0 582 29467 3

Democracy and Reform 1815–1885
D G Wright

0 582 31400 3

Poverty and Poor Law Reform in Nineteenth-Century Britain, 1834–1914:
From Chadwick to Booth
David Englander

0 582 31554 9

The Birth of Industrial Britain: Economic Change, 1750–1850
Kenneth Morgan

0 582 29833 4

Chartism (Third edition)
Edward Royle   0 582 29080 5

Peel and the Conservative Party 1830–1850
Paul Adelman   0 582 35557 5

Gladstone, Disraeli and later Victorian Politics (Third edition)
Paul Adelman   0 582 29322 7

Britain and Ireland: From Home Rule to Independence
Jeremy Smith   0 582 30193 9

TWENTIETH-CENTURY BRITAIN

The Rise of the Labour Party 1880–1945 (Third edition)
Paul Adelman   0 582 29210 7

The Conservative Party and British Politics 1902–1951
Stuart Ball   0 582 08002 9

The Decline of the Liberal Party 1910–1931 (Second edition)
Paul Adelman   0 582 27733 7

The British Women's Suffrage Campaign 1866–1928
Harold L Smith   0 582 29811 3

War & Society in Britain 1899–1948
Rex Pope   0 582 03531 7

The British Economy since 1914: A Study in Decline?
Rex Pope   0 582 30194 7

Unemployment in Britain between the Wars
Stephen Constantine   0 582 35232 0

The Attlee Governments 1945–1951
Kevin Jefferys   0 582 06105 9

The Conservative Governments 1951–1964
Andrew Boxer   0 582 20913 7

Britain under Thatcher
Anthony Seldon and Daniel Collings   0 582 31714 2

INTERNATIONAL HISTORY

The Eastern Question 1774–1923 (Second edition)
A L Macfie   0 582 29195 X

The Origins of the First World War (Second edition)
Gordon Martel   0 582 28697 2

The United States and the First World War
Jennifer D Keene   0 582 35620 2

Anti-Semitism before the Holocaust
Albert S Lindemann   0 582 36964 9

The Origins of the Cold War, 1941–1949 (Second edition)
Martin McCauley　　　　　　　　　　　　　　　0 582 27659 4

Russia, America and the Cold War, 1949–1991
Martin McCauley　　　　　　　　　　　　　　　0 582 27936 4

The Arab–Israeli Conflict
Kirsten E Schulze　　　　　　　　　　　　　　0 582 31646 4

The United Nations since 1945: Peacekeeping and the Cold War
Norrie MacQueen　　　　　　　　　　　　　　　0 582 35673 3

Decolonisation: The British Experience since 1945
Nicholas J White　　　　　　　　　　　　　　　0 582 29087 2

The Origins of the Vietnam War
Fredrik Logevall　　　　　　　　　　　　　　　0 582 31918 8

The Vietnam War
Mitchell Hall　　　　　　　　　　　　　　　　0 582 32859 4

WORLD HISTORY

China in Transformation 1900–1949
Colin Mackerras　　　　　　　　　　　　　　　0 582 31209 4

Japan faces the World, 1925–1952
Mary L Hanneman　　　　　　　　　　　　　　　0 582 36898 7

Japan in Transformation, 1952–2000
Jeff Kingston　　　　　　　　　　　　　　　　0 582 41875 5

US HISTORY

American Abolitionists
Stanley Harrold　　　　　　　　　　　　　　　0 582 35738 1

The American Civil War, 1861–1865
Reid Mitchell　　　　　　　　　　　　　　　　0 582 31973 0

America in the Progressive Era, 1890–1914
Lewis L Gould　　　　　　　　　　　　　　　　0 582 35671 7

The United States and the First World War
Jennifer D Keene　　　　　　　　　　　　　　　0 582 35620 2

The Truman Years, 1945–1953
Mark S Byrnes　　　　　　　　　　　　　　　　0 582 32904 3

The Origins of the Vietnam War
Fredrik Logevall　　　　　　　　　　　　　　　0 582 31918 8

The Vietnam War
Mitchell Hall　　　　　　　　　　　　　　　　0 582 32859 4